The Hour which cometh, and now is:

SERMONS,

PREACHED IN

INDIANA-PLACE CHAPEL, BOSTON,

BY

JAMES FREEMAN CLARKE.

BOSTON:
WALKER, WISE, AND COMPANY,
245, Washington Street.
1864.

Entered, according to Act of Congress, in the year 1864, by
WALKER, WISE, AND COMPANY,
In the Clerk's Office of the District Court of the District of Massachusetts.

BOSTON:
PRINTED BY JOHN WILSON AND SON,
5, WATER STREET.

PREFACE.

THESE Sermons, having been mostly written in the course of the last three years, during the great American conflict of freedom against slavery, are necessarily frequent in allusions to this war. Surrounded with those whose sons, brothers, and friends were fighting and falling on so many bloody fields, this dark background is seen behind the figures in each discourse.

I suppose that repetition of ideas and thoughts may be sometimes noticed by the reader. Such repetition is a defect in works of pure theory or intellectual science; but, in practical and spiritual works, we need, as in music, frequent variations on the same themes.

It only remains to say, that these Sermons are affectionately inscribed to the Church of the Disciples, in whose service they have all been preached.

JAMES FREEMAN CLARKE.

MAY 19, 1864.

CONTENTS.

SERMON I.

SERMONS.

SERMONS.

I.

THE HOUR WHICH COMETH, AND NOW IS.

John iv. 23: "THE HOUR COMETH, AND NOW IS."

THIS remarkable phrase is used twice by our Master, — once in regard to the true worship of the Father, which he declares to be coming, and to be already present; and, again, in regard to those who are in their graves hearing his voice: they shall hear it, he says, and they hear it now. In somewhat the same way, he says of the harvest of faith which his disciples are to gather in, It will be harvest-time in four months, you say. Look! I see the harvest ready to be gathered now.

This blending of future and present is in the very nature of prophecy, which sees what is coming in what now is; which sees the fruit in the flower, the flower in the bud; which sees the action to be in the motive which now is at work; which perceives that an idea is potent enough to develop itself into a long series of actions; which recognizes the antitype in its type; and, in one lightning-flash of spiritual perception, sees a whole landscape leaping out of the darkness of the future into the momentary illumination of the present.

There is a future of which we know nothing till it has arrived: there is another future, which we know before it comes. Some things can be foreseen almost as if they were seen. Some things are here already, potentially, before they are here actually,— are here in their seeds and roots, before they are here in their fruits and results. "There is a field of grain," says the farmer. "Grain!" you reply. "I see nothing there: there is only black earth."—"Yes," the farmer answers: "it is sown with grain." When the seed is there, the grain is virtually there.

Therefore we celebrate the birthdays of great men, regarding each of them as the seed of a great future. We keep the 22d of February, and close our banks, fire cannon, listen to orations, because, on that day, a little child was born, in whose coming came the deliverance of America from European vassalage. Fifty years passed from the birthday of the child before he did his work; but we celebrate not the day when the work was done, but the day when the child was born to do it. The whole nation goes back to the cradle of George Washington, and says, "The hour comes, and now is, when America shall be free." So we celebrate Christmas, the birthday of Christ. So all Christendom goes, on that sacred morning, with the Eastern Magi, to offer its gifts of grateful love to the little unconscious infant. So, in Catholic prayer-books to-day, we find prayers addressed to the infant Jesus; that is, prayers to a purely ideal being, — to a being who does not exist: for surely there is no infant Jesus now! Yet so clearly do we see that the essence of a great event is not in the thing done, but in the power which is to do it, that, when Christ is born, we regard Christianity as established.

With the same ideal tendency, the same disposition to put the idea of a thing above the actual thing, we keep the 4th of July as the day of National Independence. But we did not become independent on the 4th of July, 1776: we became independent not till some years after that. All that was done on the 4th of July was the enunciation of the idea of independence. The purpose, the resolution, the determination, were born that day: so we celebrate the birth of Independence on that day.

There are some things, no doubt, which are not here till they are accomplished; but other things are really here when they are begun. That which depends on outward circumstances, on contrivances, on outward force, or will, is not here till the circumstances take place. The discovery of America, the invention of printing, the landing of the Pilgrims, carry their chief importance in the events themselves, — not in the idea lying back of them. But every thing which depends on spiritual insight and moral purpose virtually comes when the truth is seen and uttered, when the moral purpose is declared. When Martin Luther fixed his paper against the door of Wittenberg

Cathedral on the Eve of All-Saints, 1517, the Reformation came. We date the Reformation from that day; not from the day when the reformers agreed upon their creed at Augsburg, in 1530. When the idea is born, the events flowing from that idea are born.

In fact, there are certain truths which are so commanding and convincing, that, when they are once seen and uttered, certain consequences are already logically certain. Such truths are so adapted to the human reason, conscience, and heart, that they must be accepted sooner or later. Such truths are mighty powers introduced into human affairs, which will produce inevitable consequences. No matter what is the resistance of unbelief, the obstinacy of prejudice, the bitterness of opposing interests, the rage of party madness; no matter what falsehood, calumny, slander, assail their champion, — these truths are mighty, and must prevail, though it may be, as the poet describes it, by means of —

> "A friendless conflict, lingering long
> Through weary day and weary year."

The prophets of the Old Testament were men to whom God gave the favor of seeing the future in the present; of seeing the hour which was coming, as if it were already arrived. Standing on the mount of vision, they overlooked the large panorama of the future; they saw the waving forests near at hand, the blue valleys below, the fields farther on waving with grain, the rivers winding like lines of light through the distance, the pale sea on the horizon, the faint mountain-lines far away. They saw in the principles and motives, in the ambitions and purposes, already at work, the results that must inevitably follow. Not by any mere political sagacity, which is a very short-sighted affair, but by that spiritual insight which sees the real beneath the accidental, the inevitable law working amid all varying circumstances, the prophets saw, in grief and anguish of heart, the national woes which were to come from national sins, and the restoration which would follow national repentance. They saw more still: they saw, in all the mysterious workings of events, the preparation for a higher revelation of truth and love. They saw in the whole Jewish law the preparation for a gospel higher than the law; in all the Jewish ritual, the preparation for a worship of truth and love. They saw the coming of the Son of man; the approach of—

> "That far-off, divine event,
> To which the whole creation tends."

Some kind of prophetic sight akin to this supports all great reformers, — all those who are struggling to establish spiritual ideas, moral principles. They see the thing they are to do almost as if it were already done. Trusting themselves to the simple power of truth, having faith in God and in the human heart, they feel strong enough to battle alone against a world. The Jesuit, who has made a great ecclesiastical machine; who has built up, cunningly, a system of checks and balances; who has organized an army of monkish soldiers, which he wields in the cause of Holy Church; who induces rich people to leave him their money, in order to save their souls; who manages statesmen and kings through their confessors, and lays his hand on the colleges and schools of a nation in order to proselyte little children, — he has his hour too, but it is only the hour of success. When his plans fail, when his schemes are detected, when his cunning is baffled by a deeper sagacity, he has no resource. His failure is certain. But the man who trusts in truth never fails. Savonarola and Huss, on the scaffold and at the stake, were just as sure of victory as if they saw it present. We are no more certain now of the coming end of slavery than Follen and Channing were when they died; though then slavery seemed triumphant. All these could say, "The hour cometh, and now is." All saw the future in the present. Touissant L'Ouverture, in his dungeon, was more sure of the success of his cause than Napoleon of his. Wordsworth well said to him, —

> "Live, and take comfort. Thou hast left behind
> Powers that will work for thee, — air, earth, and skies.
> There's not a breathing of the common wind
> That will forget thee: thou hast great allies.
> Thy friends are exultations, agonies,
> And love, and man's unconquerable mind."

When Jesus said, "The hour cometh, and now is, when the true worshippers shall worship the Father in spirit and in truth," he only on the surface of the earth knew what true worship was. Men worshipped God, as though he loved sacrifices; as though he took pleasure in seeing his creatures torment themselves;

as though he were far off, and could not easily hear; as though he were angry, and had to be appeased; as though he loved to be praised; as if he were capable of being teased, by much speaking, into consent; as if a solemn form were agreeable to him. But Jesus saw in his heart that diviner worship, the love of a child to its father and mother; the trust of a weak creature in a perfectly wise, good, and great Being; the confidence of a sinful creature in one all mercy and compassion; the worship which does not need to speak in order to be heard; which is the motion of a hidden fire that trembles in the breast; that worship, which, when it comes, will make every place a church, every day the Lord's day, all work devotion, all joy thanksgiving, all events blessings, and all of nature and life full of God. Jesus, feeling this worship in his own soul, and knowing its beauty, majesty, and power, saw that all other worship; all of mere form, ceremony, ritual; all of worship born of fear, anxiety, doubt; all prayer to which men are dragged by conscience or led by custom, — must cease and determine, when this divine and heavenly worship is once known. So he said, "The hour cometh, and now is."

And so, on the other occasion, when he said, The hour cometh, and now is, when all that are in their graves shall hear the voice of the Son of man, and come forth, to the resurrection of life or the resurrection of judgment. Come out of their graves, — the graves of ignorance, error, sin; out of the graves of selfishness, sensuality, falsehood; out of the graves of worldliness, covetousness, cunning, and fraud, in which they have buried themselves. He saw that his Father would one day reach every soul; in this world, or in the next world, or in some world, would reach every soul of man. He saw, that sooner or later, as long as in every man there is heart, reason, and conscience, the reason must at last see the truth, the conscience must feel it, the heart must love it. And so *all* in their graves shall hear his voice and come up, — the faithful to see their own faithfulness rewarded with entrance into fuller life; the unfaithful to be judged, to know at last the evil of their evil, and so take also the first step back toward good: therefore a resurrection, a rising-up, for all, — a rising-up of the good into *love*, a rising-up of the evil into *truth*. He saw that distant day as though already here, because he had once for all spoken the immortal truth, to which sooner or later every knee should bow, of things in heaven, and things on earth, and things under the earth. And so, dying on the cross; disgraced, defeated, conquered; forsaken by his friends, betrayed by his own disciples, leaving not one on earth who understood him, — he could say to his Father, "I have glorified thee on the earth; I have *finished* the work thou gavest me to do."

If he saw it then, surely we may see it now. If every one of the "glorious company of the apostles, the goodly fellowship of the prophets, and the noble army of martyrs," saw, each in his prison, at his stake, in his lowly, thankless toil, amid hatred, persecution, and opposition, — saw the day of triumph coming, as though it had already come, — we surely can see the day of a purified Christianity, of a freed Church, of the marriage-supper of nature and revelation, reason and religion, works and faith, morality and piety.

Yes, the hour cometh, and now is, when Christian doctrine shall be redeemed from the Jewish and Pagan errors which have clung to it, and so be brought back to the simplicity of Christ; when men shall no more be taught to be afraid of God, as though he were angry, and had to be appeased by a bloody sacrifice; no more be driven from their dear Father by Pagan doctrines concerning his need of some expiatory victim, before he can forgive his children. They will no more be taught that man is all corrupt and evil, — nothing but sin: they will be taught to see in every soul something good, something allied to God, some conscience, some heart, something of holy fire lingering under the ashes of vice and sin. THE HOUR COMETH, AND NOW IS, when men shall learn to respect human nature, and not despise it as wholly corrupt; and then they will love each other. THE HOUR COMETH, AND NOW IS, when they will look on the vicious and the criminal with pity, not contempt, and try to help them out of their evil; when those who have been abandoned, and left without any sympathy or brotherly aid, shall be sought out and taught and saved. Then the Christian Church, united by the holy spirit of humanity and brotherly love, will come together, and be at one; the Catholic no longer hating the Protestant, nor the Orthodox despising the heretic, but all working together in the great cause of human improvement. THAT HOUR COMETH, AND NOW IS.

It is told of Michael Angelo, that, when he had spent two years in painting the frescoes on the ceiling of the Sistine Chapel, he had acquired such a habit of looking up, that he could not look down; and, if he wished to read a letter, he had to hold it *up* above his forehead in order to see it. The Christian Church has placed Christianity so entirely in the worship of God, who is *over all*, that it has lost the power of seeing the same God, who is *through all*, and *in us all.* It only sees God *above* us, not God in nature around, not God in man's human soul. Its religion, therefore, has all gone into worship, into churches, into Sundays. BUT THE HOUR COMETH, AND NOW IS, when Christianity is to be seen in the street, in the shop, in all human life, and God to be felt as "all in all."

Certainly we may say, that the hour cometh, and now is, when a rational and humane religion shall take the place of a religion of form and dogma. Do we not see how every man, who preaches and teaches in any way this religion of love, takes hold of the hearts of all men, even those who seem the most rigid and the most closely imprisoned in their creeds? See what a general respect and love have come around the memory of Theodore Parker! — not because of his opposition to the supernatural part of Christianity, but in spite of that opposition. It is because of his broad humanity, his generous love of truth, justice, and right. See how such men as Robertson in England, and Beecher in America, guide the hearts and the thoughts of tens of thousands, because they are prophets of this great future, — of the day when God and Christ shall be seen to be the friends of all human beings, and reason and revelation be wholly at one! And see the universal expression of esteem and love which has risen from the whole land like a cloud of incense, honoring the heroic and generous soul of our own brother Starr King! The "New-York Independent" forgets that he was a Unitarian and Universalist, and honors him with warm tears of affectionate sorrow. The Democratic papers forget that he was antislavery and Republican, and give the truest and best testimonies to his character and worth. It is because he was a youthful prophet and example of the HOUR WHICH COMETH, AND NOW IS; of the future day of the Church and State; of the religion of reason, justice, humanity; of the Christ who is to come, and is already here.

There are those, who, taking a literal view of Scripture, teach that Jesus Christ is coming back to earth in some particular year, in outward form, and in some particular place. No doubt, he is coming. His hour cometh, and now is. He is coming more abundantly, just as he has come already, in a greater inspiration of faith, a greater sense of the nearness of God, a greater love for God and man, a universal outflowing of humanity and brotherhood to all. That is the second coming of Christ, and the only second coming that has any significance or value to us. If he *should* come outwardly in the sky, with the noise of a trumpet and a great light, that would be only a portent, a wonder, — something to excite astonishment, fear, admiration; but it would not make a single man any more of a Christian than he is now. That was the sort of sign which the Jews wanted, and of which Christ said, "An evil and adulterous generation seeketh after a sign; and there shall no sign be given them but that of the Prophet Jonah."

Jesus comes as his truth comes, as his love comes. He comes with his Father to dwell in us, and we in him. As he comes so, every knee bows. Sin is conquered. The last enemy, death, is overcome. Christ comes to redeem us from the power of all evil. Then heaven cometh, and now is. Then, God's will being done on earth as it is in heaven, heaven begins here. It is here already in its seeds and roots; and we have the foretaste of the world to come, the first-fruits of a higher life, while we are yet dwelling in this.

And so, lastly, we realize that death is nothing; that we are already immortal; that the hour of immortal life cometh, and now is. Death ceases to exist to a Christian. He looks forward to the time when he shall fall asleep, and wake again, surrounded by all whom he loves, and who love him; by the spirits of the just made perfect; and shall find the truth of what Plato and Milton said, — that what we call life is death, and what we call death is life. For Plato says in a striking passage in his *Gorgias*, "I should not wonder if Euripides spoke truth when he said, 'Who knows if to live is not really to die, and to die really to live; and that we now are, in reality, dead? Our present existence is perhaps our death, and this body our tomb.'" And so Milton says, —

> "Meekly thou didst resign this earthly load
> Of death, called life, which us from life doth sever."

That which Plato and Euripides *thought* possible, Jesus *saw* to be real; and so he said, "He who liveth and believeth in me shall never die." So he always called death sleep; so his disciples said that he had abolished, annihilated death; so he took away its terror out of their hearts; and they felt, that though to live was to be with him, yet to die was to gain more than they lost.

Thus it is that immortality and heaven are coming, because they are already here. Thus it is that true worship, pure Christianity, humane religion, are sure to come in their full and ripe harvest, because they are already here in their seed and germ. So it is, that the living experience and the deep convictions of the human heart are always a sure word of prophecy of the glory which is to be revealed; and the life which comes now from God and Christ is the promise and assurance of the life which is to come hereafter.

II.

THE LETTER AND THE SPIRIT.

2 Cor. iii. 6: "WHO ALSO HATH MADE US ABLE MINISTERS OF THE NEW COVENANT: NOT OF THE LETTER, BUT OF THE SPIRIT; FOR THE LETTER KILLETH, BUT THE SPIRIT GIVETH LIFE."

Rom. ii. 28, 29: "HE IS NOT A JEW WHICH IS ONE OUTWARDLY: BUT HE IS A JEW WHICH IS ONE INWARDLY; IN THE SPIRIT, AND NOT IN THE LETTER; WHOSE PRAISE IS NOT OF MEN, BUT OF GOD."

THE chief distinction between man and man, in any pursuit or occupation, is this, — that the one sees the SPIRIT of a thing, and works in that; the other, only the LETTER, and sticks in that.

For in every thing there is a spirit and a letter. It is not merely in the Bible, but everywhere. Every thing which exists, exists literally and spiritually; in its form and its essence; in its body and its soul.

For example: Suppose a man should undertake to describe a landscape, — a scene in the White Mountains, or in the heart of the Mississippi Valley. He might give you the height and position of the mountains; state accurately the size of the trees, and the position of every thing in the foreground, the middle distance, and beyond: but he would not give you any thing, after all, but a number of details. Another man, with a few suggestive words, would place you in the scene itself. You would feel the majestic presence of the mountain, with its varying shades of sombre, dusky green, or its purple tints melting into aerial blue. You would feel the air stirring among the great multitude of leaves, and waking the deep silence of the forest. You would feel the life of the great sycamores, reaching out their white arms over the lazy streams. The one description, though perfectly accurate, would awaken no interest, suggest no picture, and be forgotten in an hour: the other would fill your imagination with the presence of Nature herself; and years after, when it came up to you, you would scarcely know whether it was some place you had heard described, or some place where you had been yourself. The one gave you the letter of the scene; the other, its spirit. I recollect several such descriptions which I read in childhood; and they seem like something I have seen. Some of Walter Scott's descriptions are of that kind. Shakspeare's are all so. Take, for example, his description of a brook: —

"The current that with gentle murmur glides,
Thou know'st, being stopt, impatiently doth rage;
But, when his fair course is not hindered,
He makes sweet music with the enamelled stones,
Giving a gentle kiss to every sedge
He overtaketh in his pilgrimage:
And so, by many winding nooks, he strays,
With willing sport, to the wild ocean."

The peculiarity of this description is, that the brook is alive all through: it "glides gently;" it "rages impatiently;" it kisses the sedge; it is a pilgrim, straying with willing sport to the ocean, which is also alive and "wild," untamed by man. So Milton, so Wordsworth, so Tennyson, so all great poets, describe Nature; not as in an auctioneer's catalogue, or as on a surveyor's map, but discovering everywhere its soul. Milton describes the sun, —

> "Who, scarce uprisen,
> With wheels yet hovering o'er the ocean-brim,
> Shot parallel to the earth his dewy ray;"

which gives you an image of Apollo in his car. But he describes the same sunrise elsewhere by making him a king: —

> "Right against the eastern gate,
> Where the great sun begins his state,
> Robed in flowers and amber light."

And so he makes the moon a traveller through the sky, —

> "Like one that had been led astray
> Through the heaven's wide pathless way;
> And oft, as if her head she bowed,
> Stooping through a fleecy cloud."

It is not the chemistry of Nature, which is its letter, not the proportions of silex and alumina in the landscape, which touch us most, and are most valuable: but the soul of Nature, the glory and beauty which no tongue can describe, which poetry only can suggest, never catalogue; the soul of peace, of harmony; the soul which seems almost to speak to us, —

this is what brings us near to God, and gives the outward world its highest value. Neither the Greeks nor the Jews saw much of this soul in Nature. Christianity has enabled us to feel it, and has created in us the power by which, in modern times and in modern poetry, man and Nature come into communion and harmony. This is a part of the atoning work of Christ, — to make man at one with Nature around him. Nature was terrible to the Old World, — full of a demoniac spirit. Lucretius traces all Pagan religion to a fear of natural portents. Christianity has reconciled man and Nature, and made us feel that she is our mother and our friend.

So, in every man, there is the letter and the spirit. You can describe him by enumerating his actions, and giving his phrenological tendencies, — so much conscientiousness, so much reverence, so much combativeness; but a deeper sagacity goes below all this, and finds the man's soul, that which gives unity to his life. Love is more sagacious still: it feels, by a sure instinct, the inmost character, and is wiser than wisdom. You cannot know any one till you love him; because, till then, you only know him externally: the secret of his life you do not know. We feel that no one understands us who does not love us: for beneath all our actions and all our opinions, all our outward life and character, there is the inward stress and tendency of our nature, our aspiration, our longing, our struggle; which is so deep down, that no one knows it unless by sympathy.

Look at two portraits: one gives the features; the other, the soul. One is after the letter; the other, after the spirit. In one, you have the outside of the man,—his husk, his shell, the mask he wears: in the other, there is a revelation of his inmost nature. The last is the only kind of portrait of a friend I ever care to have.

I recollect very well the first time I ever saw those wonderful portraits, by the great masters of art, which thus give us the soul of the man they paint. I recollect a picture of Ignatius Loyola, by Rubens, at Warwick Castle; one of Grotius, by Rembrandt, at the Bodleian Library in Oxford; one by Titian, at Hampton Court. It seemed as if I could never see enough of them. I went on, and returned again to look more and more. In these pictures, there was told the whole history of the man's life,—all its stormy adventure, all its earnest longing; agonies of thought, patiently endured; the soul refined by fires of suffering, by infinite toil, until, at last, it had reached the summit of self-possession and peace. I had supposed, till then, that portrait-painting was an inferior domain of art; but, after seeing such revelations of character accomplished by portraits, I felt there was nothing higher.

And so, when we come to truth, we see how this also has a letter and a spirit. The letter of Judaism, says the apostle, was its rites, its sabbath, its sacrifices, its priesthood, its temple. That was all of Judaism that the Greeks and Romans saw,—all that the scribes and Pharisees saw. But Paul says, "He is not a Jew who is one outwardly; neither is circumcision that which is outward in the flesh: but he is a Jew who is one inwardly; and circumcision is of the heart, in the spirit, and not in the letter." Socrates was a better Jew, in this sense, than Caiaphas: Seneca was a better Jew than Herod.

But it took clear insight and strong courage to say this. "What! this great system of ceremonies, this great sacramental and sacrificial system, which Jehovah had instituted, in order to separate the Jews from all mankind, — is this all nothing? and only the inward spirit, that no one can tell any thing about, — is that every thing? This is doing away with all distinctions, this sort of transcendental talk!" Conceive what the Pharisees must have thought of it.

The old covenant had its spirit and its letter, and the letter was only for the sake of the spirit. The spirit of the Old Testament is its constant sense of one God, supreme, eternal, all holy, all good; who requires of man justice and mercy; whose law forbids all wrong from man to man; protects the feeble, the poor, the stranger, and looks forward to the triumph of good over evil, truth over falsehood; foresees a perfect world to come at last, in which there shall be no more oppression, cruelty, or sin; in which all shall know God, from the least to the greatest.

That is the spirit of the Old Testament, from Genesis to Malachi, — a spirit of justice and faith. All the rest is its letter. Just as God surrounds the juicy fruit of the palm with a hard shell, and, outside of that, with a fibrous husk; so that the milky pulp shall slowly sweeten and ripen till the time comes for the nut to fall, and then the husk is torn off, and the shell broken; so he surrounded the immature convictions of the Jewish nation with this hard shell of ceremony, this tough husk of sacrifices, meats, and sabbaths. It kept them to themselves. It placed an element of mutual aversion between the Jew and the Gentile. So the inward spirit ripened slowly, from the days of Moses, when the nation was almost Egyptian and Pagan; through the times of Elijah, when they worshipped the stately idols of their Syrian neighbors, the sun-god Baal, and "Astarte's bediamonded crescent;" on through their Assyrian and Babylonish captivities, when they learned some truths from Persian Magi; on through the times of Ezekiel and Zechariah. The prophetic Muse of David sang to his harp some melodious anticipations of Jesus; and Isaiah, "rapt into future times," announced a religion of the spirit as above all forms. At last, the fulness of the time had come: the husk and shell of the Jewish religion were broken away, and the fruit ripened out of the law into the gospel.

But if he is not a Jew who is one outwardly, much more, surely, he is not a Christian who is one outwardly. If sacrifices and priesthood did not make Judaism, neither do baptism and church-going make Christianity. The new covenant also has its letter and its spirit; and, when we stick in the letter, we lose the spirit. Paul says of the new covenant, "God hath made us able ministers, not of its letter, but of its spirit; for the letter killeth, but the spirit giveth life."

All the forms of Christianity are means, and not ends: we need them as helps, not as results. Going to church does not make a Christian. Being baptized does not make a Christian. Professing Christianity does not make a Christian. Only loving God and man makes a Christian. Yet there are many people and teachers who lay such stress on baptism and the Lord's Supper, and the letter of the Bible, that they really see less of the spirit of Christianity than Isaiah or David saw. A thousand years before Christ was born, David saw more of Christianity than those see who hesitate as to whether an infant can be saved who has not been baptized, or whether God can love a good heathen after he dies. Jesus, though a Jew, was less particular in keeping outwardly the Jewish sabbath than many Christians are in an outward keeping of what they call the Christian sabbath; which is no sabbath at all, but the blessed day of our dear friend, in which the best thing we can do is to be loving and generous, thankful and good-natured, cheerful and happy.

Truth has its letter and its spirit. Dogmatists and bigots lay all stress on the letter. They pack it up in certain words; they string it on articles; they lock it up in a chest of drawers which they call a creed; they worship it in the text of the Bible.

They say, "If you do not believe it just as we express it, you shall, without doubt, be damned everlastingly." But truth cannot be kept in any forms: it is a conviction in the soul. You express it so to-day; otherwise, to-morrow.

Every doctrine has its letter and its spirit. The letter of a doctrine is its logical meaning, or that which the words literally imply. The spirit of a doctrine is that which is intended by those who hold it; the deep conviction in their minds which they attempt to express thus, of which this is the outward symbol. For, as all language is imperfect, no verbal statement can ever adequately express the human thought. The best statement is only an approximation. A doctrine, therefore, may be false in its letter, but true in its spirit; false in what it says, true in what it tries to say.

No doubt, there was truth in this sense in all the great doctrines which have been held by large multitudes during long periods. The letter of the Trinity is false; but the spirit of the Trinity seems to have been the desire to unite the different views of the Deity held by the Jew, the Greek, the philosopher, and the child. While the Jew had seen the unity of God and his holiness in revelation, the Greek had seen his wisdom and power in nature, and the philosopher had found God also in the instincts of his soul. All these different convictions were felt to have some substantial reality, and the doctrine of the Trinity grew out of an attempt to unite them in a single statement.

The attempt has not been successful; but its spirit was sound, and, in some form or other, may yet be found also true in the letter.

But we should do an equal injustice to Paganism, if we regarded only its letter, and forgot its spirit. The spirit of Paganism is that which the Apostle Paul described in his noble speech at Athens, when he told the Greeks that they already worshipped, though ignorantly, the true God. The spirit of Paganism is feeling after God in nature; trying to find Him who is not far from any one of us; having vague irrepressible longings after an infinite truth and beauty.

Christian missionaries, who go to convert the Heathen, are often moved by seeing the profound earnestness of their devotion. They feel that there is a substantial truth in all these religions in the midst of their formal errors. The poet Schiller has well expressed this truth in the play of "Wallenstein," where Max speaks of the belief of the great duke in astrology: —

"Oh! never rudely will I blame his faith
In the might of stars and angels. 'Tis not merely
The human being's pride that peoples space
With life and mystical predominance;
Since likewise for the stricken heart of love
This visible nature and this common world
Is all too narrow: yea, a deeper import
Lurks in the legend told my infant years
Than lies upon that truth we live to learn."

Mr. Coleridge was once a Unitarian, afterward a Trinitarian; but he did ten times more for Liberal

Christianity after he became a Trinitarian than he did before. He taught the Orthodox Church one great idea, which has penetrated it through and through, — that truth is not a statement of opinion; that faith is one thing, belief another; and that no man is ever saved by a doctrine, but only by an insight. So that now it has become all but impossible for any Protestant teacher, however Orthodox, to believe that any one will be damned for disbelieving a creed. As long as truth was confounded with belief, people could think so: now they cannot. The whole system of Orthodoxy is saturated throughout by this doctrine. It is like the ice on the river in the spring. It is floating there still, a foot thick, and seems solid ice: but it is water-soaked; and, one morning, it will sink, and be all gone. For all men have now come to see, more or less distinctly, that truth has its letter and its spirit; and that the letter kills, while the spirit alone gives life.

So also with morality. *It*, too, has its letter and spirit. There is a logical morality, which says, "This is right, and that is wrong;" but back of all that is the spirit, the motive, the aim, which makes a thing right or wrong. "Is it wrong to lie?" Certainly, we answer. "Is it wrong to commit sacrilege?" Surely. "Is it wrong to assassinate?" No doubt. "But I," says Jacobi, "am that atheist, that godless person: yes, I am that wretch who would lie, as the dying Desdemona lied; deceive as Pylades, when he pretended to be Orestes, that he might die in his stead;

commit sacrilege as David, when he ate the show-bread; be an assassin like Brutus, and a sabbath-breaker like the disciples, who plucked ears of corn, because they were hungry, and because law was made for man, and not man for the law."

The letter of morality kills: the spirit of morality, which is the love of right, the love of truth, an inward truthfulness of soul, a fidelity to one's own highest nature, an aspiration after whatever things are pure and lovely and noble, — this it is which fills the soul through and through, at once with magnanimity and humility, at once with courage and modesty; makes us faithful without pedantry, and holy without cant and pretence.

This, then, we say, is the chief difference between man and man. Some people, in whatever they do, follow dead routine; others, a living law: some see only what is customary; others see always what is needed: some are bound fast to what is usual and what is proper; others are made free by the sight of what is beautiful and good.

No man is a master in any work till he works according to the spirit. A man cannot be an able mechanic if he is a man of routine. The able mechanic is one whose mind is wide awake, and who is open to the incoming spirit of discovery; who is hoping to do better than he has done. So he makes a high art of any work. Such men as Stephenson and Bramah, Fulton, Ericsson, and Nasmyth, were greater poets, and lived a more imaginative life, than the parrot poetasters who rhyme like Tupper or Dobell. The grimy workshop of these men is all transfigured with music, song, and ideal lyrics.

Every occupation has those who follow it after the letter or after the spirit. The first do their best to kill their calling, and destroy all the respect that is felt for it in the minds of men: the other class elevate it, — give it dignity and worth.

There is, for example, the physician after the letter, who follows blindly the traditions of his school, whatever it may happen to be. He degrades his profession, in the minds of men, by the way in which he uses the terrible instruments in his hands; until at last men say, "Our chance of recovery is better without the doctor than with him." Thus the letter of medicine has killed medicine.

Then there is the pedantic scholar, who lives among dead words; who studies languages, not for the sake of the great literatures to which they are the portals, but for their own sake. Languages, being taught so, at last lose all their interest for the human mind; and so young men study Latin and Greek for six or eight years, and end by not being able to read a Greek or Latin book. The letter of scholarship has killed scholarship. Teachers, thus teaching after the letter, invariably destroy all interest in the subject which they teach. Meantime, the teacher who teaches with enthusiasm, because he is interested in the substance and spirit of what he teaches, excites a like enthusiasm in the mind of the scholar. Every thing thus learned is remembered; and the whole subject, thus vitalized, is thoroughly and deeply known.

During the last century, history was written according to the letter. Excellent, painstaking men collected all the facts, dates, and names belonging to a period, put them together, and called it all "history." It was only dead annals. Who took any interest in these histories? Who cared for them? The letter of history had killed it. Then came historians in France like Michelet and Thierry; in England, like Carlyle and Macaulay; in America, like Bancroft and Motley. Then the curtain was lifted from before the Past. It came up before us with its tragedy and its tears. It was as when Eliphaz saw in his vision the spectral form: "In thoughts from the visions of the night, when deep sleep falleth on men, fear came upon me, and trembling. Then a spirit passed before my face." We saw men, like ourselves, on the stage where these great dramas were performed. We saw the wild, stormy promise of the French Revolution, and its pathetic end. We saw the poor King of France flying under the dewy night to Varennes. From earlier centuries came forward the living forms of stern Keltic chiefs and Druid priests; of Norman sea-kings, cruel and terrible; Cromwell and Hampden, earnest Puritan deliverers of English liberty. The spirit had once more returned into history, and it was again alive.

We see by these varied examples the truth of the

apostle's statement, that the letter kills. We should hardly have ventured so bold a statement. We might have said that the letter without the spirit was inadequate. We might perhaps have gone further, and declared it useless. But to call it positively pernicious; to say that the letter of religion, of the Bible, of worship, *kills* religion, the Bible, and worship,— we should scarcely have ventured to do that. It would have seemed a dangerous statement. But an insight and experience like that of Paul enable one to say what would be thought dangerous by one standing on a lower platform. Now that he has said it, we also can see it. In every thing, the letter kills, and the spirit makes alive. The mere letter of the Old Testament and the New Testament kills piety. The mere letter of morality kills goodness. The letter of our daily work kills our interest in life. Edmund Burke says, "There is an unremitted labor, when men exhaust their attention, burn out their candles, and are left in the dark."

But when we are open to the spirit, and let that flow into all our work, thought, and life, then every thing is once more vitalized; then the Bible becomes a new book, full of intense interest; nature is new, being full of God; and man becomes a new creature, with a new heaven and a new earth.

III.

PROPHETS WHO HAVE BEEN SINCE THE WORLD BEGAN.

Luke i. 70: "PROPHETS WHO HAVE BEEN SINCE THE WORLD BEGAN."

A PROPHET is not merely one who foresees, who knows the future, who beholds events as they draw near: he is this, and more. He is not merely one who rebukes a nation's sins. Prophets do that; but that is not all they do. He is not merely one who teaches truth. The essential thing which makes him a prophet lies deeper than any of these partial definitions take us. A prophet is one who goes back of all traditions in religion to the original reality; behind all creeds, to the primal insights out of which they grew; beneath all expediency, to the creative law of justice and eternal right. This makes him a prophet; this helps him to foresee; this charges him full of noble indignation against all falsifiers of truth, and betrayers of justice. Such men are naturally and necessarily the teachers of their race. They do not teach officially as a profession, but from the need of utterance. He who sees, must say what he sees. "We also believe, and therefore speak."

The prophetic element, therefore, is not necessarily any thing miraculous or exceptional. The prophetic faculty is the natural, not the unnatural, condition of man. All men foresee and foretell in proportion as they have any manliness of soul, and force of intellect. Half of the conversation of every day turns upon what is to happen to-morrow. Farmers ask each other what sort of weather it will be the coming week. Merchants inquire what will be the condition of the market three months hence. Brokers foretell the effect of such and such events on the money-market. No man lives, who does not constantly look forward to foresee and to foretell what is to come. People often make mistakes: but that does not prevent them from trying again; for the instinct of the soul compels them to look forward. We may say, therefore, that prophecy is one of the natural faculties of the soul, just as much as reason or imagination.

You think, perhaps, that I am confounding different things, — natural sagacity, which foretells events by knowledge of the laws which produce them; and spiritual foresight, born of inspiration, which foretells the events sent by God. But is there such a distinction? Are not all events sent by God? Our Saviour blames the Jews because they could not foresee the spiritual events about to come, when they could foresee the weather to-day or to-morrow. "He said to the people, When ye see a cloud rise out of the west, ye say, There cometh a shower: and so it is. And, when ye see the south wind blow, ye say,

There will be heat; and it cometh to pass. Ye hypocrites! ye can discern the face of the sky and of the earth; but how is it that ye do not discern this time?" As though he had said, "The same sagacity which, applied to temporal things, enables you to foresee earthly changes which are to come; if applied to spiritual things, would enable you to foresee spiritual events which are to come."

Jesus called them "hypocrites," because they professed to be the religious leaders of their nation, and yet had no such perception of coming religious events as they had of every-day affairs. It was their business to foresee the coming of the Christ, and to notice the signs of his coming; and they did not do it. This shows that they did not really care about it as they professed to care. Every one can foresee in his own department of thought in which he is really interested. Napoleon could foresee just what his enemy would do, because he was interested in the game of war. Before he left Paris for his last campaign, which ended at Waterloo, he said, "Wellington lies with eighty thousand men in front of Brussels. Blucher lies with a hundred and twenty thousand Prussians on his left. These two armies are intended by their commanders to support each other, and their two wings to come together; but they probably do not. Probably they have left a vacant space of four or five miles between them. I will throw my army into that space, and strike them separately, first one, then the other, before they can combine." He found it exactly so. And half of his success in war lay in this power of military prophecy, by which he could throw himself, in imagination, into the position of his enemies, and so foretell exactly what they would do. Every man is thus a prophet in the things he cares for. Those who care most of all for religious truth, for the spiritual progress of mankind, for the advance of a great moral cause, can foresee in that direction, and are prophets to other men. Jesus therefore blamed the Pharisees, and justly, for not being prophets in religion, when they could prophesy so easily in regard to common things.

Therefore the Jewish prophets were not the first nor the last prophets in religion: there were prophets before them, so our text declares, — "prophets who have been since the world began." Not only all men, as we have said, have something of the prophetic element in them, but God has other prophets, mighty forelookers and foretellers, who have been since the world began.

For example: Nature is "a prophet who has been since the world began." The facts of nature look forward to a result, as well as backward to a cause. Nature contains both the law and the prophets, — universal divine laws, yet these laws tending always to sure providential ends.

I go in the spring to a seed-store, and I buy packages of flower-seeds. They come from Germany. I open a package, and I find twelve little papers containing twelve varieties of some flower, — asters, for example. There are a dozen little seeds in each paper. They look alike; but I know, if I plant them apart, when they come up, each seed will produce its own flower, with its own color, — white or purple or scarlet, as the case may be. Each little seed is a prophet, foretelling what is to come out of it. Each seed, bearing fruit after its kind, has, since the world began, been a prophecy and promise to man, that, if the sowing does not fail in the spring, the harvest shall come in the autumn.

Look at the human eye. Consider its wonderful formation, its lenses adapted to refract light, and bring it to a focus on the retina, yet without dispersing the ray. In the first human eye was a prophecy of all that the eye was to do, — a prediction and promise of sunlight, moonlight, twilight, — of all the forms of beauty and wonder which cover the earth. When God made the eye, he foretold light; he predicted sun, moon, stars; he announced the coming of beauty, grace, symmetry, — every glory of sunrise, every magnificence of evening. And, when God made the human hand, he foretold in its construction all it was to do, all the human arts which were to come from its use.

All nature is strewn with prophecies, had we but intelligence to read them. The very form of the continents, with their seas, mountains, plains, foretells the course of human affairs. Geography foretells history. The great level plains of Central Asia foretold the nomad tribes of herdsmen and shepherds who were to wander over them. The great river-valley of the Nile foretold the civilization of Egypt. The indented coast of Greece foretold Hellenic culture. All nature looks forward to man, and foretells his coming and his destiny.

So nature around us, and reason within us, have been prophets since the world began. Reason, allied to nature, foresees evermore. Great inventors and great discoverers have in them this element especially, because their reason is fed by the knowledge of nature. In the Book of Samuel, we read that he who was afterward called a prophet, or foreteller, was originally called a seer,—one who sees. Sight leads to foresight. He who sees well can easily foresee. Every great invention and discovery is a prophecy. Columbus foresaw America long before he set sail for it. Fulton foresaw his steamboat, and beheld it in vision sailing up the Hudson, against wind and tide, before the keel was laid. All great moral reformers are supported by the spirit of prophecy in their breasts. They rest secure on the eternal laws of God's government, and know certainly, that, because God reigns, the right must triumph. What would Luther have done, standing alone against all Christendom, attacking a church which had governed Europe for a thousand years; which had its thousands of priests and bishops in all lands, before which kings and emperors trembled; which held in its hand the knowledge, the wealth, the power of Europe, — how could he, a poor, lowly monk, venture on the audacity of attacking such an awful power, had not God in his heart given him to see that the eternal laws of truth and justice were on his side, and that, therefore, he must at last be conqueror; whispering to his heart that his friends —

"Were exaltations, agonies,
And love, and man's unconquerable mind"?

All great souls, who have done any noble work in the world, have been supported by this divine power of prophecy within them. They have looked forward in hope, assured hope, to a future success, of which the present gave no signs. The true prophets of God have not been men of abstract thought or abstract piety; but they have been the real workers, the real moral and religious leaders and chiefs, who have lived by faith in a better future while doing the hard work of to-day.

It is quite a mistake to suppose that the Jewish prophets were merely or essentially foretellers of the future, or writers of books: they were the great reformers of their time, — men who lived in the midst of strife. The first, and perhaps grandest, of them all, after Moses, Samuel, was at once an heroic ruler and general, and a wise statesman. He was the first who brought order out of anarchy. Till his time, the whole land was torn with petty guerilla warfare. Some such state of things prevailed as in Mexico now. A succession of leaders had arisen; but they brought no order out of chaos. The reason was, that they were mere fighters, — captains, not prophets. "The word of the Lord," it is said, "was precious in these days: there was no open vision." The men of action were there, but not the men of deep religious thought, not the men of open vision. Then Samuel arose, a great statesman, a great commander, a great prophet, all in one; an awful, majestic figure, who has come down to us through all these intervening centuries, surrounded with a strange halo of mystery and grandeur. He first united the elements of action, moral conviction, and spiritual insight. He was the first of the long line of Hebrew prophets; all of whom, like him, were more men of action than of devotion. They fought against the evils of their hour, — Isaiah, Jeremiah, Ezekiel, and, greatest of them all, Elijah; they rebuked kings and people, and stood up for justice and humanity in the midst of an evil generation. What gave them this power? Not the belief of a creed, not any traditional religion. No; but the fresh and living sight of justice and truth with which God inspired their hearts. They saw the right: they did not merely believe in it. They saw God: they did not merely reason him out by a chain of argument. They were seers, therefore they could be doers; for no man can do any noble thing but the man who sees something nobler, — even immortal and infinite truth.

This leads me to another point. The lowest kind of prophecy is sagacity, based on observation of outward laws. It is thus that —

> "Old experience doth attain
> To something of prophetic strain."

But this is only the lower kind of prophecy. The higher and better prophecy comes not from the region of the understanding, but from a deeper depth. The reason of man, indeed, as we have seen, has been a prophet since the world began. But God has had other, nobler, surer prophets of the future than the mere intellect. The conscience sees further than the understanding; the heart is wiser than the head. These, also, have been God's prophets since the world began.

Deep in the human breast, God has placed this solemn prophet, whom we name Conscience. He looks evermore at the eternal law of justice, deeper than any outward law:—

> "Which doth preserve the stars from wrong,
> And (by which) the most ancient heavens are fresh and strong."

No man but hears its voice. It speaks to us of right that we ought to do, of wrong that we ought to resist. It foretells a judgment to come. It speaks of a sure retribution for all evil, sometime or other, somewhere or other. It is the sword of Damocles, hanging over the head of Louis Napoleon in the Tuileries. It scared Herod when he thought of John the Baptist. It makes the weakest man strong who is acting from conscience. It frightened the slaveholders, who held the whole power of the nation in their hands,—Presidents, Congress, the Democratic party at the North, the whole bench of Judges,—and made them wish to hurry out of the Union, so as to escape the conscience of New England; for they knew that this New-England conscience was stronger than they all. In it they foresaw —

> "The vanward cloud of evil days,
> With all their stored thunder, laboring up."

For conscience always speaks as one having authority. By the voice of Joan of Arc, from her burning scaffold, calling on Jesus, it frightened the soldiers into hysterics. It compelled Gov. Wise, looking on John Brown, to say that he was the bravest and most honest man he ever knew. From the prison of Jeremiah, its voice reached the ear of the King of Israel, and struck terror into his heart. From the cross of Christ, it seemed to darken the sky, and rend the graves, and raise the dead. It may be that truth is for ever on the scaffold, and wrong for ever on the throne; but it is also true, that truth on the scaffold not only sways the future, but awes and terrifies the seemingly triumphant present. Almost before the ashes of Savonarola had been swept from the great square in Florence, Raphael was painting his serious face among the doctors of the Church in the frescoes of the Vatican.*

---

* "At Rome, Raphael was the first who undertook his apotheosis by placing him among the most illustrious doctors of the Church in the dispute on the Holy Sacrament. Ten years had then elapsed since the death of Savonarola. Pope Julius II., who was worthy of appreciating such a genius, had succeeded Alexander Borgia on the pontifical throne; and thus were terminated the scandals with which

The human heart, also, has been one of God's prophets since the world began.

The heart, I just now said, has a deeper wisdom than the head. Its faith, its hope, and its love predict and assure a better future than the mere intellect can foresee. Every thing that is greatly good in the world has been accomplished by the power of faith, not resting on outward evidence, but on the inward evidence of the heart. How has Christianity triumphed? Not by its miracles. Our books teach us to believe in Christ because of his miracles; but who really believes in Christ because of his miracles? We believe in him because we love him. Love leads to knowledge. He "draws all men unto him." "His sheep hear his voice, and follow him." The head believes in God by means of argument: the heart sees him. "Blessed are the pure in heart; for they shall see God." The intellect reasons about immortality: the heart knows it. The intellect proves Christianity to be true. The heart of man, in all ages, feels the truth of that generous faith which brings God near to us as a Father; which reveals man as a brother; which restrains the tyrant, and breaks

---

this infamous family had appalled Italy. The severe and despotic character of this pontiff will not allow us to suppose that Raphael would have ventured to place the portrait of Savonarola in one of the Stanze of the Vatican, unless the idea had been suggested to him by Julius himself, who, no doubt, preferred this kind of reparation, as affording the best guaranty for present publicity and future perpetuity." — Rio : *Poetry of Christian Art.*

the fetters of the slave; which supports the head of the feeble and sick, and opens heaven to the dying eye.

Is it all an illusion, — this grand hope, born out of love? Let us look at it. A desires a partner in business, and finds B. He exercises his best judgment in the selection; he takes advice, and asks references, and inquires into his antecedents: yet B often turns out, after all, not the man he thought him to be. But, as long as two friends love each other, their love is a sure foundation for mutual trust. Love does not deceive. Love, which beareth all things, believeth all things, hopeth all things, endureth all things, is the one thing which *never faileth.* Nothing is so solid as love. It sometimes seems to be the only substantial thing there is in the universe. Perhaps it is so; for God is love, and God alone has real self-existing being. We live from him, as we receive his love into our souls.

Therefore is love also a true prophet. It foresees and foretells a better future. It looks through the darkness of the present, — through pain, disappointment, trial, sorrow, bereavement, loneliness, — and sees all things working together for good. The true optimism comes to us when we love. When we forget ourselves, and love others; when we forget our selfishness, and share in God's interest in mankind; when we throw ourselves into life, and follow Christ in his trust in God, his hope for man, — then the heavens again smile. Then the day dawns peacefully, and the night closes serenely. Then we look through all anxiety, and see good beyond. Then, when we lay our beloved in the damp grave, we have a hope full of immortality in our hearts. Mortality is swallowed up of life. Our faith in God is faith in good. Let the heathen rage, let the rebels succeed, let tyranny seem to triumph, let our hearts be wrung with bitterest disappointment and sorrow, we have within us a sure word of prophecy, to which we can continually resort till the day dawn and the day-star arise in our hearts.

Such are some of the words which God speaks to the human race by the mouth of his holy prophets who have been since the world began. Not in Judæa alone, therefore, not in Palestine alone, are God's prophets found, but in all lands, and in all times, where the reason, the conscience, and the heart of man exist. These are always inspired to prophesy. The inspiration may be of a higher or a lower order; from that of Baalam, the son of Beor, to that of Jesus of Nazareth. But, differing in degree, it is one in nature: it is always the inspiration which flows from God into the soul which opens itself to him.

IV.

STEPS OF BELIEF.

John iv. 42: "NOW WE BELIEVE, NOT BECAUSE OF THY SAYING; FOR WE HAVE HEARD HIM OURSELVES, AND KNOW THAT THIS IS INDEED THE CHRIST, THE SAVIOUR OF THE WORLD."

THE woman went out of the city that morning, one of the most forlorn creatures of earth. She was despised by her neighbors, and she knew that they had a right to despise her. She was living with a man who was not her husband: she had been false to others, or had been abandoned by them. Affection, pure affection, was dead in her heart. It was ulcerated by sin, remorse, and shame. She was bitter toward men, defiant toward God. She believed that men had been unjust to her; that God had not given her a fair chance.

So she went out that morning from the ancient city of her fathers, situated in the beautiful and sequestered glen at the base of Gerizim. Above her head rose the great cliffs, whose gray rocks were half hidden in the masses of foliage, and whose purple shadows rested on the valley through which she passed. The blessings of Gerizim had passed her by: the curses of Ebal had fallen on her forlorn head.

So she followed the foot-path, her water-urn on her head, till she saw before her the old stones surrounding the Well of Jacob. On one of them a man was sitting; and she knew him, by his dress, to be a Jew.

One would think that two nations who differed from all the world, and were despised by all the world, would stand by each other. One would think that races having the same blood, speaking almost the same language, having nearly the same sacred books, both followers of Moses, both worshipping the same God, would have some sympathy for each other. But such is not human nature. We can pardon those who differ widely from us, — not those who almost agree with us. "Since they almost agree, why not quite?" we say. The Catholic king could not pardon the man whom he thought a Jansenist; but when he found he was not that, but simply an atheist, not believing in any God at all, he gave him an office.

Besides, the men or the race who are despised like to find something lower than themselves to despise in turn. The scorn of mankind fell on the Jew. He turned against the Samaritan with a still greater contempt. Juvenal, the Roman poet, tells us, in his sharp, stinging verse, what people in his time thought of Jews. "He is the son of a Jew," says he: "so the poor fellow has been taught to worship clouds, and to consider it as bad to eat pork as to eat a man. He obeys what Moses has written in his mystical book, and makes the seventh day one of pure laziness." And so a wiser man than Juvenal, Tacitus, says that the Jews "nourish a sullen and inveterate hatred against mankind: their ceremonies are gloomy rites, full of absurd enthusiasm, — rueful, mean, and sordid."

The Jews were thus thought by the Romans to be the lowest of mankind: they thought the Samaritans infinitely lower than themselves. The Samaritans despised and scorned the woman who went on that eventful morning, her heart full of rage and despair, to the sacred ancient well. There she saw a Jew. She went to the open mouth; did not look at him as she lowered her urn into the deep well, and drew it up, ready to meet his contempt with cold indifference; when he quietly asked her for water: "Give me to drink."

Then she turned, and looked at him. We know what she saw, — not the face which painters have made so familiar to us, the ideal of art; not a face all gentleness and weak humility. No: Jesus never looked so. There beamed upon her from his eyes a light, penetrating to the depth of her mind, — a light of calm insight, of generous good-will, of manly strength; a look which contained in itself the promise of comfort, guidance, support, wherever it fell.

I shall not go through this strange, magnetic, electric, soul-creating, and wonderful conversation with any paraphrase of mine. The woman went from her home that morning in despair: she went back full of new hopes. She had seen with her own eyes him, the long expected, long-predicted one. He had read her inmost thought; he had touched her most secret experience; he had filled her heart with a faith in God and herself. "The man who has told me all things that ever I did — is not he the Christ?"

He who shows to us all we ever did, he who reveals to us our own heart, — he comes always in the name of Christ. Unless Jesus comes to us so, he has not really come to us at all. Until he shows us what *we* have done, shows us what our life really is, what we are before God and before the eternal laws of right and truth, we do not see him as the Christ, as our Master and King. We see him, perhaps, as Jesus of Nazareth, — a good man; a wonderful teacher, considering his circumstances and opportunities; but nothing more: not as the Christ, the Son of God, the Saviour of the world.

It is only love and insight which show us all we have ever done. Cold sagacity misjudges us: mere sympathy, feeble good-nature, soothes, but does not essentially help us. But love illuminated by truth, truth warmed through and through by love, — these perform for us the most blessed thing that one human being can do for another. They show us to ourselves: they show us what we really are, what we have been, may be, can be, shall be.

So the words of Jesus found the poor soul in her despair, and, not excusing her past folly and sin, showed her the noblest truth and good, — the living water of God, the pure worship of the Father, transcending all forms and ceremonies, uniting all sects, breaking down all partition-walls; lifting earth to heaven, and bringing down heaven to earth. We hear no more of her: she passes out of the history, never to return. But to-day and for ever the wonderful and sublime words which Jesus spoke to her, the highest words ever uttered by man, the prophecy of a great future, are a part, and for ever a part, of the story of this poor woman.

I wish to indicate here, from the words of the text, the *five steps of belief* through which we pass in our human experience. The men of Samaria began by believing in Jesus in consequence of what the woman told them: they ended by believing in him in consequence of what they themselves had seen. "Now we believe, not because of thy words; for we have heard him ourselves, and believe that this is the Christ, the Saviour of the world."

All our belief begins with the testimony of others. We first believe on testimony. God has made us to rely on the truthfulness of others. The little child believes every thing which is said to him, and so learns fast; because ninety-nine things of a hundred said to him are true. So nations and races take their belief from their ancestors. The man born in China believes in Confucius: if you had been born there, you would have believed in him. Every one born a Turk believes in Mohammed. Had you been born in Italy, you had been a Roman Catholic, to begin with. The vast majority of Trinitarians, Unitarians, Episcopalians, Methodists, Quakers, are so because they were born so. Their parents were so before them. This is a good thing. We begin with a traditional belief, which we accept without a doubt, and in which is always contained a great deal more truth than error. So we all learn something. God has graciously shielded little children from the wretchedness of doubt. But though childhood is good for children, it is not good for men. We must pass from traditional belief to something beyond it.

Now, the fault with many sects and churches is, that they try to make this traditional belief a permanent end. They try to fasten it, and rivet it, and to make any progress out of it impossible. The Roman Catholics do this openly and on principle. They make an idol of their traditions, and refuse to let themselves hear the other side of any question; but, in doing this, they cease to believe in testimony, and believe with their will. This, then, is another way of believing. The first method of belief is belief from testimony; the second, belief from will.

But, to a certain extent, God has made us to believe with our will; and, to a certain extent, it is right to do so. That is, when we have seen a thing to be right and true and good, we ought to cling to it. That truth which, in our calm and sober hours, we have accepted, we ought not to let go, because, in hours of trial and darkness, we cannot see it. Cling to it still, and you will see it again by and by. There is such a thing as loyalty to truth, which is noble.

It is good to stand by the flag in the storm of battle, and when all around seems defeat and disaster. It is good to trust in God, in goodness, in eternal right, in the triumph of truth over evil, when we do not see how, or understand why. So, having believed from testimony, we may go on, and all persons do go on, and believe from will. All persons do and ought to cling for a while to their traditional belief, to the religion of their fathers, to the convictions of their people and land, and not be in any hurry to give them up.

Still we cannot stay for ever in this belief from will. After a while, the intellect claims its rights. We have to think about our belief, and examine it; and then comes in the belief from reason, which is the third step.

Christianity is, no doubt, a reasonable religion. It encourages inquiry. It is not afraid of any amount of investigation. There is no sort of harm, nor any danger, in the freest exercise of thought. To cry out against heresies, and to persecute heretics, is itself unbelief: it is being afraid that the truth cannot stand. Think as much as you will, inquire as freely as you choose; there is no sort of objection to this. It is our duty to examine and criticise and reflect; for how otherwise can truth advance? The church and world can never be one in faith except by free thought. By keeping where we are, we keep apart: by going forward, we may come together. So that it is right to believe from reason, and to believe with a clear and active understanding. This is the third stage of belief.

But these beliefs need to be all merged into another and higher belief; that is, the belief from experience. We must say to Tradition, "Now we believe; not because of thy words; but we have seen him ourselves, and know that this is indeed the Christ, the Saviour of the world." Knowledge only comes through experience. Belief passes into knowledge when we live it. To live the truth we believe, is, therefore, the only way to be certain of it. It is always so.

The certainty we have of our own existence, and of the reality of the outward world, came by experience. It is so long ago, that we have forgotten the process. But the infant, gazing with blind wonder on the world, reaching out its feeble hands to touch the sky, knows nothing certainly. His own being, and that of the world around, are confounded in one. But God puts into his heart an instinctive and irresistible activity; and, in his incessant movements and play, — handling every thing, touching every thing, examining all things, — he is coming to a clear knowledge of the world about him. It is activity, born of desire, which makes us know every thing. Knowledge is thus born of love, through experience.

I know those whom I love, and I know no one else. Those who love me, and no others, know me. Sharp, cold, criticising intellect knows nothing as it ought to know it. Its knowledge is empty; it rings hollow; it is as sounding brass and tinkling cymbal.

You cannot know any thing of nature and the world around you except by loving it. The naturalist is he who takes a joy in nature; who is happy in roving, day by day, through the summer woods, or by the sounding sea; who is not studying in order to become a great man, but because Nature herself is beautiful and dear to him. She haunts him, she attracts him, she fascinates him: he can never leave her. So, at last, every feature of her lovely face grows familiar, and he is full of knowledge, and always running over with it; and you cannot speak to him in the street, but he will tell you something about Nature you did not know before.

And so we know men when we love them. Jesus knew the Samaritan woman because he loved her. He saw in her, beneath all her sin and shame, a heart still capable of true goodness, of pure worship, and sincere adoration. His sympathy brought him close to her soul; and so he knew her as no one else did.

It is not enough to know the outward facts of a man's life in order to know him. His actions are the smallest part of him. Beneath all his acts is the man himself, with his hope, his aim, his purpose, his conviction, his longing, his sin and remorse, his faith and struggle. *This* is the real man; and you can never know him till you have begun to love him; and then he lets you into his inward experience, and you know him well. So, too, we cannot know God till we love God. Jesus teaches us to know God by showing him to us as our Father and Friend. It is by coming to him day by day, and trusting in him, and leaning on his help, and believing in his providence, and conversing with him in throbs and aspirations of prayer, that we come at last to be as certain of God's presence and love as of our own existence.

And so we know Christ by loving him. When we take him as our Master, Friend, Saviour; when we seek to obey his divine law, and help him in his present work in the world, — we come to know him. He who sympathizes with Christ in caring for the poor, the ignorant, the suffering, the sinful, and seeks to help Christ in this his great work, comes to know Christ. In looking for his poor, we find him; in visiting his prisoners, we visit him; in speaking words of truth and love to the sinful and weak, we find ourselves in secret intimacy and sympathy with our Master. We do not know Christ only by reading about his life and miracles, but by having him formed in our hearts, by making ourselves Christs to other souls, by letting his spirit act in and through us, and so leading others to him.

And so, at last, we also know immortality. That ceases to be belief, and becomes knowledge. We begin by believing in a future life on outward evidence: we end by knowing it by instinctive conviction. We experience immortality every time that we live and act from an immortal motive. Whenever we go out of ourselves and our own self-interest, we *are* immortal: we have eternal life abiding in us. The more we live so, the more certain we are of our own immortality and that of others. "He who liveth and believeth in me shall never die," said Jesus. He did not see death: he could not see it any more than the sun can see a shadow. All high, generous motive obliterates death from the pure vision. It is not our duty to think of death: our duty is to think of life. We are to live as though there were no such thing in the world as death, either for ourselves or others. Think of God, of Christ, of duty, of immortality, of love, and you shall realize the truth of the saying of Jesus, "I am the resurrection and the life. He that liveth and believeth in me shall never die."

So, my friends, it is our privilege and duty to pass on from the belief of testimony, in which we are born and nursed, to the belief of experience and personal conviction. Step by step, life leads us on, and deepens every conviction, changing opinion into knowledge. Doubts and fears vanish one by one; uncertainty and scepticism pass away. So the storm of yesterday, which darkened all the sky with a triple canopy of clouds, and threatened us with a rainy Sunday, has gone by, and left a serene, cloudless heaven. And so, too, shall this awful hurricane of war, which has burst upon our land, also pass by, leaving us a clearer atmosphere than before, and a purer air to breathe; leaving us righteousness in the place of iniquity; true peace instead of a false one; real union instead of hollow compromises; in place of a nation hampered and fettered by evil institutions, a great and noble Christian republic, with its face lifted to the future, and the rising sun of coming centuries of human progress glowing around its brow as an immortal halo of glory.

V.

THE THORN IN THE FLESH.

2 Cor. xii. 7: "THERE WAS GIVEN TO ME A THORN IN THE FLESH, THE MESSENGER OF SATAN, TO BUFFET ME, LEST I SHOULD BE EXALTED ABOVE MEASURE."

WHAT this "thorn in the flesh" was, no one knows. There has been no end to conjecture; but it leads to nothing. All we know is, that something in his soul, which he compares to a thorn sticking in the flesh, pained him and weakened him. Like a thorn in the flesh, it was a foreign substance introduced into his soul and life. Like a thorn in the flesh, it often gave him intense pain. Like a thorn in the flesh, it disabled him, in some way or at some times, from doing his work. Thus much we know: also we know that he earnestly prayed three times, but without any success, hoping to get rid of his trouble; and that he found, at last, that the trouble was good; that, when humbled, he was exalted, when weak strong, according to the everlasting Christian paradox. From all this we may learn some useful lessons.

For, first, we all have something which goes with us, stays by us, hides itself away in our soul, and which is like a thorn in the flesh. It is a foreign substance; something unnatural, by no means a part of our true lives. It is something which opposes our best progress, interferes with our sincerest efforts to do right; a messenger of Satan, therefore; and yet it is somehow sent by God,—"given us," says the text; and which God finds to be for our good, and refuses to take away. It is something which makes us weak, yet strong in our weakness; which humbles us, yet gives the very humility we want in order to rise.

Let us consider some of these thorns.

Sickness is a thorn. Some fine brain, like Pascal's or Robert Hall's or Buckminster's, has a fibre which makes discord; and the whole economy of thought stands still. Some spirit ready to devote itself to great duties, a young man just entering the ministry of Christ, a noble woman like Mrs. Browning, an inspired teacher of the race like Dr. Channing, a child of genius like Mozart or Raffaelle, from the weakness of an ill-assorted body, die at the beginning of their work, or are hampered and checked all the way through by the poor body. The sweet bells of their soul make no adequate music, but are jangled, out of tune, and harsh; or else they fall into silence just as the awakened world listens for their wide-rolling melodies. A son, longing to support his widowed mother; a daughter, perfectly trained in intellect and heart to help and bless those who need her care,—is smitten into palsied helplessness by some inexorable disease. "How mysterious the Providence," we say, "that these should be thus arrested! while some hard, tyrannical husband, some stolid, selfish worldling, some reckless spendthrift and swindler, says, 'What's the use of anybody's being sick? *I* never knew a sick day in my life.'" The man who uses his health as a despot is healthy: the man who would use it for boundless service to his race has it not. Legree's nerves, muscles, and sinews are all perfect; but the angelic Eva fades before the moth. So that this pathetic minor crosses our ears in all the world's music: this is the sad refrain of all our poetry, singing evermore, —

She was of this world, where the things most sweet
Pass soonest away;
And Rose met the fate which other roses meet, —
To bloom for a day.

Another thorn in the flesh is the unexpressed soul. It is homeliness, awkwardness, inability to express one's self easily and adequately. How many poor souls, full of noble sentiments and ideas, are hemmed in and shut up by these barriers! They sit like the prince in the "Arabian Nights," with half his body black marble. Young people feel this thorn very keenly. They cannot pass for what they are worth, they cannot have what they have a right to have, just because the cruel step-dame, Nature, has not loosened their tongue, — has put on them a strait-jacket of *mauvaise honte*, — has given them a poor, homely face or figure. It is a perpetual thorn in the flesh, and a barrier to their usefulness. The beautiful soul is put into the homely body, and sees some very commonplace soul dwelling hard by in a lovely, all-attracting form. From these lips, the magic of grace makes the silliest sophism charming: in those, the repelling austerity of manner deprives the purest truth of its power.

Then there is another thorn, worse than this,—the black drop of blood which has got mingled in our circulation from some alien source. Inherited depravity, the sin of the parent visited upon the child by some mysterious but inevitable law of descent, makes us struggle, all our lives through, against a messenger of Satan in our own bosom. If Satan could send his angel into the soul of Paul, and Paul could not get rid of him, we need not wonder that these angels of darkness come to buffet us. These thorns stick fast in the fibres of the mind and heart. Pity those who thus suffer,—pity, and do not blame. Perhaps you meet every day an overbearing, dogmatical person, who, you are sure, is perfectly satisfied with himself, and who despises every one else. You feel yourself justified in despising him. But this very man is perfectly conscious of his faults. He struggles against them; he hates himself for them. Though bearing so brave a face outwardly, he is inwardly dissatisfied with himself as much as you are with him. Pity him, therefore. And here is one who is sharp, cynical, bitter, critical, fault-finding. It is in his blood to be so. He finds fault all day with himself for being so. Cannot we try to pity him, instead of hating him? And here is a fretful person, or a morose person, or a grumbling person. You cannot avoid him more than he would like to avoid himself. What faults of temper are sticking in us like thorns! What habits of thought, of feeling, of speech, for which we abhor ourselves the moment we have spoken the sharp word, done the hasty act, indulged the unworthy desire! How we cry to God to help us out of this misery! and cry, as it seems, in vain.

"Where Sin's red dragons lie in caverns deep,
And glare with stony eyes that never sleep,
And o'er the heavenly fruit strict ward do keep,—

There our poor hearts, long struggling to get free,
Torn by the strife, in painful agony
Cry out, 'O God, my God, deliver me!'"

Sometimes the thorn seems to be, not in ourselves, but in our circumstances. How happy we might have been, how good we might have been, but for this unfortunate lot! Poverty is the weight which rests on some lives. They feel that their best powers are wasted in a mere struggle for existence. They have no leisure for improvement,—no time for thought, for good society, for hopeful and humane endeavor. Poverty is the angel of Satan sent to buffet them. They grow bitter against their condition, they rebel against the hardship of their lot. Or else there is a disappointed hope, a chamber of the heart closed and barred, and left without a tenant. Oh, if that dear child had lived; if that friend had not gone, whose soul lifted ours into another world,

— how different we should have been! We hug our bereavement, with bitter determination not to be comforted. We press the thorn into our heart. There is a happy street for us in the world above, where we may meet our lost friend again; but no happy street shall we ever find here.

What deeper thorn in the heart than the sense of an irreparable loss? But within these two years we have seen the best blood of the land, the purest and noblest children born in our Northern homes, go out to die, with their fathers' blessing and their mothers' kiss. These children, for whose coming God prepared this fair land, that they might open their infant eyes on the beauty of its hills and valleys, its lakes and forests; for whose childhood, past generations of thinkers, from Plato and Aristotle down to Pestalozzi and Horace Mann, have been providing methods of education, — these young men, purified in the calm atmosphere of virtuous homes, developed by the training and discipline of schools, of study, of books, of travel, the costly fruit of the latest century and the most advanced race, go to die in a field of unavailing slaughter. Well, I visit their mothers or sisters, their fathers or brothers, when the fatal news arrives. I go with fear, dreading to meet such a great and hopeless anguish. I find heaven there. I find the peace of God in their souls. It is the happiest place in the city to go to. I cannot bear to leave such a divine atmosphere. I go to carry sympathy, and perhaps words of comfort; but I receive instead inspiration, and the influences of angelic joy. Together with the deep sense of bereavement, the thorn penetrating the depth of the soul, the lethal arrow not to be taken from the heart while the heart beats, there is this strange serenity, sent down direct from God. And the boy, falling on the battle-field, renews all the tales of Greek and Roman heroism. We can burn our "Plutarch." We do not need to read hereafter the stories of Themistocles, of Aristides, or Leonidas. These Boston children, your brothers and sons, are to be spoken of in history for ever, and are to be the illuminating lights of the coming age. This is the thorn in the flesh, — deep as death, but changing into the most divine beauty and life for all time.

The old painters delighted in taking for their subject the martyrdom of St. Sebastian; perhaps because it gave them an opportunity of painting a beautiful manly figure, who in Christian art corresponds to the Antinous in Greek sculpture; but also, I think, because it gave them the occasion to attempt that high problem of artistic genius, — the representation of outward suffering passing into a deep inward peace and joy. This youthful form, all aglow with life and health, with no saintly emaciation, is bound to a tree, and pierced with arrows, with crimson blood oozing from the wounds; but the face is radiant with celestial joy, to which the suffering gives relief. So on a summer day, a dark background of shadowy hills, with a purple thunder-storm passing behind, relieves and enhances the sunny glory and beauty of the nearer valleys, waving in green luxuriance beneath the blue sky. So the thorn in the flesh becomes the test and sign of the highest life.

But perhaps the worst of these thorns of circumstance are to be found in the ill-assorted home, where the sweetest ties of life become fetters and manacles; the daily cup of blessing becoming a cup of poison, from mutual misunderstanding, or want of adaptation. In a true home, hearts tend to each other in confidence, by a natural attraction, as the pendulum to its centre. The soul expands into fullest development in that genial atmosphere. I think the home shows itself a true one as it takes off restraint from the soul, and removes reserves, while preserving tender thoughtfulness and mutual deference. Love teaches respect without reserve. This is its formula. In the world, and in most places, we are like glaciers, half thawed only, our thought flowing at the rate of a foot a day, — a little brook of utterance dripping from beneath the superincumbent frozen mass. But, in the true home, this glacier is melted in the summer influence of love and confidence, and flows down into a lovely river; every sharp, self-possessed particle turning into a liquid drop of perfect adaptation. This is the joy of society, — entire freedom, born of entire confidence in one another. But how often does it happen otherwise! The soul, fluent abroad, freezes at home. There is no confidence between parents and children. The father thinks it his duty to be stern and unsympathizing: the sons carry elsewhere their confidence. Brothers and sisters are ignorant of each other's interests. The husband is a tyrant, the wife a slave. He, possibly, is a genteel, courteous tyrant; she, doubtless, a luxuriously cared-for slave. Or he is intemperate, and a brute; she a patient angel, working herself into her grave to support the children whom he neglects. Or perhaps it is the reverse, — he patiently toiling to support the home, and she idly wasting in careless dissipation the fruits of his labor. This is the deepest thorn in the flesh; this "the objection" (as Jeremy Taylor says) "which lies in one's bosom."

What soul is there that does not have its thorn? What heart that does not know its own bitterness? What society, however graceful, beautiful, where conversation flows in brilliant sweeping floods of eloquence, or flashes in ripples and waterfalls, or moves calm and serene, —

> "A river of thought, that, with delight,
> Divides the plain," —

that has not its jealousies, its *ennui*, its weary sense of emptiness, and often envies the day-laborer his healthy work? What dark, locked-up chambers of mystery are in every household, every heart! But these implacable demons, sent, as it seems, from hell below to torture us, turn to smiling angels when we cast our care on God, and surrender our will to his will. They purify the soul; they deepen it; they make life more serious, earnest, joyful.

We find, by our text, that there are some limitations to the effectual fervent prayer of the righteous man. Prayer avails much, but does not remove these thorns. Three times Paul besought the Lord to remove his, not because of its anguish, but because it deprived him of power to do his work; but God said to his soul, "No." It was revealed to him that he needed this thorn to humble him, and to make him lean more wholly on God's truth and love. "My strength is made perfect in thy weakness." The strong, determined energy of the apostle would have become arrogant self-reliance but for this thorn. Its sting cast him more wholly on God.

And so it may always be with us. If you have any trial which seems intolerable, pray, — pray that it be relieved or changed. There is no harm in that. We may pray for any thing, not wrong in itself, with perfect freedom, if we do not pray selfishly. One disabled from duty by sickness may pray for health, that he may do his work; or one hemmed in by internal impediments may pray for utterance, that he may serve better the truth and the right. Or, if we have a besetting sin, we may pray to be delivered from it, in order to serve God and man, and not be ourselves Satans to mislead and destroy. But the answer to the prayer may be, as it was to Paul, not the removal of the thorn, but, instead, a growing insight into its meaning and value. The voice of God in our soul may show us, as we look up to him, that his strength is enough to enable us to bear it.

The sickness may be not to death, but to life. We, in our sickness, may do more than in our health. Our poverty, which seems such a manacle, may unite us in deeper sympathy with our race, and throw us more wholly on God. The rich man is tempted to lean on his mortgages and stocks: but the poor man is induced to lean daily on God for daily bread; and, as it comes day by day, his trust grows cheerful and confident. The man who trusts in his investments is frightened with every financial panic: the man who trusts in God is always brave. And so it often happens, that the man of millions, unless he keeps up his courage by giving away freely, is afraid of poverty; but the man who has nothing but God is afraid of nothing, and so possesses all things.

We pray against our besetting sin. But God may answer this prayer, not by removing the temptation, but by giving us more confidence in him, more sense of his pardoning love in Christ, more of a sentiment of steadfast reliance, more of habitual living with God. Instead of removing the temptation, he comes and dwells with us. God and Christ make their abode by our side. "Most gladly, therefore, we glory in our infirmities, that the peace of Christ may rest upon us." God does not take away the Red Sea, nor the wilderness, nor Jordan, but goes with us through them all, — a cloud by day, a pillar of fire by night. Nothing brings us so near to God as the sense of our spiritual and moral needs.

According to one theory of life, the true progress

of man consists in removing all obstacles, making all conditions harmonious, all work attractive, all relations agreeable and suitable. Following out this theory, we strive to break away from all inharmonious relations. But the poor Irish woman, who clings to her brutal, drunken husband, and says, "He was good, ma'am, once, and he's my husband," can teach these philosophers a lesson. I do not say that she is right, or that they are wrong; but I do say, that true human progress often consists rather in taking the good of our position, and bearing its evils, than in breaking away from inharmonious relations. The world advances through shadow as well as through sunshine. The heart grows great and noble by manfully meeting and bearing the great trials of life. When we are weak, then we are strong.

This nation of ours, amid all its prosperity, has had its thorn in the flesh. The institution of negro slavery in the United States has been the one thorn in our destiny, the one difficulty of our situation. All good men have sought for years, and prayed, that this thorn might be removed. We have tried to get rid of it by colonization, by emancipation, by debate, and all varied efforts, — in vain. God has left this thorn in the flesh of the nation to sting it into humility, and reliance on him; and now it has humbled us indeed. It has destroyed for a time our Union, taken away our prosperity, involved the present in doubts and the future in darkness, and caused all Europe to shake its head at us in derision. But this humiliation the country needed; and this thorn is allowed to remain, till we learn to lean on God and truth, on justice and humanity, not on our own strength, energy, wealth, and abundant power. Nothing else, perhaps, could have taken out of the national mind that egregious vanity and self-esteem which was growing more colossal every year. We seemed to suppose that it was our own energy and ability which had prepared for us the continent. We took credit to ourselves for the richness of our land, the extent of our soil, the treasures of minerals and vegetables which we possessed. We felt a little proud because our rivers were so long, and our States so large. As for our prosperity, we attributed it wholly to our own enterprise and talent. No wonder that the Old World listened to us with some disgust; and so now, in our trial, we do not obtain its whole sympathy. It might have had sympathy with our cause, if not with us. But better for us, perhaps, to learn to stand alone, and fight our own way back to union and peace.

"Leaves fall; but, lo, the young buds peep!
Flowers die; but still their seed shall bloom.
From death the quick young life will leap,
Now Spring has come to touch the tomb.
The splendid shiver of brave blood
Is thrilling through our country now;
And she, who in old times withstood
The tyrant, lifts again her brow.
God's precious charge we sternly keep
Unto the final victory:
With freedom we will live, or sleep
With our great dead who set us free.
God forget us, when we forget
To keep the old flag flying yet!"

VI.

FAITHFUL OVER A FEW THINGS.

Matt. xxv. 21: "FAITHFUL OVER A FEW THINGS."

IT is a peculiarity of Christianity to lay stress on little things. It cares more for quality than for quantity. One man "may bestow all his goods to feed the poor;" and yet the gospel shall pronounce him devoid of love to his neighbor, and of less account than the poor widow who puts her two mites into the treasury of God. It is not, "How much have you done?" but, "In what spirit have you acted?" not, "How long?" but, "How well?"

Every man's life has a law which governs it. All that he does unconsciously, he does according to that law. Is his ruling motive ambition, pleasure, conscience, love of truth, love of God? Then that ruling motive colors every act; and every word he utters in his most careless hours partakes of that general determination. And therefore for every idle word shall he give an account, because his idle words are all polarized by the central magnetism which governs his soul. In the English marine, it is said, there is a thread of scarlet which is woven into all the cordage, from the largest cable to the smallest line. It is the mark of government property. So a line of red runs through all of our thoughts, words, feelings, and actions. It is the stamp of our character upon each one of them. So Shakspeare never introduces on the stage a character that is not qualified by an individuality. If he speaks a second time in the play, you may know that it is the same person who spoke before.

If there is such a law of unity pervading our lives, some of us are not very well aware of it. We think that we can act one way in small things, another way in great ones: that in small matters we are not under law, but that in great things we are. So we come to despise or to neglect small matters. We trifle with truth in little things, with honesty in little things, with the law of reverence or of love in little things.

But what is the meaning of the word "integrity"? It means thoroughness, entireness; putting the same quality of soul into every thing, great and small. No one is a man of integrity who does not do every thing with the same undeviating honesty, the same unbending principle. The man of real integrity puts the whole energy of conscience, faith, love, into the smallest act as into the greatest. So the steam-engine in a factory exerts the same tremendous power to cut in two an iron bar, or to stick a pin into a card.

Christianity does not allow us to trifle with any thing. There is nothing trivial to the illuminated eye and heart of faith. He who says to his brother, "Thou fool!" is in danger of hell-fire. He is, in fact, already in hell-fire; for the feeling of contempt for his brother, the scorn and disdain which can thus reject from its sympathy a fellow-man, is itself the spirit of the pit.

"He who hateth his brother," says the apostle, "is a murderer." His hate may vent itself in no deadly act, in no word of injury: but the hatred in the heart is murderous; it is tending that way. It is the arc of the curve, the return of which is deadly.

A similar error leads us often to say, "How much good I would do with my money, if I were as rich as this man or the other!" How much good do you do *now* with what you have? "Oh! if I had only time, what would I not learn and do!" says another. How do you spend the time *you have?* If you do not spend well the small time you have to spend, the little money you have to use, why do you think you would do better with more? The astronomer turns his glass to the heavens, and fixes three little points of the comet's course, and so finds a small arc of its curve. From that arc he can predict the whole. And so there may be an angel looking down this moment on you and me, seeing what we have done yesterday, the day before yesterday, and to-day; and, from these three positions of our soul, he may infer the path in which we are moving,—inward toward the sun of life and light, or outward into darkness, coldness, and death.

Here is a man who is a petty tyrant. He bullies the weak, he dictates to the submissive. If he is a coarse and ignorant man, he beats his wife: if he is a refined and educated man, he civilly and politely tyrannizes over her. If he is a master, he is harsh to his dependants; if a lawyer, he badgers the witnesses, particularly if they are women and children. Now, because this man happens to live in a free State, is he any the less a slaveholder? Because he has no opportunity to torment whole communities, is he any the less a Nero? Here is another man, who cannot bear to be contradicted in argument, and gets angry with his opponent when he cannot convince him. In him dwells the spirit of a Dominic or a Torquemada. Give him the power, and he would straightway put on the rack a man who differed from him. Here is another, who indulges his appetites, his passions, his desires, a little way, and then stops short of debauchery and intemperance, because he is afraid of the consequences. In his heart he is nevertheless guilty of the acts which his hand may never perform.

I once heard of a colored preacher, who used this plain but striking image in a sermon: "You think, my brethren, that you can go a little way out of God's road into the Devil's field, and not be caught, provided you do not go too far. But the Devil is not such a fool, when he spreads his nets and sets his traps for you, to put them away in the middle of his field. No: he puts them *close to the road:* so, if you mean to go a great way or only a little way, he is sure to have you in either case." The illustration was homely; but the doctrine is sound.

Perhaps we can best see how the moral difference between men consists in a quality of conviction and purpose, running into all they do, by comparing together different persons in the same walk or pursuit.

I can conceive that there may be two men, equally active, laborious, and eminent, in the same profession or trade; and one shall be doing a great work by his occupation, while the other shall be really doing very little. I may illustrate this by describing two law yers, two physicians, two merchants, and two clergymen.

There are two lawyers, Counsellor A. and Counsellor B. Counsellor A. studied law, believing human law to be founded on divine law; to be an attempt to organize justice, truth, and right in human institutions. He considers it his business as a lawyer to protect the weak, to restrain the injustice of the powerful, to search out the truth in intricate and dark cases, so that the innocent may be proved innocent, and the guilty punished. He trains his intellect to be acute, penetrating, comprehensive, and full of resource, in order to hunt the flying footsteps of truth, and pour light into the tangled maze of error and sophistry. With the authority of insight, he makes peace between litigants, by showing each where he is in error; and he stands among men as a judge, though he may not have the title or the office. He does a great work for society; and, when he dies, Justice and Truth weep over his grave; for, with him, God's law always reigned supreme.

Meantime Counsellor B. is a different sort of a man. He is a great lawyer too. He entered his profession to make money, to get influence, to acquire reputation; and he has got them all three. He regards all laws as equally arbitrary and accidental, resting on no basis of absolute justice; and therefore all, good or bad, to be equally deserving of respect. His business, as a lawyer, is to get his case. He will use any argument by which any jury-man can be persuaded. If he cannot convince, he will confuse; if he cannot prove, he will puzzle; if he has no arguments, he has plenty of sophisms. He is a great orb, raying out darkness. Such a man may work very hard all his life, and yet die at last, having done no real work for mankind.

Then there are two physicians, Dr. C. and Dr. D. Dr. C. feels a strong sympathy for human suffering, and a desire to alleviate it. He believes that it is God who has given wonderful healing properties to plants and minerals; and he studies patiently and carefully symptoms and remedies. Every case is sacred to him. The sickness of the beggar has his attention, like that of the prince. He is humble enough and wise enough to admit that he does not know every thing. He confesses his ignorance, and is ready to receive light. He does not go blindly and dogmatically according to his theory, but patiently interrogates Nature, and sits at her feet waiting. He also asks God's blessing on all that he undertakes, and enters his patient's chamber with prayer. What a great work does not such a man do in the world! He carries health of mind as well as of body to a thousand homes; and to such a one we may apply the words of the poet: —

"I have lain on the sick man's bed,
Watching for hours for the leech's tread,
As if I deemed that his presence alone
Had power to bid my pain begone;
I have listed his words of comfort given,
As if to oracles from heaven;
I have counted his steps from my chamber-door,
And blest them when they were heard no more."

But Dr. D. is of another school. He is a pedant, and prescribes according to some little theory. He is conceited and vain, — vain of his own science, vain of his profession and clique. Very bitter is he against innovators and interlopers. He had rather a man should die under the regular practice than get well by an irregularity. He has no awe, no fear, no great sense of responsibility, no tender human love. He is not living to be useful, but living to be successful; and his work is not really work, — it is idleness.

And here are two merchants, Mr. E. and F. The first regards commerce as a great means of civilization. The ship which carries goods carries ideas; and the minds of nations are woven together by the winged shuttles which cross and recross the resounding ocean. He enlarges trade by an infusion of generosity and magnanimity. His ships go as missionaries; his sailors are treated as men. Such large and generous views elevate a trade to the dignity of a mission; and the princely-minded merchant does a great work in the world, even though his means be small.

But Mr. F. I shall not describe, because it is not necessary. There are in business too many men who merely ask how they can make money, not how they can do good by their business. We know the result of this, — how mind and heart are narrowed, and how the great business may turn out at last a mere waste of life.

What more blessed work than that of a good clergyman? — one who is modest but manly, whose heart is in his work, whose life is given to making men happier and better. He sees all sides of life. He is welcome in the homes of the rich and the poor, the intelligent and the ignorant. He goes from the wedding to the funeral, from the gay dinner-party to the bedside of the dying. To him men bring their confidences: he sees human nature from the inside as well as the outside. Men of the world think they understand human nature because they know men in their business-hours, — because they know them in the street and shop, in the court-room and on change. But in these places they see just so much of them as the fencer or boxer sees of his opponent. Men meet each other there armed for battle. We see the fighting-side of men at such times. But the minister, if he is a man of sense, no pedant, nor made morbid by a gloomy theology; if he is a man in whom others place confidence as sincere and conscientious, — has opportunities of knowing and helping men which few others can obtain. He has enough to do, enough to learn, enough opportunity for loving and being loved. What more does he want here or anywhere?

But a clergyman who is ambitious for success outside of his work; who is aiming at worldly position or literary renown; who loves pleasure or ease; who is narrow in his views; is a bigot or a partisan,— such a one may do more harm than good. He loves his creed more than truth, he loves his sect more than Christianity, and himself most of all. If the interests of his church are identified with some abuse, then he comes at last to apologize for or defend the abuse. Thus we have seen, in our day, the example of Christian ministers, servants of him who came to break every yoke and let the oppressed go free, defending slavery, and opposing the roused conscience and heart of mankind with arguments drawn from the curse of Noah. They —

> "Torture the pages of the blessed Bible
> To sanction crime and robbery and blood;
> And, in Oppression's hateful service, libel
> Both man and God."

Would it not be better if such men had been shoeblacks or day-laborers, — better for themselves, and better for mankind? Would it not have been better for Christianity if they had never been born?

Some men toil and groan to be orthodox,—to have every point of their creed, and of the creed of everybody else, exactly sound and square. But one single effort to get the truth is more than years of such painful orthodoxy. One hearty, earnest, genuine longing for light, and struggle toward it; one conscientious putting-aside of prejudice, party feeling, private interest, in order to correct our possible errors,— is valued, no doubt, far more by God than a lazy assent to a whole bushel of propositions, be they never so sound and true. Yes, there is more faith in honest doubt than in ever so much cowardly and indolent acquiescence; and, in the day of judgment, I am sure there will be many a man who passed for an infidel here, and was lashed by all the Orthodox pulpits, rostrums, and newspapers for his heresies, who will shine forth as the sun in the kingdom of the Father; for his soul was white, and he kept his mind unspotted from the world.

These things may teach us the grandeur and majesty of our lives. There is nothing common, nothing unclean, in man's being below. Vast principles are involved in all that we do, or omit to do, each day. Every day we rise to a great career, a grand opportunity. Into the smallest word and act we may put the most divine or the most devilish spirit. We may walk every day into heaven as we walk down the street, or we may walk into hell.

According to the state of our soul every day, we shall keep company with devils or with angels. If we allow ourselves to be cold, selfish, hard, and worldly, we shall draw around us a company of evil spirits impure as our own. If we resolve on a noble and generous direction of our life, then angels and archangels, thrones and dominions, holy and pure spirits, angels of light and love, cherubim with many eyes, and seraphim covered with wings from the nearer glory of God's presence, — these will be our companions and inward monitors; for as we are inwardly, in the centre of our being, so shall we be surrounded outwardly.

And now, as we have looked at the working of this law on its dark and threatening side, let us turn the picture, and see it on its bright and encouraging one.

It is not any great amount of work which is required of us in order to be good and faithful servants: it is to be genuine and true in what we do. For example, take the subject of prayer. What does Christ ask of you? To pray a great deal? To pray so many times a day? To pray morning, noon, and night? Not at all. On the contrary, we are told not to be like those who expect to be heard for their much speaking, and who, for a pretence, make long prayers. "When ye pray," says the good and generous Master, — "when ye pray," pray so. Pray more, or pray less, as your needs impel you: he leaves that to you. Only, *when* you pray, pray in spirit and truth. Then be sincere. Ask God for what you really want, not what you think it proper to ask for. Do not say a word till you really can put your heart into it.

Pray in that way, sincerely, earnestly, ever so short a prayer, and that will be the same in the sight of God as if you read from a breviary, like a Catholic priest, so many hours every day. If you are faithful in the least, you will be faithful in much. If, when you *do* pray, you pray with the heart, and from the heart, you will then have the spirit of prayer; which is the main thing. If you can say once, from the heart, "God be merciful to me, a sinner!" you have in you the same spirit of penitence, the same essential humility, which was in the soul of Peter when he repented and was forgiven. Divine pardon you have tasted in that moment, and know its sweetness. You are in unison with the lowliest and loftiest saints who sing praises to God nearest the throne.

So, if you are faithful in the smallest duty when tempted to do wrong, you have in you the spirit of all virtue. The smallest child who resists a temptation to disobey is in the same sphere of spiritual life with the heroic souls of confessors and martyrs. It is therefore that we are so moved by all narrations of fidelity, generosity, conscientiousness, no matter how small the sphere of action, or how humble the actor.

We are not obliged, then, to pass our lives in anxiety; in anxious thoughts about our duties, or in gloomy thoughts about our sins. Keep in the generous, kindly, loving spirit of Christ, and then "all things are yours." One throb of love is worth more, in the sight of God, than a life filled with anxious, conscientious, laborious, but hesitating and imperfect obedience. He does not ask *much* of us, but asks that this shall be right.

I saw in Overbeck's studio, in the Cenci Palace in Rome, among many drawings of a somewhat conventional character, some in which he had allowed himself to follow Nature rather than the traditions of his Catholic masters. Among these, there was a sketch of the woman who brought her two mites to the treasury of the temple. A burly Pharisee was pressing forward, ostentatiously emptying his purse into the opening of the great iron-bound chest on the floor. The poor woman, with two darling little children clinging to her, and hiding their faces in her dress, was modestly reaching forward her humble gift. On the other side stood Jesus, with his disciples near him; and half turning, with a smile on his face, he seemed to say, "See there, again, what I have told you so often! It is not the gift, but the spirit in which it is given, that makes its value. She has given more than all of them." Or, as Crashaw has versified it, —

"Two mites, two drops, — but all her house and land, —
Fell from an earnest heart, but trembling hand.
The others' wanton wealth foamed high and brave;
The others cast away: *she* only, *gave.*"

The reward for being faithful in small things is the opportunity of serving God in things of more importance. Such is the divine law. He who has made himself ready, and has put on the wedding-garment, may go into the marriage-feast of truth and love. He who has strengthened, by diligence, his powers of soul here, shall have opportunity, ample and grand, of using them there. This life is, in one sense, all preliminary and provisional. We are in a studio of the great Artist, and he gives us little pieces of clay to model. One may have a better piece than another; but when the Artist comes, and looks at the work, he does not think of the quality and size of the clay, but of the skill, patience, and fidelity displayed on it.

I have heard many definitions of "art;" but I know, on the whole, no better one than this, — to do faithfully what we do. Any thing, done perfectly well, becomes a work of art. Any thing, finished thoroughly in all its details, affects the mind as art; and any high or beautiful work, thoroughly done, becomes fine art. It is the perfect finish of poetry, the exact proportion of architecture, the regular modulation of music, the delicate precision of painting and sculpture, which make them all works of art. Any thing which can be done in a slovenly way, where a little more or less makes no difference, is not art. Shovelling gravel, or digging potatoes, cannot be carried to that precision, and so cannot become works of art.

But life becomes a work of art when it is all directed to one aim, all arranged according to a plan, and all thoroughly executed. Christianity alone can make life high art, because it alone fulfils these conditions. It gives high aim to all our activity, fills it with a noble spirit, and teaches us to execute it thoroughly and perfectly.

It is a grand and glorious truth that is taught in our text. Let us only be genuine, honest, true, in any thing, however small, and we have in that the sign and pledge of an entire consecration of heart and life to God. He who is able to deny himself the least pleasure from a simple sense of duty has in him the spirit which would enable him, if the necessity came, "to give his body to be burned." He who feels the least throb of genuine, sincere love for his fellow-creatures has the spirit born in his soul which would make him equal to all generosities and philanthropies, if these should be called for. He who fulfils his duty well in any sphere is preparing himself for the highest. What does it matter to God what material we work in? We are his journeymen, his apprentices, learning our trade in his workshop of life. He gives one a piece of common wood, another a piece of mahogany, another of ivory, to try his skill on; but he looks not at the material, but sees how we have done our work

So it is. A single act of genuine, sincere, thoroughgoing fidelity raises us at once to a higher plane; and our whole life proceeds henceforth by a nobler, manlier measure. We have seen many instances of this. We have known men make what seemed a hard sacrifice for duty: but, after that hour, their mind, heart, and whole nature were elevated and ennobled; they were henceforth new creatures. A genuine good action has a transforming efficacy on the character. We are not the same men afterwards as before. Pray for the opportunity of doing such an act; pray for the chance of making some great sacrifice; or, rather, find such an opportunity for yourself. Look for it, for it is very nigh thee now; for angel-opportunities come to us every day, and we entertain them unawares.

Sometimes I meet with people weary of life: they think they have nothing to live for, nothing to do in the world, nothing to enjoy; they have lost their interest in every thing, and the world is to them a thrice-told tale. They think they wish to die. They are mistaken: they wish to live. They think they wish to go away from mankind. They are mistaken: they wish to come near them. Those are most weary who do not know this; who have been trying to gain, not to give; who do not taste the bliss of bounty; who do not pour out their life on others, to have it given back again, full measure, pressed down, and running over, into their bosoms.

"Two hands upon the breast,
And labor's done;
Two pale feet crossed in rest,
The race is won;

Two eyes with coin-weights shut,
And all tears cease;
Two lips where grief is mute,
And wrath and peace:
So pray we oftentimes, mourning our lot;
God, in his kindness, answereth not.

Two hands to work addrest,
Aye for his praise;
Two feet, that never rest,
Walking his ways;
Two eyes that look above
Still through all tears;
Two lips that breathe but love,
Nevermore fears:
So cry we afterwards, low on our knees:
Pardon those erring prayers! Father, hear these!"

VII.

MORAL PERSPECTIVES.

Matt. xxiii. 23: "YE PAY TITHE OF MINT, ANISE, AND CUMIN; AND HAVE OMITTED THE WEIGHTER MATTERS OF THE LAW, — JUDGMENT, MERCY, AND FAITH."

WHOEVER has noticed a china plate will have observed, that, with all its economic merits, it has grave defects as a work of art. The chief of these consists in an entire absence of what we call perspective. The house in the foreground is no larger than that in the extreme distance. The water-fowl several miles off are as large as the little children close by. The Chinese have not yet learned to discriminate, in their work, the effects of distance on the size of objects, their forms, and their color. That department of art known as perspective they have not yet attained; but it is a very important one. I recollect that Hogarth has a picture in which he represents some of the absurdities resulting from ignorance of the laws of perspective. A woman, leaning out of a window, is lighting her candle at a fire on a distant hill. A flock of sheep, going up the road, grow larger as they recede; and a horse in the foreground is somewhat smaller than a man a quarter of a mile off.

Now, there are in the world of thought and action certain laws analogous to those in the domain of art, forming what we may call moral perspective. Some men's thoughts, for example, obey these laws; and we call these men sagacious and wise. They recognize what is near and what is distant. They see what is practically important, and what not. A merchant once told me that the secret of success in business was to know what thing ought to be done first, and what should be postponed. You are listening to a trial in a court of law. Obscure and conflicting testimony has confused the case. A great lawyer rises, and all that he does is to call the attention of the court and the jury to the important points in the case. He brings these out in a clear light, and places them in the foreground; letting secondary matters recede into the middle distance, and unimportant ones disappear in the background. He has made a great and successful argument simply by applying the laws of perspective to the matter in hand.

So it is with the great statesman, politician, essayist, or writer in any department of literature. So it is in all practical life. The great general is he who sees the pivotal points of the campaign or the battle; who is strong on these, not confused by the multitude of details. This is always one of the secrets of success.

On the other hand, we feel at once the absence of

intellectual perspective in a book or a man. The book is uninteresting because it has no method, no progress, no leading thoughts, no beginning, middle, or end. The man is tiresome in whose conversation all things are of equal importance; who emphasizes equally the gossip of the street and the crisis of a nation. The minds of some men are like Alpine scenery, where vast mountains, piercing the sky with snowy peaks, alternate with valleys, whose falling waters, green meadows, and luxury of foliage, make marvellous contrasts with the terrific scenes above. But other minds are like the dead level, in which the monotonous outline and stagnant waters make a dreary waste, dull and flat and empty.

These laws of perspective also apply to the moral world, to good and bad, to right and wrong. It is of this that I wish chiefly to speak.

The text tells us that the Pharisees had no perception of moral perspective. They went beyond the Chinese plate, and reached the absurdity of Hogarth's picture. The tithing of mint was not only as important as justice, but *more* so. It hid it entirely. Their picture was all a foreground, filled with ritual observances; and all the higher duties were omitted or forgotten. The little ceremonies in front eclipsed the great duties behind.

One of the most common diseases of the conscience is this want of perspective, — this confusion of duties small and large, near and distant, important and insignificant, primary and subordinate. It is the state which the Apostle Paul defines as a "weak conscience." The Corinthian Christians shrank with horror from the idea of eating meat offered to idols: but they were sectarian, and quarrelled about religious opinions, — one saying, "I am of Paul;" and another, "I am of Apollos." They were exclusive and aristocratic, and could not eat together at the Lord's Supper, but sat apart.

Paul respected the conscientiousness even of a weak conscience, and said, that though an idol was not any thing, yet as long as it seemed to them to be something, and they were conscientious about it, they ought not to eat the meat offered to idols, lest "their weak conscience should be defiled." And so, now, people observe days and times, and consider it a sin to take a walk on Sunday, or for little children to enjoy themselves. They think it a very dangerous thing to doubt concerning the Trinity, or to question total depravity, but no sin at all to buy and sell little children, to tear husbands from wives, and keep back the hire of the laborer who has reaped their fields. It is no sin, they think, to be grasping and sharp and mean in business; no sin to be censorious and bitter against all out of their own church and party; but a dreadful sin to go to a church which does not hold the opinions they happen to believe themselves, or to think they believe.

A great many people are unnecessarily tormented because they cannot have technical evidence of their conversion. They torment others in the same way.

If they would only be contented with Scripture evidence, how happy they would be! Here are some of the tests of true religion laid down in the New Testament: —

"We know that we have passed from death to life, because we love the brethren."

"If any man believe that Jesus is the Christ, God dwells in him, and he in God."

"He that loveth is born of God."

"He that dwelleth in love, dwelleth in God, and God in him."

"If we confess our sins, he is faithful and just to forgive us our sins, and to cleanse us from all unrighteousness."

Now, is it not strange, that, with such passages as these before their eyes, people shall still insist that to be baptized, or not to be, makes the difference between salvation and damnation? Thus speaks Frederick W. Robertson, the wise Church-of-England minister, concerning this Church-of-England superstition: "The superstitious mother baptizes her child in haste, because, though she does not precisely know what the mystic effect of baptism is, she thinks it best to be on the safer side, lest her child should die, and its eternity should be decided by the omission. And we go to preach to the Heathen, while there are men and women in our Christian England so bewildered with systems and sermons, so profoundly in the dark respecting the Father of our Lord Jesus Christ, so utterly unable to repose in Eternal Love and Justice, that they must guard their child *from* him by a ceremony, and have the shadow of a shade of doubt, whether or not, for omission of theirs, that child's Creator and Father may curse its soul for all eternity."

One English writer, who encourages this superstition, is Miss Yonge, the author of many excellent books for children and young people. Her books are almost always sensible, wise, and Christian; but she fails in this point of moral perspective. She represents some very little things as though they were very large. She sometimes intimates that it is a terrible thing for an unbaptized child to die; thus making of baptism a magical charm by which to save the child's soul from God. She does not exactly say that an unbaptized child will be lost; but she seems afraid that it may be so. She thus encourages a heathenish superstition, which neither Christ nor the Bible authorize. The Bible speaks of the "washing of regeneration, and renewing of the Holy Ghost." It is regeneration which washes us, not washing which regenerates us. The object of Christian baptism is this life, and not the other. Baptism is an introduction into the Christian Church in this world, not a preparation for the next. Miss Yonge, therefore, reverses the true view of baptism; and, in the same way, she represents the rite of confirmation as so important, that the neglect of it fills her young people with great terror.

A little child was dying of a cruel disease, whose

only comfort was in listening to reading. They were reading to her out of a book called "Ministering Children." Her father came in, and proposed to read to her. She said, "I don't wish to hear that book, papa: take the other one on the shelf." Afterward, her cousin said to her, "Why did you not wish to hear more out of that book? Why did you ask your father to read from the one you had already finished?" — "Because," said the dear child, "it made papa feel badly to read in that one: so I asked him to read from the other."

Now, I should like to ask Miss Yonge, whether, if this child, who forgot her own suffering to spare her father a pang of grief, — whether, if this angelic child should die without being baptized, God would not receive her? That generous love in her little patient heart would make her dearer, in my opinion, to the heart of the Saviour, than if she had been baptized by the Archbishop of Canterbury, and confirmed by the Pope of Rome.

The other day, I read an account of a lady who went to Corinth to look for her husband, after the great battle there. Searching, she found his body. "Now," says the narrator, "if I were writing a romance, if this were a sentimental story, I should describe how she sat bathed in tears from morning till evening, unconscious of every thing. But it is better than a romance: it is a noble reality. So the fact was, that, after shedding some natural tears, she turned from the dead body of her husband to the wounded soldiers of his company; and, instead of indulging sentimental sorrow, she found comfort, for two long days, in taking care of the wounded and dying."

But suppose that this lady had never passed through any technical conversion: could she possibly have any better evidence of God's love in her soul than that which helped her to leave her own sorrows to care for others' woe? God's life was in her heart *then*, if never before or after. She was born again at that time, because she loved the brethren.

Yet many people forget all that Christ has said of obedience, humility, and love being the essence of religion, and place this in some opinion, some ceremony, belonging to some church, adhering to some religious usages. To Jesus, life, a holy life, is the one thing needful. To them, profession, ritual, emotion, conformity, are much higher.

What shall we say of such persons? Only this: That their consciences are weak consciences, and have no sense of spiritual perspective. If their opinions concerning religion and morals were put into a picture, it would be like the picture on a Chinese plate.

Much harm is done in these ways. Much harm also is done by a confusion of great and small in regard to common duties and common faults. People make sins out of mistakes, and grave crimes out of pardonable errors. Children are taught, that to break a dish is as wrong as to tell a lie, by the indignation the mother shows when that accident occurs. No doubt, it is inconvenient to you to have your best cup or glass dropped and broken; but, if you show a high indignation at what is at worst carelessness, what will you do when your child commits a serious offence? Your child has torn its clothes, or soiled them in playing in the dirt. Now, this is, no doubt, a bad thing for *you* who have to mend them; but you have no right to treat it with the same gravity as though it were an act of cruelty, falsehood, or selfishness. You sophisticate your child's conscience in doing so. Or, if the child's sense of justice is too clear to be sophisticated, then you destroy your own influence. Treat such things as misfortunes, not as sins. Let them have their evil consequences if you choose. Say to the child, "How sorry I am that you have torn your frock! Now, I don't know what we shall do. I am afraid you cannot go to the picnic." But do not say, "Oh, what a naughty child! How *could* you do it? You shall not go to the picnic."

We are very apt to make great sins out of what only happens to be troublesome to ourselves. Remember, when you do this, that you are confusing the moral sense. Grave, austere reproach and solemn rebuke are precious, and should be kept for great occasions. Do not waste them on small matters. They ought not to be used in a family or in a school more than a few times in a year. By applying them every day, we destroy their effect. Treat small matters lightly, troublesome mistakes cheerfully; and use stern and severe reproach and censure only for real sins. Then your censure will be remembered as long as your child lives.

One of the great advantages of true religion is, that it gives this perspective to life. A religious person, laying all stress on the essential vital facts of the soul, is able to look with proper allowance and charity on the smaller faults of men. To him there is "one thing needful;" one only. To him all virtue, all duty, is briefly comprehended in this one thing, — LOVE. As, by a law of perspective, all the lines of the picture perpendicular to its surface have the same vanishing-point; so all the lines of duty, being parallel, converge to this point of love, which is always before the Christian eye; and are all fulfilled in that. This constant conviction of the supremacy of love gives unity to thought and life, — gives a tone of united earnestness and charity to all judgments and all appeals.

I was reading, this week, a recent book by a very intelligent Englishman, Arthur Helps; in which I noticed the want of moral perspective in his judgment of the present American crisis. He says that the English would have sympathized with the Union in its present distress, had it not been that "Americans were such a boastful people." And so, because we have this fault, which is offensive to the good taste of our polished English neighbors, they cannot take any interest in a great struggle on which is staked the triumph of slavery or of freedom, the salvation or the destruction of a great Republic! Because Americans boast, and chew tobacco, and eat with their knives, therefore the English will not care for the defeat or the triumph of right, liberty, and humanity! Is not this tithing mint, and forgetting justice?

In the same way, among ourselves, in the struggle of great principles, in the conflict of mighty ideas, men allow themselves to take one side or the other because of some petty partiality or prejudice. "This man is distasteful to me: so I will not stand by him in contending for the right." "That man is, I think, influenced by personal ambition or interest: therefore I will not help him to fight the battle for truth and justice." "These people are not to my taste: so, though God is with them, I will go against them." God, fortunately, is not so fastidious; and he stands by his oppressed, his poor, his despised ones, though they may be Jews defiled with leprosy, or Africans with big lips and crooked legs.

All great souls rise above this petty Chinese narrowness. Before all noble minds, every thing in the picture of life assumes its proper proportions. Primary duties, mighty truths, the master-lights of our being, the essential vital essences of things, come forward into the foreground, and occupy the chief and constant interest. Back into the middle distance fall the minor interests and lesser duties; and into the shadowy background, where the soft aerial tints melt the outlines into ineffable beauty, and blend sky and land in one sweet flood of happy light, pass all the remoter interests of life; on to the distant horizon-line, where heaven and earth become one. This is true greatness of soul, — to recognize the relative proportions of all truths, all duties, and all interests. When we meet persons thinking so, in whatever society or condition of culture, we feel respect for them. We draw near to them. They do us good. In all that they say, we feel the presence of serious things. We see that their life is earnest. They talk of what is important. They do not gossip about trifles, or dispute about insignificant matters. They make life seem worth living; they add interest to every hour. As they speak, our heart burns within us; and, though they may not talk in sanctimonious phrase of religious subjects, we feel the profound religion which has its home in their souls; and so they bring us nearer to God, to immortality, and to heaven.

Nearer to heaven; for heaven, too, has its perspective laws. To us, living in a little point of time, on a little spot of space, heavenly things, as well as earthly things, must be seen, not as they really are, but as the laws of optics require. The heavens bend around us, and touch the earth, — a dome of deep azure by day, a dome of stars by night. But this is only appearance. The heavens everywhere extend into infinite distances, unbent and uniform. Before a north-east storm, the clouds form themselves into great fan-like diverging masses, rising from the north-east and south-west points of the sky. The vast auroral columns of fire, shooting toward their vanishing-point in the zenith above, seem converging to a point there.

But this is all a perspective illusion. The clouds which seem to converge are parallel; the auroral streamers which seem to converge are parallel: they only *seem* to converge and to bend.

And so the lines of love, which run parallel in this world, seem to have their vanishing-point in death. The cloudy and fiery pillars of Divine Providence seem to vanish in disaster and evil. The progress of truth, justice, and humanity, appears to vanish in the triumph of evil and wrong. But all this is only apparent. This is the perspective effect of our short-sighted vision. Loving hearts shall go on side by side for ever. Truth and justice shall move forward on their vast orbits through all space. Good shall be triumphant over evil, right over wrong, peace over war; and all things in heaven and earth shall work for good to those who love God.

VIII.

"IF HE SLEEP, HE SHALL DO WELL."

John xii. 12: "LORD, IF HE SLEEP, HE SHALL DO WELL."

IT is curious how large a part of every man's life is passed in sleep; more than a quarter of it; probably, on an average, a third. So that, if a man lives to be seventy, he has slept for more than twenty years. He has slept as long as Rip van Winkle, only not all at once. No matter how industrious, how active, how ambitious, how full of enthusiasm for what he has to do; after every few hours he becomes unconscious of all these vivid purposes, and drops away into entire indifference and ignorance of them all. People may be as different as you please in character, taste, temper; but they must all sleep six hours out of the twenty-four. The rapt saint, just caught up into the seventh heaven in an ecstasy of prayer, comes back to earth, and goes to bed, and falls into some foolish dream. The most virtuous man in Boston, and the coarsest criminal in the penitentiary, at one o'clock to-night will be equalized in sleep; the good man having subsided into a merely passive and negative virtue, and the sinner returned for a few hours to the innocence of childhood. Newton, just about to discover the great secret of the universe; Shakspeare, with "Hamlet" half written; Milton, with the music of paradise half sung; Stephenson, with the locomotive almost invented; Lord Bacon, with the "Novum Organon" nearly thought out; Rafaelle, with the final touch which is to charm the world in the Dresden "Madonna" not yet added, — must all go to sleep, and lose for six hours all consciousness of their great work and mission.

It seems a great loss.

Even the earth needs to go to sleep once a year. The earth around us, so full of activity and life a little while ago, folds its arms over its bosom, and sleeps the dreamless sleep of winter. The trees, which lately shook their multitude of leaves in the warm air, made sweet music in the rapid breeze, and lashed their branches angrily in the summer storm, now stand with all their life gone to sleep in their roots. But, amid this winter sleep, Nature is nursing her powers, and re-collecting her forces, and preparing to come forth anew in full and varied life with the next year. It seems like death; but it is only sleep. Had we never seen a spring, we should say that it was quite impossible for this dead grass ever to revive; for these cold, clattering branches to be covered again with tender, delicate leaves; for new blossoms and flowers to hang tender and fragrant on bush and tree; for the children to go out again, and gather sweet fruits and berries from these dried-up and withered sticks. But as what seems like death in nature is only sleep; so that which we call death, Jesus called sleep.

Did you ever stand by night on a housetop, looking down upon the roofs of a sleeping city? Here and there, a light shows where men are still awake,— some immersed in study; some lonely watchers by the bed of pain or death; some in gay, protracted revelry; some obliged by poverty to cheat the body of its needed rest to supply food and clothing to starving children. All the rest of the vast population sleeps. From every height of wisdom and holiness they have gone down, from every depth of passion or sin they have come up, to this tranquil, neutral land of peaceful repose. The transcendental philosopher, who has been, in his lamp-lit cell, fathoming the last mysteries of being for his admiring disciples; the sublime poet, who has been weaving, with a smile, a tale of woe; the preacher, who has finished his best sermon for to-morrow; the orator, who has committed to memory the last fiery paragraph of the speech which is to shake a nation's soul,— these have all gone down into that unconscious sphere, the only sphere of real democratic equality. There they lie, side by side, with the burglar, who has arranged his plans for robbing his neighbor's house; the disloyal editor, who has finished the paragraph which is another stab of his poisoned dagger at the heart of his struggling, tormented mother-land; the drunken child of sin and shame; the worldly man or woman, planning poor triumphs of a selfish success. They sleep beneath the kind curtains of night, beneath the watchful stars encamped in the heavens above, beneath God's ever-open eye. All seem to sleep the same sweet, dreamless sleep of the just, — the innocent children in the dormitory of that convent-school, the two hundred prisoners in the jail near by.

And, "if they sleep, they shall do well."

The words were true in a deeper sense than the disciples thought. It was a sagacious remark in that sense. "Nothing," say the works on physiology, "is so refreshing during sickness, or so conducive to rapid convalescence, as quiet sleep." Balmy sleep is kind Nature's sweet restorer. It serves to equalize all the functions of the frame, distributing the vital power to all parts, repairing all damages in the delicate machinery of the body; so that, when the will-power is put on again in the morning, it may go to work as before. Perhaps Nature goes on the maxim, that "a stitch in time saves nine," and mends up all the little microscopic lesions in her tender tissues before they attain the dignity and danger of a case for the doctors.

What is sleep? Nobody knows. One essential character, however, of sleep, is, I think, the suspension of will. Man ceases to be active, he becomes passive, in sleep. All the operations independent of will go on; as respiration, circulation, digestion, and the like. All that depend on the will, as attention, perception, direction and management of thought, control of muscles, are suspended. Man, while awake, is always in a state of active will. We do not know it perhaps, but, when we stand still, we are holding ourselves up. We are not merely seeing and hearing, but listening and looking, all the time; we are always holding our thoughts, and guiding them. When we fall asleep, it is by gradually letting off the control of will from body and mind; and, if you ever noticed yourself just when you were falling asleep, you will have observed that you took off the directing power from your thoughts, and let them go where they would. So they begin to move of themselves, by their own associations; and at last you begin to dream. Meantime, as the active power ceases, the passive and automatic powers go on more energetically. The breathing becomes fuller and deeper, as we can notice. The nutritive operations are so intensified, that most physiologists say that all nutrition takes place in sleep. The body, indeed, becomes a little colder in sleep; but that is because, the activity being suspended through body and mind, there is no such consumption of fuel required in the lungs, and a small fire is kept up there.

Therefore, as to the body of a man, "if he sleep, he shall do well." Sleep comes as a physician and inspector-general, and examines the whole body all through, and repairs and renews it. We make a mistake in trying to do without sleep, as students and scholars do sometimes. Work as hard as you can, provided you can sleep hard too. An eminent preacher once gave me an account of his way of doing so much mental work, and his method in writing sermons; and he concluded by saying, that a great deal of it was done by good hard sleeping. Said he, "I sleep as much as I can every night; for I am persuaded, that, if the preacher does not sleep during the week, the congregation will sleep on Sunday." And I think he was right. I think it is partly the preacher's fault if the congregation sleep at church; for how quickly we rouse up when any thing is said which is real and vital! A clap of thunder will not stir a man so quickly as an arrow of thought shot directly into his conscience and heart. Partly the preacher's fault, therefore, but not wholly; partly it is the architect's fault, who has not ventilated the church; and partly it is no one's fault. A minister said to me the other day, that when he preached in the country, and saw the farmers, who had worked in the open air all day during the week in their shirts, come and sit, dressed in thick cloth, in a hot church on Sunday, he was pleased to see them dropping asleep, and getting a little nap; "forty winks of sleep," as Napoleon used to say; and then waking up bright, and ready to listen again. Dean Swift once preached a sermon on the text in Acts where it is stated that there were many lights in the upper chamber where the disciples were gathered, and that "there sat in a window a certain young man named Eutychus, being fallen into a deep sleep; and, as Paul was long preaching, he sunk down with sleep, and fell from the third loft, and was taken up dead." Dean Swift begins his sermon by saying, The fate of this young man does not seem to have been a warning to his successors who go to sleep in church; except in this, that they choose safer places in which to indulge themselves; and, instead of sitting in the window, they compose themselves more comfortably in the corners of the pews.

But the dean might have bethought himself that this text was as much to the address of the preacher of long sermons as to the sleepy hearer; and that, if Eutychus could not keep himself awake even to hear Paul, there must have been some physical cause for his drowsiness: probably his being in the upper part of the room, where the bad air from the people and the lights was collected.

But sleep rests mind as well as body. Sleep rests the conscience and the will. The sense of responsibility reposes in sleep; and we sometimes do in our dreams the wickedest actions, without feeling any remorse.

There are mysterious blessings also attending sleep. We wake with better, wiser thoughts. We wake from good sleep with a more loving heart. So God sent a deep sleep upon Adam, and out of it came Eve. Inspiration comes in sleep; as when a deep sleep came on Abram, and in it came the promise, to him and to his children, of the land of Palestine. To Jacob came in a dream a vision of heaven, and angels ascending and descending; and a clear promise, that "in his seed all the families of the earth should be blessed," and not merely the Jews. So that, in sleep, sometimes come to us glimpses of truths we are unable to see when awake; perhaps because in sleep we are more passive and open to influences, and not so shut up in our own opinions and belief. So that, when Jacob arose from that sleep, he said, "Surely the Lord is here, and I knew it not: this is none other than the house of God, and the gate of heaven." Daniel's visions, which came to him in sleep, have exercised the waking thoughts of men ever since; and still they do not know very well what to make of them.

Wilkinson says that "man is captured in sleep, not by death, but by his higher nature. To-day runs in through a deeper day to be the parent of to-morrow; and the man issues from sleep every morning, bright as the morning, and of life-size."

All this teaches us of other spiritual sleeps, not unconscious, but conscious; of the higher sleeps of the soul, when we sleep to care, to anxiety, to sorrow, to sin, to fear, to death; falling asleep in God. Let us look at these.

As natural and automatic sleep refreshes the body by the suspense of the active will; so the sleep in which the soul casts itself on God, suspending, for a time, strength, effort, and all conscious goodness, is just as necessary for the repair and health of the soul.

We must rest even from duty and effort sometimes; but the true rest from these, the true sleep to refresh conscience and spirit, is to come near to God in nature or the Bible, or the closet of prayer. Work and prayer should alternate like day and night in the Christian life; and bodily sleep and waking seems to be the exact analogon of this spiritual sleep and waking. There are two spheres, — one of duty, the other of devotion, — into which man needs alternately to go. They ought not to be confused. They are distinct. When a man says, "To work is to pray," he confuses them. To work is not to pray: it is to work. When a man makes prayer his work, and gives his life, like the monks of Paganism, Mohammedanism, and Christianity, to a mere abstract, mystical devotion, he confuses them. You cannot work well, except you stop working sometimes, and pray. You cannot pray well, unless you stop praying sometimes to work.

I know Paul says, "Pray without ceasing:" but by that I believe him to mean, "Do not confine yourself to regular hours of devotion, — three times a day, or seven times a day; but pray all the time, as you feel the need of prayer." And this corresponds with the Master's saying, that true worship is to worship in spirit and truth.

Here is a man harassed with anxiety and care about his business, about his health, about his family. Here is a woman harassed with care about her sick child. She thinks she ought to be anxious: he thinks he ought to be anxious. They try to be anxious, rather than not to be. They never throw off the burden, and go into God's glad presence, sleeping to care, sleeping to anxiety, as the little babe in its cradle sleeps. They should give all their thought for a time to their duties, put their whole heart into them, and then take an hour of rest in God's blessed love, and cast all their cares on Him who cares for them. Thus could they work better, and conquer their difficulties better: for care and anxiety unnerve the soul; and to try to live in anxiety is like trying to live without sleep.

The Christian world rests on Sunday. I am no sabbatarian. I do not believe in keeping the Jewish sabbath. Saturday is the sabbath; and, if any one wishes to keep the sabbath, let him keep Saturday. I believe that the Lord's Day is a day of freedom, not of constraint; of joy, and not of gloom. I believe in the Catholic view of it, not the Puritanic. The Catholic Church never allows fasting on Sunday, not even in Lent. It has always been a rule of the Church to make Sunday a festival, — never a fast. In Lent, no member of the Roman-Catholic, of the Greek, or of the Oriental churches, is allowed to make Sunday a day of fasting. I should like to see Sunday made in every family the happiest of days, — a day of domestic joy and love; a day for doing good; a day in which no gloom is allowable; a day on which every one of the family should bring all his gifts of good-humor, and inventions of kindness, to the rest.

But it is not a day for common business, for going to and fro. It is a day in which to stand still, and consider the wonderful works of God. All life should cease its bustle and confusion, and grow calm. That is the beauty of our mode of keeping it. The world stands still every Sunday throughout Christendom, — stands still, and thinks; and I believe an immense access of power, thought, and character, comes to Christendom from this one source. We do not keep the Lord's Day as well as we might, or as well as our children will keep it; but, even now, it is a source of great blessing to mankind.

So also God has sent his Son to teach us to sleep to sin as well as to care. We are not bound to be always troubling ourselves about our sin. We are not bound to be awake to sin. The Bible says, "Be awake to righteousness." It does not say, Be awake to sin. We are to see our sin, and repent of it, and bring it to God, and lay it down before his footstool, and then accept the righteousness which is by faith. Open your hearts to God's forgiving love. Trust that your Father forgives you when you are penitent; and you are forgiven. Receive the sweet sense of reconciling love into your heart, and repose in him, — the dear Friend who sent his Son to save you, not merely hereafter, but now; not merely from punishment, but from sin itself.

Jesus, you will have noticed, always speaks of death as sleep. He does not choose to call it death; for he came to abolish death, and those who believe in him do not expect to die. They expect to pass through a sleep into a fuller life. Therefore he said of the young girl, "The damsel is not dead, but sleepeth;" and of Lazarus, "Our friend Lazarus sleepeth." And so the disciples, afterward, were fond of the phrase, and spoke of those who were asleep in Jesus. They said that a part of those who had seen Jesus "remain, but some are fallen asleep." — "They which are fallen asleep in Christ." — "We would not have you ignorant concerning them that are asleep." — "Since the fathers fell asleep." Their choice of this expression was not accidental, nor was it a mere figure of speech. They saw, in sleep, the image of death; meant to show us, that as we sink away every night into unconscious but happy repose, and awaken refreshed, so it will be at the end.

The most remarkable use of the phrase, however, is in the case of Stephen. To the Jews he seemed to die a horrible death of anguish: to the disciples he seemed to drop into a pleasant slumber, his mind full of visions of Christ and heaven. "When he had said this, he fell asleep."

Jesus calls death a sleep. The ancients and moderns have called death the sister of sleep. Lewes, in a scientific work, says this is a mistake; that sleep has nothing in it like death. Yet perhaps there is a deeper analogy than science can perceive. Death is not destruction; it is repose. It is going to rest with God and Christ, and the dear spirits loved and lost, in some of the many mansions our Father has in his great house, the universe. Just as there is a positive pleasure in sleep which attracts the tired man, just as food attracts the hungry man; so death attracts the weary soul. This instinct is no mistake. The little child, full of wakeful life, hates to go to bed, longs to sit up later; but the tired child drops sweetly into his little bed, the flushed cheek resting on the round arm. So, when we are full of life, we hate the idea of death; but, when it comes, it usually finds us tired and ready. Almost always, men are willing to go. In all my experience of death-beds, I have met only one case of a person who was unwilling to die. Usually death comes as sweet as sleep, bringing with it a positive joy, and revealing beforehand to the soul something of the love and peace which lie beyond these shores of time.

Thus sleep is a symbol and teacher of many things. At first sight, it seems like a waste of life; but it is just as true life as the waking part. Many physiologists even declare that sleep is the natural condition of man, and wakefulness the abnormal state of the body. This, I think, is not so. The one is as natural as the other; for the two must be well balanced to make perfect health. To sleep too much is as unhealthy as to sleep too little. But sleep and wakefulness, passive life and active life, faith and works, piety and morality, love to God and love to men, — these all are the great polar forces of bodily, mental, and moral life, which act and re-act on each other, and keep us as we ought to be. The man who sleeps all the time, sleeps to no purpose: his sleep hurts him. He who wakes all the time, wakes to no purpose: he can do nothing well. He who labors for man, with no faith in God, labors to little good. He who worships God, without serving man, worships to little good: his prayers hurt him rather than help him.

Sacred is the day; sacred also the night. Holy is work; holy also is prayer.

Yes, all sleep is sacred. "If a man sleep well, he shall do well." A writer says, "Such is the power of the heart to redeem the animal life, that there is nothing more exquisitely refined and pure and beautiful than the chamber of the house. The couch! — from the day that the bride sanctifies it to the day when the aged mother is borne from it, it stands clothed with loveliness and dignity. Cursed be the tongue that dares speak evil of the household bed! By its side oscillates the cradle. Not far from it is the crib. In this sacred precinct, the mother's chamber, is the heart of the family. Here the child learns its prayer. Hither, night by night, angels troop. It is the holy of holies."

The only appropriate words with which to conclude these reflections are those which we know so well, — the words of that deep and tender woman, the Christian Muse of the nineteenth century of Christianity, — words which, though we may know them, we do not tire of hearing: —

"Of all the thoughts of God that are
Borne inward unto souls afar,
Along the Psalmist's music deep,
Now tell me if there any is
For gift or grace surpassing this, —
'He giveth his belovèd sleep'?

O earth, so full of dreary noises!
O men, with wailing in your voices!
O delvèd gold, the wailer's heap!
O strife, O curse, that o'er it fall!
God strikes a silence through you all,
And giveth his belovèd sleep.

His dews drop mutely on the hill;
His cloud above it saileth still:
Though on its slope men sow and reap,
More softly than the dew is shed,
Or cloud is floated overhead,
He giveth his belovèd sleep."

IX.

STAND STILL.

Job xxxvii. 14: "STAND STILL, AND CONSIDER THE WORKS OF GOD."

Eph. vi. 13: "HAVING DONE ALL, STAND."

THERE is a good deal of merit in being able to stand. It is merit, however, which is very liable to be undervalued. We highly prize the merit of going, and also that of doing; not enough, perhaps, the worth of standing. It is, no doubt, a great merit in a horse to go. A horse is advertised to go so many miles an hour, so many minutes to a mile; but it is considered an additional praise, even for a horse, that he can stand. He will "stand without tying," it is said. Now, if this is a merit in a horse, still more is it in a man. The man who will "stand without tying" has achieved a great moral accomplishment. I mean a man who will hold his place, and keep it, by an internal force, not an external one. I mean one who will stand to truth and principle,—not being held to them by force of outward circumstances, by the expectation of others, by the fear of being called inconsistent, by the bond of a creed or covenant publicly acknowledged, but by the simple power of inward conviction, of loyalty to conscience and right.

Nature is full of types to show us the beauty of such steadfastness. Far in the depths of the primeval forest, there stands a tree, the monarch of the woods. A casual seed, wafted by the summer breeze, found for itself a favorable spot of soil. Year after year it grew, — a little stalk, too small to support a bird; over which the rabbit leaped as he ran; — then larger, a sapling. So, year by year, rooting itself more deeply, spreading its limbs more widely, adding new rings of wood to its trunk, rising higher into the circumambient air, visited by myriad insects, by various birds, it stands and grows. At last, it reaches its maturity, and is a mighty tree, monarch of the woods. Then it stands in the same place for a hundred years, for five hundred years, unchanged. The white clouds drift over its mighty head in the infinite expanse of heaven. The glories of morning, the splendid hues of evening, the deep silence of night, pass over it. It stands, unmoved. Every thing comes and goes around it: it remains, contented in its rooted stability. Having done all it was meant to do, it stands. It does not see so much variety as the butterfly that lights on its leaf. The bird, who comes to make his summer nest in its branches, could tell it a thousand stories of the countries he has passed through in his annual migrations. But the patient tree is not sent to hear the news of what is happening in the world, but to stand. Yet what majesty in this steadfast repose! And at last the traveller comes to the place, and gazes upward into the infinite multitude of its bowery recesses, its flickering lights and shades, its million leaves waving tremulous in the summer breeze, or roaring in the storm, as it lashes the air with its thousand branches. He thinks of it, standing through so many seasons, meeting the spring warmth with tenderly swelling buds, and stripping itself in the autumn to battle with skeleton arms against winter tempests; and there comes over his mind the sense of a sublime stability, which touches some nobler corresponding element in his own soul.

Man was made, not only to see, to do, to go, to make progress, but also to stand. Until he has learned to stand, he has not learned the whole lesson of life. Amid all change, we desire something permanent; amid all variety, something stable; amid all progress, some central unity of life; something which deepens as we ascend; which roots itself as we advance; which grows more and more tenacious of the old, while becoming more and more open to the new.

Hence the importance of being able *to stand.* It is important, first, in order to see the truth; secondly, it is important, in order to retain what we have seen.

First, Mental stability is good, in order to be able to see the truth. It is good to stand still, and consider.

There are two ways of seeing things. One may go to see, or one may stand still and see. Each way has its advantages. If my object is to collect separate things, all the facts of a certain kind, I must go and look for them. To make a systematic collection of any kind of facts, we must go for them. If I want all the beetles or butterflies, all the Roman coins, all the books printed in the fifteenth century, all the best ancient pictures, all the knowledge about certain men or times or countries, so as to write a history or a biography, I must *go* for them. The history of Greece will not come to me by any inspiration, while I sit in my garden. I must go to libraries, and hunt it up out of many books. A collection of autograph-letters will not come to me as I stand still thinking about them: I must write to this man and that, inquire here and there, and so find them.

But if my object is, *not* to make a full collection, but to see some one thing in its relations, as it lives, vital and active, I can often do that better by standing still. Let me illustrate. A man takes his gun, and goes through the Western woods to shoot birds or other game. He finds what he goes for. He tramps over many miles. He pushes through wet thickets, where the long-billed woodcock flies up, or the pheasant whirs with sudden flight. He finds in the deep forest the tree to which the pigeons come at night to roost. The startled rabbit runs across the open meadow before him; the gray or black squirrel springs lightly from the end of one long swinging branch to another. So the man comes home at night with what he went for,—a bag full of game. But he has seen none of these creatures in their natural state. Terror went before him. The squirrel hid behind the lofty limb, or ran affrighted up the other side of the tree-trunk; and the birds, with panic-stricken bosoms, hid themselves among the leaves. He has got some birds; but he has not seen their life.

Now, another man goes into the forest. Perhaps you have so gone yourself. You sit on a stone in the shade, and wait, perfectly still, to see what will come. As you sit, all the timid creatures come out, and you see them in their domestic life. The diligent birds bring sticks and strings to make their nests; and, while they work, chirp to each other about their amazing architecture. The squirrel hops out of his hole, bringing a nut to eat in the fresh air; and chips the shell with the air of an artist, spreading his bushy tail over his back like a shawl. All sorts of creatures come and go that one never sees at any other time. All natural history reveals itself to patient waiting and watching. These wonders of God, hidden from the wise and prudent, who know all that books teach, are revealed to the babes of simple, patient, attentive, open-eyed waiting.

I once had occasion to wait ten minutes at one of the corners of the Common for a gentleman who appointed to meet me there. I discovered, while standing still, what I never had discovered in walking by that place,—that it was a place of general appointments. Several little dramas occurred while I waited. Several persons came, and stopped, and looked up and down, and strolled to and fro, and came back; and, at last, their friends met them, and they went away. A young woman came, and sat down on a bench very quietly. After a while, a young man arrived; and each took the other's arm, and they departed.

Now, I had been by that corner five hundred times without noticing these things; but when I stood still there, and waited a few minutes, I saw them all.

Travellers in Europe often fail of seeing what they ought by not standing still. They hurry with inconceivable rapidity from one place to another. They put themselves into the hands of a courier, and go all over the Continent. They give a day to Florence, and two days to Rome, and think they have seen Europe: hardly more than if they had staid at home, and read a guide-book. I saw a man in Venice, who had arrived there that morning, and was going away in the afternoon. He thought he had seen every thing. We were sitting in a little *café* on the great square of the Duomo. He sat by the window, with his back to it. He did not even turn round, so as to look at the strange beauty of the scene outside the window, — the oriental front of the Cathedral of St. Mark, with its domes and mosaics, and the groups in the old historic square. A man must *stand still* to see any thing. Some of our American and English travellers never stand still long enough to receive a single deep impression of any place they go to.

Now, it is the same with truth. We must stand still in order to receive truth in any living and profound way into our minds. It is different with us and with a locomotive or steam fire-engine, which, by running, makes a draft for its fire to kindle. The fire in man's heart kindles while he stands still. "While I was musing, the fire burned." That is the difference between the way of getting theology and getting religion. If I want to get theology, which is dead truth, "the skins and skeletons of truth stuffed and set up in cases," then I must go about, and seek for it in books, in sermons, in this church and the other. I must listen to all the statements and arguments which I can hear: so, by and by, I get my theology. But, if I wish for religion, it is different. Then I must stand still, and consider the wonderful works of God. I must see God in the glory of morning, and the beauty of descending twilight; in the charm of earliest birds; in herb, tree, fruit, and flower glistering with dew. I must stand still each day, and think of what God has done for me; how he has blessed me with home, friends, love, opportunity of knowledge, and rich influences of culture. I must consider how he has sent to me wise teachers, and generous, loving hearts, to stand by me amid the storms of life. I must remember how he has put dear little children in my arms, and holy wise men and women near me for my emergencies; how he has borne with me in my wilfulness and pride and folly, and restrained me from going into irremediable evil. I must recollect how often, when I have gone to the very verge of some fatal wrong, he has put forth his hand, and held me back, and saved me from being an utter castaway; or how, when I have prayed, because I could not do any longer without prayer, he has hastened to meet my ignorant supplication, and answered it, — oh, so sweetly! filling my soul down to its very depths with the peace of God passing all understanding!

So, too, I must see Christ, if at all. People perplex themselves and others with infinite questions about him, which never have been answered, nor can be. Was he God? Was he man? Did he pre-exist? What is the hypostatic union, — two natures in one person? They quote texts for and texts against. "I and my Father are one." "My Father is greater than I." "Before Abraham was, I am." They tear these poor texts from their places in the living Scripture in order to fling them at our heads. Such texts, in their place, in the life of Jesus, are like flowers and fruits in a garden full of sweetness and charm. But the apples, peaches, and roses which are plucked from their stalks soon decay, and become something very different. So are texts plucked from their context. Take that famous text, for example: "I and my Father are one." How was it spoken? Some Jews wished Jesus to issue a proclamation that he was the Messiah. "Tell us plainly if you are the Christ?" they say. He answers, "See my life; see my works. Do you love them? Do you see any thing of God in them? If you do, you will follow after me, because you belong to me. You cannot help following me, and keeping by me; and all the powers on earth cannot take you from me, because your heart will perpetually draw you to me and to my Father. It is one and the same thing. If you come to me, you come to God; because my life is to you God's truth and love revealed. We are one; and if you are bound to me by loving my works, and sympathizing with them, then you are bound to God, and no one can separate you from God."

This is the way to know Christ, then, — to stand still, and look at him, not to argue about him. Look at his majestic holiness, so grand, yet so simple and unpretending, which came up in Judæa, and lasted a few years, and then filled the centuries with its light and beauty. Look at his religion, so human, yet so divine; a religion for this world, and the other world too; a religion which loves God by loving its brother; a religion not of any dogma, any ceremony, any anxious fears, but of trust, obedience, and generous affection. Look at Jesus himself, the perfect revelation of God in man; a man so manful, and, if I may say it, also so womanful; a man harmonizing the best traits of man and woman. He was calm, deep, brave, a leader of men; also tender, childlike, pure, and gentle as the best of women. Stand still, and look at him. Come to his feast of love, and think about him. Sit at his feet, and thank God that he has lived, lifting us above the terror of death and sin, and showing us heaven here and heaven hereafter.

Next, stability in man is LOYALTY. It is not merely a passive and indolent conservatism; it is an active adherence to certain convictions, duties, and affections. Even the tree has a *live* hold of the earth: its roots are as living as its branches. It is not held to the ground, passively, by the law of gravitation; but *clings* to it actively, by the law of life. Much more, man's stability is an active, and not a passive virtue. To keep to what is old, merely from an indolent reluctance to change, is less meritorious than the stability of a tree; but to cling to the past, to the known, the loved, the dear, from loyalty, from gratitude, from conscience, — this alone is noble. We must stand actively, not passively. We cannot even stand on our feet passively. It requires a constant effort of will and great balancing power to stand, as the human being stands, on two feet. The culmination of creation came, when the animal, which had floated, upborne in water or air by wings or fins; which had crawled on the earth, or had walked on four feet, — finally arose, and stood on two, and was able, having done all other things, to stand. I suppose it would be impossible for the most skilful sculptor to make a statue of a man which should stand on two feet. In almost all other instincts, some animals excel men; but, in this of balancing himself, man excels them. It is easier to walk than to stand. In walking, we are partly passive, falling forward: in standing still, we are constantly holding ourselves upright.

No doubt it is the destiny of man to make progress in truth; to forget things behind, and reach out to things before. But, unless he stands on something, he cannot go forward. There must be something solid beneath his feet, else he cannot walk. It is not progress to throw away all I know to-day, in order to learn something else to-morrow. To advance in knowledge is not wholly to forget the past, but to take it with us. We drop much, we put away childish things, we leave the form of truth behind us, as the snake his skin; but we must not leave the substance of truth. In all mental progress, there are some great convictions —

"Which wake, to perish never."

There are some mental convictions which only deepen and strengthen while all other thoughts change. There are ideas of God, freedom, immortality, justice, truth, eternal right, infinite love, to which we must cling as the tree clings to the soil; on which we must stand, in order to move on.

This is the distinction between real mental progress and that which only simulates it. We too often imagine that change is progress. We see people who go from church to church, from creed to creed, dropping all their past at each step they take. This may sometimes be necessary; but it is an unfortunate necessity. To lighten itself off from a rock, a ship may have to throw its cargo overboard; but this is not a good thing to do, if it can be helped. True intellectual progress is to add new thoughts to the old ones.

The reason why so many men stick in a few opinions, and take no new ones, is, that they are not rooted in any thing. They are afraid to move, for fear of falling. They have not learned to stand; so they cannot go. It is not because they believe the old so strongly, that they fear the new; but because they believe it so feebly. The man who is *rooted* in certain convictions is not afraid to move forward; for he knows he shall not lose them.

Nothing is so beautiful and noble as this power of persistency and progress in one. It is beautiful to see the ship, with all sails spread, running before a favoring breeze,—one cloud of white canvas; plunging forward into the dark sea, and throwing it from its bow in sparkling drops, and masses of foam: but still more beautiful it is to see the same ship lying to, its head to the wind, holding itself against the storm, without cable or anchor; compelling the blast which tries to drive it back to hold it in its place. So noble is it to see the man lying to in the storm of life. He is unable to make progress; but he compels the very blast of adverse circumstance to hold him in his place.

The weakest of all things, perhaps, is scepticism. Unless a man has some fixed, clear convictions, he drifts helplessly through the world. He has no force in himself. He can do nothing. The sceptic is a cipher in action, because he is a cipher in conviction. The tree which, at any rate, stands for a thousand years, is nobler than he. Pity him, however, and help him. He is in a morbid state. He is a sick man: be tender to him. Do not despise the sceptic; but, if you have any faith, help him to it. Sympathize with him; for some of his disease is in us all. We all of us are obliged to pray, "Lord, I believe: help thou mine unbelief!"

But one source of scepticism is in the false idea that we are wholly passive in our belief. It is not so. When God shows us a truth, it is our duty to cling to it. When we have seen any great idea, we must not let it go, but stand to it firmly and loyally. A man can be loyal in thought no less than in action. He is disloyal, if, having seen a truth, he lets it go through indifference; if curiosity is stronger in him than conviction; if he loves novelty more than reality.

Again: he who can stand firm in his convictions, and be loyal to his insights, is able to be also loyal to his duties. Having done all, he can stand.

In the ruins of Pompeii, after they have shown you the great amphitheatre, the streets, the forum, the shops, the houses, the villas, they take you through the gate, and show you the stone sentry-box, where were found, buried in ashes, the rusted remains of the helmet and cuirass of the Roman sentinel. When the black cloud rose from the mountain, and the hot ashes fell around him, and the people rushed by him from the city in their frantic flight, he could do nothing else, but he could *stand;* and so he stood, and died in his place, suffocated by the sulphury air. He was buried deep beneath the ashes; and so, after fifteen hundred years, his disinterred remains testify to the nobleness which stands to its post when it can do nothing else.

It is perhaps the highest kind of courage, this of standing to our post, no matter whether we seem to succeed or to fail. For this, we dwell so often, with tearful eyes, on the story of the heady fight, when young men stand firm at their post, though conscious that it is in vain. The three hundred at Thermopylæ, the six hundred at Balaklava, the Fifteenth and Twentieth Massachusetts at Ball's Bluff, — these are more heroic instances than the men who shared the triumphs of victorious days. Having done all, they stood, and stood to die. They stood, hour after hour, while the long waves of battle rolled up against them; stood, hearing the wild yells of the overwhelming masses brought up to crush them.

> "Not theirs to reason why,
> Not theirs to make reply;
> Theirs but to do, or die."

Such moments of heroic courage indicate to us all what is the real nobleness of life. It is to do all, and then stand; to stand firm to our duty, loyal to right, faithful to justice and truth, whether men hear or forbear. This makes it worth while to live. If a man only lives for success, he is poor and cowardly when disaster comes. Then we hear him finding fault, complaining, lamenting, fearing every thing; throwing doubt on every thing; talking like the book of Ecclesiastes, not like the book of Revelation. "There is no good thing," he says, "under the sun. All men are rascals; all life is vanity. Every thing goes wrong. There is no hope for the world." The man who thus talks is one who has never lived for duty and right at all, only for success or show.

But he who has once seen the majestic face of Duty, who has once for all taken her as his queen, with submission and service, feels a stern joy in the midst of all disaster, a strange hope born in the bosom of disappointment, a joy of success amid failure. He says, "When I am weak, then I am strong." God is on his side: what shall he fear? "He is troubled on every side, yet not distressed; perplexed, but not in despair; persecuted, but not forsaken; cast down, but not destroyed." Nothing shakes his solid mind. And if this is noble; if it is a grateful sight to the higher powers to see the good man struggling with the storms of fate,—why is it not also grateful to God and the angels to see the man, who is not triumphantly virtuous, struggling against inbred sin, against habits of evil inherited or self-formed? He is unable to conquer, perhaps he is unable to be wholly good; yet he will not yield. He will stand against evil, if he can do no more.

There is yet another loyalty, another kind of persistence, as deep as these other two, — loyalty to love. To stand firm, rooted in pure and true affections; to love the noble, the generous, the good, without regard to any return on their part, — this is also excellent.

When I see persons, who, having had friends, have lost them, and who complain of having been deceived and mistaken, I think they never loved aright. The true affections are as permanent as God himself. That which I have really loved I continue to love for ever. I may not see my friend for many years. I may be separated in life and action. He may leave me for another world. He may be tired of me. But if I have really loved in him any thing good; if I have ever seen in him any thing truly excellent, beautiful, and noble, — it is there still; and I must love it still, in order to be true to myself. The heart which has not this persistency of affection is superficial and cold. Of all the beautiful things in this world, one of the most beautiful is the undying affection of father and child; of brother and sister; of friends who have been friends from childhood to manhood; of those who, through long years of prosperity and disaster, still work together, go on together, pursue the same aim, live the same life. This unselfish love is itself the germ and beginning of the love of God. This love, so steadfast to the good and right in man, leads us up to the sole Fair and the sole True. It is comfort; it is joy; it is heaven. It gives unity of purpose to life, and strength to the weary in soul.

Perhaps this war will be the means of developing a higher national life in this people, by teaching us to stand; and to stand, not on prosperity and success, but on principle. We have had our great prosperity and success, and have been elated. We are now denounced and opposed by the whole civilized world. It has happened to us, as it happens so often, that our punishment for sin was postponed until we had begun to repent and to do right. It often happens so. While men are going wrong, every thing prospers. As soon as they begin to go right, the consequences of their previous sins begin to fall on them. Perhaps it is because the nation or the men who begin to do right have begun to be strong, and are better able to bear their punishments.

But now, if God deals with us as with sons, and is chastening us, it will be for our profit. We as a nation, in our hour of darkness, will perhaps grow inwardly more strong. We have learned in past times to grow, to act, and to go forward. We have been a very fast people. We have always wished to go ahead: now perhaps we shall learn how to *stand.* The old loyalty to our national history, which we thought dead, broke forth in 1861, in a flame of light, at the siege of Sumter. We rose as a people to stand by the flag. Having learned to stand by the flag, we may also learn to stand by what the flag symbolizes; to stand up for equal rights, for universal freedom, for justice to all, for a true democracy, for general rights.

Thus man, the microcosm, resumes in himself all that is to be found in nature. He stands rooted, like the tree, in principles; he moves, like the bird, in the element of freedom; he is fed, like the flower, by the sunlight and air and rain from the skies; and, like the round globe itself, he hangs poised in the eternal heavens, moving on in the orbit of duty around the everlasting Sun, which is God himself, the same for ever and for ever.

So, my friends, life goes on. Let us live it as we ought; standing still, from time to time, to see and consider God's works, and then going out to do them; standing in our place, and looking from our place, and always loyal and faithful at our place. God sends times for work, and times for consideration. He sends us homes, where we may go and rest and consider. He sends calm evening and dewy night, the companionship of wise and loving hearts, and the peace of this holy day. Into these oratories of thought, love, and prayer, let us go to consider and ponder; and then let us take hold of life, and do the great will of the Master, and let life be better for our being in it; and when we are old, if God grants us to be old, we shall look from that mountain-top of age into the promised land of a rejoicing and happy future.

X.

GROW UP.

Eph. iv. 15: "SPEAKING THE TRUTH IN LOVE, GROW UP IN ALL THINGS INTO HIM WHICH IS THE HEAD, EVEN CHRIST."

ONE object of life is to grow. If any one grows, if he grows up, if he grows up in all things, if he grows up in all things into Christ, then he has attained one great end for which God placed him here. This seems a different statement from the old catechism statement, that the end of man's being is "to glorify God, and enjoy him for ever." Yet it is only the same thing in another form. For how do we glorify God? By praising him, by singing hymns to him, by calling him omnipotent and omniscient? Certainly not. "Herein is my Father glorified, that *ye bear much fruit:* so shall ye be my disciples." That is what Christ says, that we glorify God when we bear much fruit; and we cannot do that unless we grow. Therefore, to grow up vigorously and symmetrically, and in all things, into Christ, *is* to glorify God.

Pope gives still another definition of the object of life. It is happiness: —

> "O happiness! our being's end and aim, —
> Good, pleasure, ease, content, whate'er thy name;
> That something still which prompts the eternal sigh,
> For which we bear to live, or dare to die."

But this also comes to the same thing. For what surer way to happiness than lies in the unfolding of all the faculties, the exercise of all the powers, the development of all the capacities of our nature, the various accomplishment, the daily progress, all of which are included in the word "growth"? To grow up is happiness; to grow up is to glorify God.

The Bible, therefore, is full of indications and similitudes drawn from growth. "The righteous," says David, "shall grow like a cedar in Lebanon." Any one, who has ever seen these noble trees, will understand the force of the comparison. In my last sermon, I took a tree as the type of stability: now I take it again as a type of growth. A cedar of Lebanon is growing in the Garden of Plants, in Paris. It is a majestic tree, spreading out its great lateral branches, each sustaining a mass of deep-green foliage. But on the blue sides of Lebanon, in their own congenial climate, these noble trees made each a temple for the worship of God. Centuries of growth had hardened their imperishable and fragrant wood. Their vast limbs, each a tree in itself, spread out, heavy with leaves, making a home for all the birds of the air. What better type of Christian growth than this patient, constant, unceasing growth of one of these great forest-kings? It may be a cedar of Lebanon; or a tall elm in a New-England valley, standing in solitary grace, an urn of waving greenery; or a Norway fir, spreading its robes, like a duchess, over the white snow of its native mountains; or a live oak, sheltering with its great shadow the men and cattle on a Louisiana plantation, till the cruel bell calls again to labor; or perhaps it is a tulip-tree, covered with yellow flowers, on the plains of Kentucky; or a lofty California fir, the gigantic monarch of the forest, looking out from his snowy Sierra upon the blue Pacific. They stand firm in their place. They grow year by year, adding something to the density of their fibre, something to their expanse and elevation. Yet they become little children again every year. They renew their youth in myriad tender buds, little fragile leaves, and sweet childish blossoms. So they are the type of what is best in man, — steady growth in all that is great and strong, joined with a youth of the heart ever renewed by faith and love.

Yet it is not enough to *grow*: we must grow UP. Some trees do not grow up. If you go to the summit of Mt. Washington, just before you reach the top, you will find yourself walking on the tops of trees. They are true trees; but, stunted by the cold, and beaten down by storms which rage around the bleak brow of the mountain, they spread themselves on the ground, and cannot rise. So it sometimes is with man. Discouraged by difficulty, he loses his power of rising. He loses faith and hope. He clings to the ground. It is sad to see so many men losing faith as they gain experience; growing more worldly, and calling their worldliness good sense. It is an unnatural state of mind. Man ought to grow *up* as he grows old; to have more faith in God and man; to enlarge his horizon; to see more of the past and the future; to live more among the things which are unseen, but eternal. Such a man inspires others; elevates others; brings others to new hope; gives them new encouragement; helps them to see God in Nature, Providence, and Christ, and in their own hearts; helps them to look on life cheerfully, and on death without anxiety, as God meant that we should.

> "To each unthinking being, Heaven, a friend,
> Gives not the useless knowledge of its end:
> To man imparts it, but with such a view,
> That, while he dreads it, makes him hope it too.
> The *hour* concealed, and so remote the fear;
> Death still draws nearer, never seeming near."

Some men and trees grow DOWN, and not up. You will see trees by the side of a river, all bending down toward the running stream, stretching their arms toward it as if to bathe in the cool, rushing waters. No matter what their forms are elsewhere: by the side of running water, they all bow down to it. It is the nature of the arbor-vitæ to grow upward: but, around Niagara, it assumes fantastic forms; and there it stoops toward the torrent, leaning down, reaches its long branches into it, and becomes as strange and weird a tree as the old olive-trees of Italy, which seem half trees, half men. So, by the side of the rushing river of business which roars every day through the streets of Boston, how many men acquire a habit of stooping down, and leaning down, and reaching down, till they forget that it is the great distinction of man to stand erect, to look up to the sky, and abroad over the earth, as even a Heathen poet knew! —

> "Os homini sublime dedit, cœlumque tueri
> Jussit, et erectos ad sidera tollere vultus."

But it is not enough to grow up: we must grow up *in all things.* In a dense old forest, where the woodman has never gone with his axe, you will find all sorts of trees looking very much alike. They have lost their individuality. They all strain up and up toward the light, till they look like the pine. The elm loses its queenly grace; the oak, its manly and rugged strength; the maple, its elliptical mass of dense, green foliage; the birch, its waving, feathery branches; the beech, its pendent, flowing, glittering, sunlit surfaces: and all grow up, straight shafts, in gloomy monotony. They grow *up;* but that is not the only duty of a tree. Its duty is to spread itself out, and assume its typical form, which God gave it as a law, when it was a little seed, and told it to grow into that.

Religious people have often made a like mistake. They have thought it their only business to strain up to heaven; to drop off all their lateral branches, and cultivate a monotonous and gloomy piety. But when God made us, and put into us so many faculties and powers of body and soul, he thereby commanded us to unfold them. He did not make all men alike; nor did he mean that all men should be ascetic saints or austere pietists. He meant that we should love him, but love our brother also, and our earthly life too. God is pleased with us when we grow up *in all things* into Christ; not in one thing only. He loves to see men with well-developed bodies; with good perceptive organs; with sharp eyes and keen senses; with active and agile limbs, capable of performance and endurance; with bright intellects, capable of reasoning and judging, of comparing and reflecting. God has given men the sense of beauty, and made the earth full of it, that this sense might have exercise. He has given us poetry and imagination, wit and mirth; and do you suppose he did not mean they should be used? There is nothing profane in the human soul; nothing common or unclean. It is *all through* the temple of God; and it is sacrilege to waste or neglect or injure any part of it. If a thief breaks into a Catholic church, and steals a necklace from the doll image which stands for the Virgin, it is considered not only wrong as theft, but horribly sinful. as sacrilege. He might rob a poor family, and leave them to starve, and it would not be thought half as bad as to take this useless ornament. But this same church, and other churches too, encourage a form of religion which crushes down a large part of those faculties in man which are the ornament and glory of the human soul. They consider such repression as only a proper self-denial. But if man is the "temple of God," then why is it not the worst sacrilege to starve or crush any of his faculties,—those powers with which he serves and worships God most acceptably?

"Grow up *in all* things, therefore." True education is worship. Right development is the service of God.

This doctrine of universal development, as the aim and end of man's being, was taught perhaps more fully, and exemplified most entirely, in modern times, by the great German poet Goethe. He framed his whole life on that idea. His object was self-development. Accordingly, he was not satisfied with the triumphs he obtained in poetry and literature; but he devoted himself to science, and won new distinctions there. He also educated himself to business, and became one of the most practical and sensible of the ministers of the Grand Duke. He spent a long life in this process of self-development. Let him have the credit of it. Certainly it was a far more noble end than the mere pursuit of fame, of fortune, or of power. He sacrificed fame, fortune, and power, when they came in conflict with this object. His life, thus devoted, "without haste or rest," to this one large and deep idea, is a lesson to mankind of a truer use of genius than genius often shows.

Yet we must add that this is not all. There is something more. "Grow *up*." "Grow up in all things;" but also "grow up in all things into him who is our Head, even Christ." This is what Goethe, with all his wisdom, failed to see. This is what makes the apostolic maxim wiser than his. To grow up is an end, but not the final end. Grow up, in order to grow up into Christ. That is, since Christ is another name for generous Love, cultivate and unfold all powers in order to do good, for the sake of helping, saving, inspiring, guiding, animating, encouraging other souls. Develop all your powers, but for universal usefulness.

In my youth, I had a friend who was a woman of genius. She studied Goethe, and was thoroughly familiar with his thought. She also adopted it as her rule, and said she early learned that the only object of life was to grow. With wonderful, untiring energy, she pursued this end, and cultivated every power and faculty to the highest point. She was an extraordinary woman, yet not then altogether a satisfactory woman. There was something haughty and self-reliant, some absence of sympathy, some contempt for common people, which hurt you in intercourse with her. To her friends, she was all generosity; but, to others, indifferent and unsympathizing. But God did not mean that such a noble soul should stop there. Being so much, he meant she should be more; and so he took her through a deep experience of weakness and sorrow, through lonely days, through poverty and pain; and, at last, she had learned to add this crowning grace of human sympathy and tenderness to all the rest. She grew up into Christ, and devoted all these ripe and rich powers to the cause of *his* poor, his wounded and prisoners, his enslaved and oppressed ones; and so the woman of genius became at last also the Christian woman, risen with Christ, and sitting in heavenly places with him.

One method of growth is mentioned in the text,— "Speaking the truth in love." It is not usually thought that growth comes by "speaking:" it is thought we get our Christian growth rather by hearing truth than by uttering it. If *we* were to exhort a church now, we should be more likely to say to it, "*Hearing* the truth meekly, grow up into Christ." But Paul was not in the habit of writing without a clear meaning; and he meant what he said, that the Church should grow by speaking as well as by hearing. If hearing truth is our food, speaking it is our exercise. We need exercise, as well as food, in order to grow; and, as a matter of fact, we see that only those really grow up into a manly stature who have the courage and loyalty which make them speak the truth which they have seen. This is the daily gymnastic exercise of the Christian,— to utter faithfully, by action and word, his convictions, in the presence of those who do not share them; to testify to the truth, whether men will hear or forbear; to be a burning and a shining light in the world; and yet to do all this, not ostentatiously, but modestly; not sharply, but kindly; not in severity, but in love. If the spirit of Christ dwells in us, a spirit of truth and love, we can do it. We see men who can do it, and perhaps oftener women. We see those who contrive to be faithful, without giving offence; who can say truth, which is like a sharp sword, and yet say it so lovingly and gently that no one can be displeased. Such people are the salt of the earth; and while they keep it from decay, while they preserve society pure, and public opinion sound, they grow up themselves in all things into Christ. They become more Christ-like every day, more divine and more human, more near to God and to us. They fill us with their peace, joy, and trust. They make life more hopeful and precious to us all.

XI.

LIFE WEARINESS.

Eccles. i. 2: "VANITY OF VANITIES, SAITH THE PREACHER; VANITY OF VANITIES; ALL IS VANITY."

TO one man, every thing is vanity; to another, nothing. To Solomon, satiated with pleasure, the world seemed very empty; but to every earnest man and woman it is very full and significant. Scepticism finds no meaning in life; but faith, hope, and love find life very full of meaning. We are all of us sometimes like King Solomon, and say, "All is vanity;" but we are also all of us sometimes like Paul, and say, "All things work together for good to those who love God." In other words, life seems very empty and very weary to those who live one way; but very rich, full, and significant to those who live in another way.

I know no greater misery than this condition of life-weariness. It is not a very uncommon state of mind. It happens more often with the young than with older persons. They are tired of life before they have begun to live. Such is the state of the present generation. They are "born fatigued," as some one says. Children in their early teens write verses, in which they declare themselves to have exhausted life. They have seen every thing, and nothing is of value. "Omnia fui, nihil expedit," as a Roman emperor said. They have just come to the feast, and are already satisfied.

The pretence, the affectation, the assumption, of this state of mind is ridiculous enough; but sometimes it is considered a religious duty to take no interest in any thing. A Christian, it is supposed, ought not to care for any thing but the world to come. He should abstract himself from this life and all its interests, and think only of death and eternity. This theory of Christianity seems to assume that God did not make this world; that God is not in it; that there is no such thing as Providence arranging life, and guiding it. For if this world is God's world; if God is in it, around us, above us, beneath, within, — then life, the present life, being full of God, *is* the life eternal. Then he who despises it despises God. Such is the impiety belonging to all forms of monastic religion; to the monasticism of Protestantism, no less than that of Catholicism. A Catholic monk may live apart from the world, and yet not despise it: but how many Protestants there are, believing themselves pious because they look with austere eyes on all the joy and activity of the world; on all the gayety of youth; on all the glory of nature, the beauty of art, the achievements of genius; on all the humble pleasures of the uneducated but honest children of God, who receive life as a gift from his hands not to be despised! Because Solomon, *blasé* with pleasure, a mere voluptuary, a self-indulgent man of the world, heaping up knowledge simply for his own enjoyment,—because he found life at last empty, therefore it is supposed to be the duty of Christian men and women to despise this great gift of God to us all.

Sometimes also it is thought to be very sagacious to be cynical, and to sneer at life as stale, flat, and unprofitable. A person takes a position of superiority, as though he was acquainted with many worlds, and, on the whole, thought this a poor one. To despise the world is taken as a proof that one knows the world very well. Therefore certain persons indulge themselves in an amiable misanthropy. They are very good and kind at heart; but they love to talk of the degeneracy of the times, to say that the former days were better than these, to declare the world going to decay. I rode to town last summer, sitting fifteen minutes by the side of one of these gentlemen; and I was told more about the desperate state of the times than I had learned in ten years before. He told me that there was no virtue in public men now, no knowledge in scholars, no taste in writers, no piety or capacity in preachers, no good anywhere. I told him that there was comfort then; that such a desperate state of things must be the sign of Christ's coming. He thought not: he thought Christ would not condescend to come to a generation that had deserted all the old conservative landmarks, as this had done. So differently do we see things! I had lived among those whose faces were to the future; who saw the mighty rose of dawn in the eastern sky, like the face of God himself; and who thanked God every day for being permitted to live in such a time. Meanwhile my conservative neighbor was looking the other way into the departing night, and grieving for the secession of the owls and bats.

What makes life seem empty? and what, on the other hand, makes it seem rich and full?

Genius, the universal artist, has painted four pictures of this disease of life-weariness, and hung them in the galleries of human thought, to warn us for ever of the dangers that lie in this direction of intellectual despair.

First, The genius of inspiration has painted for us, in the book of Ecclesiastes, the portrait of Solomon, as the first type of this terrible disease. The book of Ecclesiastes is full of this dreary scepticism. Solomon had tried every thing, — riches, power, pleasure, knowledge, — and found them all vanity; and so he went about to despair of all his labor which he had taken under the sun. Why? Because of his gigantic egotism; because he had made himself the centre of all things; because he had brought every thing — wealth, knowledge, pleasure — to Solomon to try; because he had considered the world made for him, instead of considering himself made for the world. Therefore this desperate gloom, this black darkness of doubt. For it is with us in life as with the systems of Ptolemy and Copernicus. Consider your own earth in the middle of the universe, and regard all the suns, planets, and stars as moving around *you* as their centre, and the most inextricable confusion results. There is only an unmeaning going forward and backward among the planets, endless tangles of curves, without object and without result. But go out of this subjective theory, identify yourself with universal law, conceive of the sun as the centre, and your planet, as well as others, to go round it, and all becomes fair and lovely in the planetary movements; all is full of charm, and a divine order reigns in the deep heavens. So when we put ourselves morally in the centre of things, and consider every thing meant to revolve round us, all is confusion in the moral world; and not till we make God the centre, and follow his attraction in our orbit of obedience and faith, does order arise out of the seeming contradictions of our life.

I consider, therefore, the book of Ecclesiastes as an inspired picture of a great scepticism, born of a great self-seeking.

A *second* picture is given us by Shakespeare in "Hamlet." That wonderful master has shown his knowledge of human nature in nothing more than in being able to project himself out of his own time, which was one of action and endeavor, into an age not yet arrived, in which thought was in excess over life ; an age "sicklied o'er with the pale cast of thought." Hamlet belongs to our time, rather than to the day of Shakespeare. His disease is one we know very well. When he says, —

> "How weary, stale, flat, and unprofitable
> Seem to me all the uses of this world!" —

he says just what Solomon said, but not from the same motive. It was not a gigantic despair, born of a gigantic selfishness; but it was one which came from the ideal and imaginative nature being developed out of all proportion to the active. If a man is always thinking of great things which may be done, noble deeds, vast creations, a beautiful life to lead, a good character to form, and never begins to *do* any thing, then he falls at last into a condition like that of Hamlet. The cure for this is to *do* something, — some conscientious, faithful work, — some thorough, steady, regular occupation. For to be always thinking of what ought to be done, and never doing it, is sure to end in despondency and madness at last.

Then, in our day, two other highly gifted poets have given us the same picture of life-weariness, but springing from yet another root. Goethe in his "Faust," and Byron in his "Childe Harold," have painted the malady of the century then passing away. The disease of the eighteenth century was the want of faith. It did not believe in God. I do not mean that it was irreligious: it was sufficiently religious in the sense of attending to religious forms and ceremonies. It built hundreds of churches in England, precise, formal, the image of that religion, the essence of which was propriety; * but it believed in religion, not in God. As has been well said, "Instead of having God for its religion, it had religion for its God." The Father, the Friend, the Divine Providence, the Spirit which has its seat in every soul, the Love which moves in the depth of every heart, the Divinity which shapes our ends, — this God had disappeared from the faith of the eighteenth century; and therefore the nineteenth was born an orphan child, "without God and hope in the world." This state of things Goethe painted in his "Faust," and Byron in "Childe Harold." The immense popularity of these two books came from their exposing the condition of every heart. The first step toward cure was taken when the disease was fully painted. Faust, rich in all genius and knowledge, had lost his childlike faith. The Easter bells, and the Easter song of the women and angels, touch his heart only through the memory. When they sing outside of his study, "Christ is arisen, the joy of those who love!" Faust replies,

---

* "Mamma," said a little English girl to her mother, "is not Mr. A. a very wicked man?"

"No, my dear: why do you think so?"

"Because he never puts his face into his hat when he comes into his pew at church."

The anecdote gives a very good idea of the old-fashioned Church-of-England religion.

"I hear you, O heavenly tones, mighty and tender! I hear the message well; but *faith* is wanting in my heart. My tears flow; but the earth claims me again."

"Without God, and without hope in the world,"— such was the life as well as the song of the greatest English poet of the century, whose wonderful genius uttered only one long wail of despair. On him all gifts of nature and fortune were wholly wasted. To him poetry brought no calm; love, no joy; success, no peace. His human heart, made for God, and having no God, broke, because it was so alone in the world.*

We have seen what makes life empty. Now we can see what makes it rich and full.

First, plenty of work makes it full. The day-laborer, who lives close to Nature in his regularity of toil, who goes out of himself in steady, continuous action, has health and content in his heart, born of daily work. When we pray, "Give us to-day our daily bread," we may well pray that it may be given

---

* Very well to Byron applies what Mrs. Browning says so tenderly of Cowper:—

"While thus guided, he remained
  Unconscious of the guiding;
And things provided came, without
  The sweet sense of providing.
He testified the solemn truth,
  Though frenzy desolated,—
Nor man nor nature satisfy
  What only God created."

to us in healthy toil. Work is the real bread which comes down from heaven; and is gathered every morning by man, going forth to his labor. Work gives balance and regularity to all the movements of the soul. It drives all diseased fancies out of the mind. The condition, however, is, that it shall be really work, not the show of it; that we shall put ourselves wholly into it for the time; that we shall not work mechanically nor reluctantly, but with our thoughts present, our heart in it as well as our hands. To be doing one thing, and thinking of something else, is very bad for the soul. I have lately been reading the "Biographies of English Ironworkers and Tool-makers" (a most interesting book, by Smiles), in which he describes such men as Bramah and Nasmyth, who put their whole mind into what they did, and so became really heroic characters. From the smut and blackness of the forge and machine-shop, they came out the strong leaders of England, in its march of civilization. While the aristocracy of the land were wasting its strength in foolish wars of conquest, these men were adding, by industrial inventions, a hundred million of men to its power, and thousands of millions of pounds sterling to its wealth. They are the creators of the strength and wealth of England to-day.

Necessary labor is the great blessing of life to the mass of men, the great educator of character to all men. Labor, into which thought and heart go, is the moral salvation of us all. We can never do without it. In the midst of all care and trial, work keeps us healthy and happy. After Nasmyth had invented the steam-hammer, which can cut in two a log of iron, weld an anchor, or crack a nut without bruising the meat, he gave up this business, and rested himself by making a telescope, and studying the heavens; and he has already, within a year or two, made some remarkable discoveries in the solar atmosphere, which Sir John Herschel declares to be among the greatest discoveries of the time.

Work, then, makes life rich and full.

But so also does love. Passion, appetite, desire, devastate the soul, and leave it a desert; but love, which goes out of itself, which takes a hearty interest in others, which seeks every opportunity of helping those who need help, which is ingenious in resources to bless and comfort the sorrowing and needy, — this keeps "the world's unwithered countenance fresh as on creation's day." Friendship makes the earth seem rich and full. To know that there are some souls, hearts and minds, here and there, who trust us, and whom we trust; some who know us, and whom we know; some on whom we can always rely, and who will always rely on us, — makes a paradise of this great world. O solitary and bereaved hearts, who feel yourselves lonely! believe that there is this solace, if you seek it. Go and help in any good work, with earnest good will, and you will find that those who are working there in the same spirit have become your friends. Do not seek to be loved, but seek to be and do something really good, and love will come of itself; for here, as always, it is truest, that, if you "give, it shall be given you,—full measure, pressed down and running over."

That which makes this earth seem solid, and not empty, is not the rocks and mountains that are in it, but the love that is in it. The only really solid thing in this universe is love. This makes our life really life. This makes us immortal while we are here. This makes us sure that death is no end, but only a beginning, to us and to all we love. God showers this blessing on us day by day, if we will only receive it. He sends us messages of his love in the morning planets and the rosy clouds of the early day. He sends us messages of love in the fresh air which kisses our cheek; in the sweet little children around our path; in the dear friends who make life full of interest and charm; in the opportunities of usefulness, of improvement, of progress, which come hour by hour, day by day; in all the grand events of history; in the noble struggles of our nation in this hour of trial; in the grand courage of our brothers and sons, going to lay down their lives for their dear mother-land. God's infinite love comes to us daily in all these events and opportunities; and how can any one say that "all is vanity," when such inspirations are open to the soul?

Love, therefore, joining hands with faith and work, makes our life rich and full. These three, neither of them alone; work which is done in love, love which is born of faith. And it is a blessed thing, that, the longer we live thus, the more beautiful the world becomes, the more rich and precious our life seems. It is the young who are oftenest tired of life. As we live on, we seem to grow younger, not older; we find ourselves coming nearer to God and man; we grow more like little children in our hearts. Therefore we see so often that beautiful picture of old age and childhood forming the loveliest friendship; the old man with white hair, and with the wisdom of years treasured up in his large experience, being the companion and best friend of little curly-headed boys and girls, who are never so happy as with him. Beautiful is age when it does not grow hard and cold, but grows evermore full of faith and love. The old man looks backward through a life in which he has learned to know the wonders of Nature, to know the heart and thoughts of many varieties of human character; in which he has done his part in the world in his own place, doing faithfully whatever he has done. He looks back over the long perspective, and he sees how kindly God has led him on; how he has been taught by disappointment and success; how he has gone deep into his own heart, gathered up wisdom, become truly free by self-control and self-direction; he sees how he has ceased to think of God as Power and Law, and come to think of him as Friend and Father. And so he wonders that he ever could have been weary of life; so he feels the infinite riches of the universe; so he thanks God, not with words, but in the depths of a happy heart, for the gift of existence; so he looks on all things as God looked on them, when he made them; and says, "It is all good."

Thus we see how, by true living, —

> "More and more a providence
> Of love is understood;
> Making the springs of time and sense
> Sweet with eternal good."

XII.

THE FRAGMENTS.

John vi. 12: "GATHER UP THE FRAGMENTS THAT REMAIN, THAT NOTHING BE LOST."

TWO facts strike us in regard to Nature: one is its exuberance; the other, its economy.

The exuberance of Nature appears everywhere. There is everywhere a surplus, — a large margin over and above what is necessary. In what immense spaces the planets swim through the heavens! The moon, nearest to us, is two hundred thousand miles away. What vast spaces in the universe are empty of planet, sun or star, comet or nebula! Then, on the earth, what latitude is given to the ocean! What vast portions of every continent are empty! China, with its three hundred millions of inhabitants, has great forests, deserts, and mountains, where no one dwells. Massachusetts is much the most densely settled State in the Union; but, if you ride on the cars from Boston to Providence, it seems, for a great part of the way, as if you were going through an uninhabited country. New York, with its three millions of people, Pennsylvania and Ohio, each with their two millions, have enough rich farming land and woodland to give homes to the whole population of the United States, and leave room enough for twice as many more. What quantities of trees grow, stand, fall, and decay, unused and unseen by man! What flowers come and go every summer day in the thousand valleys, never noticed! What fruit ripens and falls uneaten by man or beast! What myriads of seeds are produced for one that germinates! How luxuriant is the aspect of Nature! — its infinite showers of light; its treasures of rain and snow; its abundance of every thing; its generous superfluity, —

"Wild above rule or art, enormous bliss!"

So in the nature of man is the same exuberance, the same abundance in his faculties and his experience. Our life is not tied down to any mechanical rigor of performance. We have time enough, opportunity enough, faculty enough, for every thing. What we cannot do to-day, we can do to-morrow. What we cannot do one way, we can do another. There is plenty of every thing in human nature. One thing only we need; and that is faith in it, — faith in the nature God has given us, its capacities and possibilities. Faith is the golden key which unlocks this splendid treasury, the human soul. Whatever is right and good, whatever the instinct of the heart tells us to do, believe that we are able to do it, and we *can* do it.

How much there is in man has never been discovered. The maximum of human attainments has not been reached. Napoleon did a great deal; but he seemed to himself to be idle. He might have done a great deal more. Theodore Parker, one of the severest workers we have ever had in America, declared that he had left half his faculties unused. The greatest saint is conscious to himself of how much better he might be than he is; and so he calls himself the chief of sinners. The great poet or artist knows that his noblest deed has had another, —

> "Of bright imagination born, —
> A loftier and a nobler brother,
> From dear existence torn."

One of Milton's sonnets, written at twenty-three years of age, laments his own backwardness, and his late spring that shows no bud or blossom. If he had known what he was to do before he died, he might have been patient.

Time, also, is given us in profusion. We often say we have no time for this or that; but we usually say what is not true. Every one has ten times as much time as he uses. No one has ever put into a day a hundredth part of what he might. One day would be enough to think every thing, feel every thing, and do every thing we need to in this world, if we were only fully alive, full enough of soul, to make its hours crowded with glorious life. Did you ever see a letter from any one to a distant friend, which did not begin with this apology: "I ought to have written to you sooner; but I had no time"? It is almost always a falsehood. It should be, "I had not the will, I had not the heart, I had not the confidence in myself, nor the trust that things would come to me to say. My mind has seemed empty." That is the true reason; but we make believe it is a want of time. No: time is inexhaustible to a living soul. Only let the soul be sufficiently full of life, and a moment seems like a year.

To be sure, there is a certain amount of time required for all merely mechanical work; but, for soul-work, there is always time enough, if we only find soul enough. It takes me fifteen minutes to come from the town in which I live to Boston; and I do not see how that can be abridged: but, when I reach Boston, I go to see some noble person, some dear friend, or some earnest, generous spirit; or I go to the home of sorrow and trial; and, in one minute, I live a whole year of thought or sympathy or purpose. One second is long enough to change the current of life, — to turn us upward toward heaven, or downward toward hell. The critical moments of life are not to be measured by the watch or the almanac. We look back over weary years, empty of all interest, to some few golden moments when we really lived. Those moments of pure insight, of pure love, of real action, — those made our life: all the rest is nothing. "What is the chaff to the wheat?"

We have, therefore, not only enough of every thing, but more than enough, and a great deal more than enough. The busiest person has some golden, precious moments of leisure, worth far more than the long days of the idle man.

Consider the life of Jesus. His active recorded life is thought to have been, at most, three years: probably it was not much more than one year. But because he had faith in God, and confidence in himself, his overflowing soul filled those few months so full of thought and love, that the four Gospels, the sacred books of mankind, could only take up and record for us a small part of it. If every thing had been written, "the world itself could not contain the books that should be written." That is hardly an hyperbole. Of course, it could not. Why, what Jesus said and did each day, during the twelve hours, was all memorable. We have only gathered up a few shells by the side of that ocean of truth and love. We are riparian proprietors, so to speak, dwelling on a little bit of the shore, and looking out over a small portion of the surface of the immeasurable sea which bathes all the continents of earth.

But thus, while nature and life are so exuberant, the difficulty is that we waste them both. Therefore the lesson of our text, — "Let nothing be lost." Count nothing insignificant.

This lesson is also taught by Nature, throughout whose boundless profusion and royal abundance there reigns an equally austere economy. God gathers up in nature the fragments, and allows nothing to be lost. Not a comet, escaped from its elliptic restraint, and shooting off on a parabolic or hyperbolic curve into outer darkness, but Nature reaches out after it with the long arm of gravitation, whose fingers are fine enough to catch the minutest particle of impalpable ether, and strong enough to hold in their places the enormous masses of planets and suns. Not a drop of rain, falling in primeval showers to water Eden, but has been kept safe till now. It escaped into the sod, it filtered through the sand; but it was taken into the company of other drops, and carried in hidden channels below, till it came up a flashing diamond in a mountain-spring, was tossed on the curve of a tumbling torrent, and at last went to the ocean by some old historic river, — Euphrates or Nile. Then the sun darted forth a ray of heat to meet it, a messenger sent ninety-six millions of miles, charged to gather up this one drop, and lift it again into air, and, with its evaporated tissue, to paint the edge of a cloud on some golden sunset. Every thing is transformed in Nature; nothing lost. Imperial Cæsar, turned to clay, may stop a hole to keep away the wind; but he is not lost. Decay's effacing fingers sweep away the lines of lingering beauty in flower and tree and man; but the mighty chemical affinities continually gather up all the particles, and combine them anew, and suffer nothing to be lost. I recollect in a class-recitation at Cambridge, in chemistry, the question being put about some new combination, when every thing else had been accounted for, — "But what became of the carbon?" said the professor. The student hesitated, and at last said, "It was *lost*, sir." What laughter greeted the absurd reply! for chemistry has announced to the world, as its fundamental law, that in Nature nothing is lost. All things are changed. Tennyson says in one of his poems, unpublished in this country, —

"When will the stream be aweary of flowing
Under my eye?
When will the wind be aweary of blowing
Over the sky?
When will the clouds be aweary of fleeting,
When will the heart be aweary of beating,
And Nature die?
Never, oh, never! nothing will die.
The stream flows;
The wind blows;
The cloud fleets;
The heart beats:
Nothing will die!"

And this great law of economy in Nature has its corresponding law in the moral and spiritual world. When Christ said to his disciples, "Gather up the fragments that remain, that nothing be lost," it was not because they needed the fragments of bread and fish; but it was to teach them the law of economy, — that it was wrong to waste any thing. He had just shown them that they never could need when he was near them; that he had at his beck the inexhaustible supplies of miracle. But that might make them careless and wasteful. God has limited us by need, that we may limit ourselves afterward by economy. This economy is sacred and religious, not selfish. It recognizes all things as given by God; given for use, not waste; to be treated reverently, not recklessly. When we see any one throw away a good piece of bread, we rightly feel pained. It is not because of the value of the bread, but because of the disrespect shown to what religious people, in their old-fashioned language, called "God's good creature." If a friend had made for you, with thought, love, and skill, some little gift, a pen-wiper or a book-mark, you would not throw it away when you did not want it longer, because your friend's love, time, and care went into it. But God has put into the piece of bread how much creative wisdom and providing love! the wonderful mystery of the seed and its germination; the horticulture of prepared soils, moisture, air, sun, and the changing seasons; and then the chemistry of fermentation, and the alchemy of fire. A piece of bread becomes sacred when we think of such things; and to partake of it is to partake of the sacrament. You would not throw a piece of consecrated bread from the communion-table upon the floor, to be trampled on; for it has been sanctified by love and prayer. But all nature is thus consecrated, and becomes sacred, when we see the finger of God in it.

Therefore our New-England ancestors, who themselves learned economy as a necessity on these sterile shores, taught it to their children as a religion. New-England children, down to my time, were taught economy as a sacred moral duty. I am afraid that that time has passed away. A habit of wastefulness, injurious to the character, has since come in with prosperity.

But as every thing good runs into an extreme, and so becomes a vice, our New-England economy sometimes ran into an extreme, and became parsimony. Sometimes we can save a thing only by using it, or by giving it away. We lose it by trying to keep it. You remember the epitaph on a tombstone, — "What I gave, I have; what I spent, I had; what I kept, I lost." The great millionnaire, who dies without having done any great good with his wealth, evidently loses it all in a day. He might have kept part of it by using it in some good cause, for some good end. He might have had some royal charity, some bounty that was to bless and save thousands growing up under his own living eyes; have caused the widows' hearts to sing for joy; lightened the sorrows of the orphans, and been followed to the grave by the grateful feet of thousands whom he had rescued. There are lower and higher economies: if he kept his money, he only practised the lowest.

So sometimes we lose time by trying to save it in a parsimonious way; trying to utilize every moment to some outward, visible end. Young men sometimes make this mistake when they begin to preach. They see that there is a great deal to do, and so allow themselves no relaxation, but sit all day long trying to study or to write. But this stupefies them. They would do better to expand and vitalize their souls by the good intercourse of friendship, or the glad inspiration of Nature. Then they would come back to their study, and have something to say. As it is, they only sit looking at the blank paper with a blank mind. So Milton says,—

"To measure life, learn thou betimes, and know
Towards solid good what leads the nearest way;
For other things mild Heaven a time ordains,
And disapproves that care, though wise in show,
That with *superfluous labor* loads the day."

Dissipation is waste; but recreation is economy. So that whatever time is spent in gaining new life and moral power is well spent; and that is just the rule by which to distinguish between the kind and amount of amusement which is right. That which recreates (*re*-creates) the mind is good; that which *dissipates*, wastes it, is bad.

But there is a higher economy still in this great scale. There is an economy of life, which consists in giving it away; an economy of the heart and soul, which consists in their devotion to a great good. Jesus says, "He who loves his life shall lose it; but he who loses his life for my name's sake and the gospel's, the same shall find it." He does not teach us any mercantile economy or any calculating religion: Christ's religion is not a spiritual insurance-office, by which we can secure heaven and escape hell hereafter by a certain weekly regular deposit of prayers and religious acts here. Many people think so, and are taught so. They are taught that Christ came merely to show them how to save their own souls from hell, and that this is the true thing to aim at. Christianity teaches no such selfishness as that. It teaches us that God will take care of our soul and our safety, if we go out and do his work and his will. It says, "If we will love others, God will love and bless us."

Yes: Jesus came to gather up the fragments which remain of human virtue, love, and goodness, that nothing should be lost. There are always some fragments which remain in every heart. God's great law of economy applies to these. If he does not allow a comet to wander hopelessly away into emptiness, but sends the great archangel gravitation to bring it back, he will not let a soul, made in his own image, go off on any fatal erratic curve into outer darkness. The great archangel Love shall pursue the lost souls, and find them. That is what Christianity teaches, if it teaches any thing. The Son of man comes to seek and save the lost. If he had pity on the fragments of bread, the overflowings of his bountiful good-will, will he not pity the fragments of broken minds and broken hearts? He does. He does not choose to drink the cup of joy alone in the heavenly kingdom of God. He cannot be happy there, unless you and I are there with him. He cannot be happy there, unless we bring with us our lost brethren and sisters who are perishing around us for lack of a little love. Has God sent Christ to seek and save the lost? and shall he not find them and save them? Why, not a particle of these multitudinous snowflakes which fell last night but has been made by divine fingers into lovely hexagons, and not a particle but comes to do a special work. Shall not Christ do his? Yea, verily. "As the rain cometh down, and the snow from heaven, and returneth not thither, but watereth the earth, making it bring forth seed to the sower, and bread to the eater; so shall my word be that goeth out of my mouth."

Man is made for progress; but there are two kinds of progress. One kind consists in going forward from one thing to another, — one knowledge to another knowledge; dropping the past behind us, in order to attain the future. It is leaving the good to gain the better; giving up one truth for the sake of another. It is being "eternal seekers, with no past behind us." But another and higher kind is that which gathers up the past into the present, absorbs history into life, makes all old experiences "consolidate in mind and frame." That is the only progress which endures: the other always falls a victim to re-action. Re-action in life and history is only going back to pick up something we have forgotten. So the re-action from democracy in Europe to monarchy is going back to get something good in monarchy which democracy forgot to take. Re-action from Protestantism to Catholicism is going back to get something good belonging to the Roman Church which Protestantism left behind. Re-action from Liberal Christianity to Orthodoxy is the same thing. No progress is sure that leaves any thing behind it forgotten or neglected; and so the human race will make no progress while it leaves any part neglected behind. We are members of a great body, and each needs all the rest. The English thought they could do without the Irish, and leave them behind, uncultivated, mere serfs; but the Irish have hung as a clog on the progress of England, and compelled her at last to recognize their claim. We thought we could leave the negroes behind, and neglect them, while we, members of the great American Republic, were going on, in long strides, to the acme of prosperity and greatness. But wiser fate said, "No." We have been obliged to turn round, and go back, and find the negro, to take him with us. And so there can be no real progress or peace in society while any class remains *neglected; while there are drunkards and prostitutes,* beggars and criminals, who have no care and no love extended to them. The taint of their disease comes up into our palaces and into our hearts. Let us, then, gather up the fragments, and seek and save the lost. The worst man and the worst woman have something good in them. Let us seek it, find it, and save it. The human race will not be saved till every human being is saved. The Orthodox doctrine was, that the redeemed would be made happier by looking down into hell, and seeing the torments of the damned, — their own fathers and children. The exact opposite is the truth. The redeemed are only redeemed themselves by saving the lost; and they cannot get to heaven till they bring the lost with them.

In the year 1717, from the 1st to the 6th of March, about this very time, there was the greatest snow-storm that ever happened in New England in the memory of man. The snow drifted twenty feet high in some places. In the town of Eastham, on the Cape, old Mr. Treat, who had been minister there for forty-five years, died. No paths could be cut to carry him to the grave. He lay in the house several days. At last, the Indians of Eastham, whom he had helped and taught, protected and comforted, dug an archway through the drifts, and carried the coffin of their friend on their own shoulders to the graveyard. That is the way in which we are to get to heaven: the hands of those we have helped must dig the way for us, and we must be carried on their shoulders through the drifts of our frozen life.

Many sins we commit, which freeze around the heart, and case it in an icy coat of selfishness. Many stormy and tempestuous gusts of passion rage over the human soul. But if the angel of charity stays with us; if we do not despise the poor, do not neglect the stranger, do not forsake the vicious and the prisoner, the needy and the ignorant; if we hold out a hand of help to the helpless, — these little acts of love will re-act on our own soul, and melt the ice, and warm our hearts with a strange spring-time of hope and joy. Those whose broken hearts you have healed; whose hurt consciences you have comforted; whose lost steps you have guided; whose despair you have removed; for whom you have given thought, time, strength, and life,—they are to carry you on their shoulders to heaven.

This explains the singular peace and comfort which our brave men have in the midst of their sufferings in the battle and camp, in the hospitals, and on the field. They have given themselves for the country and for us, and God blesses them. They forget themselves, and he remembers them. One wrote home to his wife the other day, that he had lost both legs; and he drew on his letter the picture of a man on crutches, and said, "That's the way I'm coming home to you, Mary: but don't mind, Mary; we will be happy yet." Such men give, and it is given to them again: full measure, pressed down, running over, does God give into their bosoms, of his comfort and of his peace.

In the mint in Philadelphia, there is a room where the gold is rolled and clipped and stamped, and cut into coin. The floor is of iron cut into holes, and the sweepings of the room fall through, and once a month are put into the furnace; and in this way are saved some forty thousand dollars' worth of gold every year that before was lost. But what are fragments of gold or diamond to fragments of love, hope, and insight?

So gather up the fragments which remain of God's wonderful gifts in Nature and in Providence, of his mysterious and beautiful gifts in the minds, consciences, and hearts of men.

You have seen the priests, after the sacrament, take care that none of the consecrated bread should be wasted, and request the communicants to distribute among them what remains, and eat it all up, to the last crumb. Do this, if it seems to you proper and devout. Tithe the mint and the anise, if you will; but forget not the weightier matters of the law. Do not forget, that far more sacred than any consecrated bread is that true bread which came down from heaven; that sacred, divine gift of the soul which God has placed in man; that power of aspiration, capacity of progress, sense of right, knowledge of infinite truth, fitness for boundless love and thought and action. Do not let even the crumbs of this fall to the ground, if you can save them; for, of all holy things on earth, nothing is so holy in the sight of God as the soul of man.

XIII.

ALL SOULS ARE GOD'S.

Ezek. xviii. 4: "ALL SOULS ARE MINE."

DURING the past week,* two Christian festivals have been celebrated by the Church of Rome, which I should be glad to see celebrated by all Christian denominations. They were instituted in days when the Church was truly Catholic, and had not become exclusive, — the days of church unity and universality; and these days are festivals of a universal Church and of a true unity. In the year eight hundred and thirty-five, the first day of November was appointed by Gregory IV. as a festival for all the saints; and it has ever since been known as All-Saints' Day. It is a day on which we may remember the saints and martyrs of every time, every land, and every creed; a day on which the war of theology should cease, the bitterness of controversy subside; which should be a "truce of God" amid warring

---

* This sermon was preached on the Sunday following the festivals of ALL SAINTS and ALL SOULS, Nov. 1 and Nov. 2.

sects. On this day, recognizing the fact that eminent goodness is monopolized by no party, that devoted piety and disinterested humanity are to be found in every denomination, all sections of the Church might unite in one great procession, to visit, with grateful love and memory, the holy tombs of all the good. Catholic and Protestant, Methodist and Quaker, Orthodox and Heterodox, might kneel together in grateful prayer around the graves of St. Francis and St. Charles, of Oberlin and Fénélon, of George Fox and John Wesley, of Milton and Priestley. On this day, the Church would be truly universal. As the first day of November is the Feast of All Saints, so the second day of November is the Feast of All Souls; and is, in its idea and spirit, even more universal, more catholic, than the other. If the first is the day of the universal *church* brotherhood, the other is a day for universal human brotherhood. It was originally established in the eleventh century, in commemoration of the souls of those who had departed during the year. It is not intended for the great and distinguished alone, not for the eminently good alone; but for all, — all souls. It is not for the holy and happy alone; but for the unwise, the unhappy, the unholy also, — those whose present lives seem to be failures. It is a feast of Christian hope, of hope for all, — hope founded in the indestructible elements of the soul itself, as made by God, and made for himself.

This last is the subject for our meditations to-day.

Let us see how it is that all souls belong to God; what it is that is meant when he says, "All souls are mine." Let us see how the despised, forgotten, abandoned children of earth still belong to God, and still are dear to him.

When we look at the world from any other point of view than the Christian, we are led to despise or to undervalue the mass of men. The man of culture looks down on them as incapable of mental improvement; the man of righteousness sees them hoplessly immersed in vice and crime; the reformer turns away discouraged, seeing how they cling to old abuses. Every thing discourages us but Christianity. That enables us to take off all these coverings, and find, beneath, the indestructible elements and capacities of the soul itself. We see standing before us a muffled figure: it has been dug out of the ground, and is covered with a mass of earth. The man of taste looks at it, and finds nothing attractive: he sees only the wretched covering. The moralist looks at it, and finds it hopelessly stained with the earth and the soil in which it has so long lain. The reformer is discouraged, finding that it is in fragments, — whole limbs wanting; and considers its restoration hopeless. But another comes, inspired by a profounder hope: and he sees, beneath the stains, the divine lineaments; in the broken fragments, the wonderful proportions. Carefully he removes the coverings; tenderly he cleanses it from its stains; patiently he re-adjusts the broken parts, and supplies those which are wanting: and so at last it stands, in a royal museum or pontifical palace, an Apollo or a Venus, the very type of manly grace or feminine beauty, — a statue which enchants the world. The statue, broken and defaced, is our common humanity; so broken, so defaced, that only the far-reaching hope, founded on God's interest in the human soul, can enable us to do any thing adequately for its restoration.

1. All souls belong to God and to goodness by creation. God has evidently created every soul for goodness. He has carefully endowed it with indestructible faculties looking that way. Every soul has an indestructible idea of right and wrong, producing the feeling of obligation on the one hand, of penitence or remorse on the other; every soul has the tendency to worship, to look up to some spiritual power higher than itself, better than itself; every soul is endowed with the gift of freedom, made capable of choosing between life and death, good and evil; every soul is endowed with reason, with a capacity of knowledge; and especially is every soul endowed with the faculty of improvement, of progress.

Compared with the capacities and powers which are common to all, how small are the differences of genius or talent between man and man!

Now, suppose that we should see, in the midst of our city, a building just erected with care and cost. Its foundations are deeply laid; its walls are of solid stone; its various apartments are arranged with skill for domestic and social objects: but it is unoccupied and unused. We do not believe that its owner intends it to remain so: we believe that the day will come in which these rooms shall become a home; in which these vacant chambers shall resound with the glad shouts of children, and the happy laughter of youth; where one room shall be devoted to earnest study, another to serious conversation, another to safe repose, and the whole be sanctified by prayer. Such a building has God erected in every human soul. One chamber of the mind is fitted for thought, another for affection, another for earnest work, another for imagination, and the whole to be the temple of God. It stands now vacant; its rooms unswept, unfurnished, wakened by no happy echoes: but shall it be so always? Will God allow this soul, which belongs to him, so carefully provided with infinite faculties, to go wholly to waste? The man who buried his lord's talent was rebuked: will God bury his own talent, having made the soul for himself? Will he let it remain hidden in the earth, by not putting it to use, and educating it in the course of his providence?

2. No: God, having made the soul for goodness, is is also educating it for goodness. The soul, which belongs to God by creation, will also belong to him by education and culture.

We send our children to school, — to the primary school to learn to read and write; to the grammar-school, perhaps to an academy, perhaps to college; we put them to learn a trade or a profession, — and then we say we have given them an education. Meantime we do not see how God is educating them, and educating us too, in this his great school, — the world. The earth is God's school, where men are sent for seventy years, more or less, to be educated for the world beyond. All souls are sent to this school; all enjoy its opportunities. The poor, who cannot go to our schools; the wretched and the forlorn, who, we think, are without means of culture, — are perhaps better taught than we are in God's great university. The principal teachers in this school are three, — nature, events, and labor. Nature receives the new-born child, shows him her picture-book, and teaches him his alphabet with simple sights and sounds. She has a wonderful apparatus, and teaches every thing, and illustrates every thing she teaches, by experiments. She lets him handle wood, water, stones; shows him animals and birds, insects and fishes; and so familiarizes his mind with a fixed order, with permanent law, with cause and effect, substance and form, space and time. Happy are the children who can go the most to Mother Nature, and learn the most in her dame school. The little prince was wise who threw aside his fine playthings, and wished to go out and play in the beautiful mud.

The next teacher in God's school is labor. That which men call the primal curse, is, in fact, one of our greatest blessings. Those who are called the fortunate classes, because they are exempt from the necessity of toil, are, for that very reason, the most unfortunate. Work gives health of body and health of mind, and is the great means of developing character. Nature is the teacher of the intellect; but labor forms the character. Nature makes us acquainted with facts and laws; but labor teaches tenacity of purpose, perseverance in action, decision, resolution, and self-respect. The man who has done a day's work well respects himself, has contentment in his heart, and knows himself, however humble his sphere, to be in that sphere essential. It is bad that men should be overburdened or broken by toil; bad that children, whom God has sent to his school of Nature, should be sent too early into the school of work: but the necessity of daily labor is a gift to the race, the value of which we can scarcely estimate. If only a few were allowed to work, and the mass of men were condemned to idleness, the world would be a Pandemonium, and life a curse; but it is a gift to all, a means of education for all souls.

Then comes the third teacher,—those events of life which come to all,—joy and sorrow, success and disappointment, happy love, disappointed affection, bereavement, poverty, sickness and recovery, youth, manhood, and old age. Through this series of events, all are taken by the great teacher,—life: these diversify the most monotonous career with a wonderful interest. They are sent to deepen the nature, to educate the sensibilities. Thus nature teaches the intellect, labor strengthens the will, and the experiences of life teach the heart.

For all souls, God has provided this costly education. What shall we infer from it? If we see a man providing an elaborate education for his child, hardening his body by exercise and exposure, strengthening his mind by severe study, what do we infer from this? We naturally infer that he intends him for a grand career. If he knew that his son had a mortal disease which would take him away before maturity, would he subject him to this severe discipline? Then, when God disciplines us by severe toil and sharp sorrow, we may believe that he is thus forming us for a great career by and by.

3. Again: all souls belong to God by redemption. The work of Christ is for all: he died for all, the just and the unjust, that he might bring them to God. He came to reconcile all things unto God. Christ did not die for the great and the distinguished only, nor for the good and pure only; but for the most humble, neglected, and forlorn. The light streaming from his cross reveals in every soul a priceless treasure, dear to God, which he will not willingly lose. The value of a single soul in the eyes of God has been illustrated by the coming of Jesus as in no other way. The recognition of this value is a feature peculiar to Christianity. To be the means of converting a single soul, to put a single soul in the right way, has been considered a sufficient reward for the labors of the most devoted genius and the ripest culture; to rescue those who have sunk the lowest in sin and shame has been the especial work of the Christian

philanthropist; to preach the loftiest truths of the gospel to the most debased and savage tribes in the far Pacific has been the chosen work of the Christian missionary. In this they have caught the spirit of the gospel. God said, "I will send my Son." He chose the loftiest being for the lowliest work, and thus taught us how he values the redemption of that soul which is the heritage of all.

Now, if a man, apparently very humble, and far gone in disease, should be picked up in the street, and sent to the alms-house to die, and then if immediately there should arive some eminent person — say the governor or president — to visit him, bringing from a distance the first medical assistance, regardless of cost, we should say, "This man's life must be very precious: something very important must depend upon it." But, now, this is what God has done, only infinitely more, for all souls. He must, therefore, see in them something of priceless value. He does not wish to lose one. We are willing recklessly to injure or ruin our own soul for the most trifling gratification; but, in so doing, we destroy that which belongs to God, and which he prizes most highly.

4. Lastly, in the future life, all souls will belong to God.

The differences of life disappear at the grave, and all become equal again there. Then the outward clothing of rank, of earthly position, high or low, is laid aside; and each enters the presence of God, alone, as an immortal soul. Then we go to judgment and to retribution. But the judgments and retributions of eternity are for the same object as the education of time: they are to complete the work left unfinished here. In God's house above are many mansions, suited to every one's condition. Each will find the place where he belongs; each will find the discipline which he needs. Judas went to his place, the place which he needed, where it was best for him to go; and the Apostle Paul went to his place, the place best suited for him. The result of life with one man has fitted him for glory and honor; another is only fitted for outer darkness: but each will have what is best for him. We may throw ourselves away; but God will not throw us away. We belong to him still; and he "gathers up the fragments which remain, that nothing be lost." In order to become pure, we may need sharp suffering; and then God will not hesitate to inflict it. In the other life, as in this, he will chasten us, not for his pleasure, but for our profit, that we may be partakers of his holiness. It is thus that God's love for the soul, and its worth, appear eminently, in that he will not let us destroy ourselves. When we pass into the other world, those who are ready, and have on the wedding-garment, will go in to the supper. They will find themselves in a more exalted state of being, where the faculties of the body are exalted and spiritualized, and the powers of the soul are heightened; where a higher truth, a nobler beauty, a larger love, feed the immortal faculties with a divine nourishment; where our imperfect knowledge will be swallowed up in larger insight; and communion with great souls, in an atmosphere of love, shall quicken us for endless progress. Then faith, hope, and love will abide, — faith leading to sight, hope urging to progress, and love enabling us to work with Christ for the redemption of the race.

"All souls are MINE." Blessed declaration of the God-inspired Ezekiel! All souls — of the great and the humble, the rich and the poor, the wise and the ignorant, the king and the slave, the pure child and the abandoned woman, the soul of St. John and the soul of Judas Iscariot, — all belong to God. He will take care of what is his: he will leave no child orphaned. Those who are trodden down and forsaken in this world, — he watches their sorrowful lives, and will cause them to bring forth fruit at last. The hardened and selfish worldling, who mocks at the higher law, and knows no rule but his own miserable rule of temporal expediency, — God will teach him yet to know and revere immortal truth and heavenly virtue.

Thus does God love all souls with a universal, unwearied, untired affection; thus did Christ love all souls, gathering around him, by his deep interest in that vital centre of life, the publicans, Pharisees, and sinners, the pious and the profane. And thus, if we are Christians, we shall love all souls; calling no man common or unclean; believing in the brotherhood and sisterhood of the race; finding something good in every one, — a vital seed of nobleness in the most deadened bosom ; and, in thus loving other souls, our own souls will be blessed. While we forget ourselves, God will remember us ; while we seek to save others, we, too, shall be safe.

Let us rejoice, friends, in these great hopes. Let us bless God for his creating, educating, and saving love. Let us rejoice that the lost souls — lost to earth, lost to virtue, lost to human uses here — are not lost to God ; that he still holds them in his hand. Let us rejoice that those who will not be led to him by blessings and joy shall be led to him by terror, pain, and awful suffering. Let us rejoice that the glory of heaven and the lurid fires of hell shall both serve God, — both work together for God. Let us rejoice in the great communion of souls ; saints and sinners, — one great family, to be led by Christ to his Father. And let the humble ones of earth, forgotten by men, know that they are remembered by God, — the nameless martyrs, the uncelebrated lives, all recorded in the Great Book above.

"The thousands, that, uncheered by praise,
Have made one offering of their days ;
For Truth, for Heaven, for Freedom's sake,
Resigned the bitter cup to take ;
And silently, in fearless faith,
Bowing their noble souls to death, —

Where sleep they ? Woods and sounding waves
Are silent of those hidden graves.
Yet what if no light footstep there
In pilgrim love and awe repair ?
They sleep in secret ; but the sod,
Unknown to men, is marked of God."

XIV.

"THE ACCEPTED TIME."

2 Cor. vi. 2: "NOW IS THE ACCEPTED TIME; NOW IS THE DAY OF SALVATION."

IT is a distinction of man to live in the past and the future no less than in the present. The discourse of reason is to look before and after. Animals, indeed, have memory and hope. When a horse whinnies at noon, it shows both memory of the past, and hope as regards the future. He remembers that he has been fed before at that time; and he is expecting to be fed again. But man can *live* in the past and the future. He can project his soul backward or forward, and dwell in memory or hope, till the present hour becomes nothing to him. To illustrate this at length would be interesting, but is not necessary, and would take a whole sermon. Pass, therefore, to a second observation.

Though it is a distinction of man to be able to live in the past and future, this is not his highest or best condition. To let the past and future pour their consenting streams into his present life is better than to carry his life into the past or the future. This proposition I proceed to explain.

The lowest condition of man is that in which he is wholly immersed in the present. This implies the absence of all culture. The man's soul is enslaved by immediate circumstances, imprisoned in this square foot of space, in these sixty seconds of time. The moment that one begins to reflect or to imagine, he goes backward and forward, and so escapes from the weight of the present. The moment culture begins, we cease to be the slaves of this Now. The child studying geography, history, grammar, arithmetic, already escapes somewhat from the limitation of the present moment. He is away into Europe, or into the time of Alexander, or into the still more remote abstractions of pure reason.

The second condition of man is that in which he lives in the past or future, or alternately in past, present, and future. It is a higher state than the first, but not the highest. To escape from the present is better than to be its slave, but not so good as to be its master. Some people escape from the present by revery. They go into Dreamland or Fairy-land, and have a good time there; build castles in the air,— castles in Spain. This gives to them a certain feebleness of character, incapacitates them for work, weakens their moral power. Some people lead a double life, putting only half their thought into their action; having another world of favorite imagination where the other half goes. So many persons walk about the world as in a dream. They take no interest in the present. It seems to them, as to Hamlet, stale, flat, and unprofitable. But duty is in the present; love is in the present; all real life is in the present; and both heart, mind, and hand must be weakened by not taking hold of the present with energy. Any thing which makes us indifferent to the dawning day, which makes us glad when time passes, which makes us wish it were good that some other time might be here, indicates a morbid state. To live in dreams of the past, or visions of the future, is sickly. You may call it religion, if you will: it is none the less sickly. To retire from life into a cloister, in order to meditate upon an eternity hereafter, is morbid. To lose our interest in the present world, thinking about another, is morbid. Any thing which disqualifies us from our duty is morbid. Symptoms of this disease are when we lose our interest in life and men, get into a habit of staying at home, living in one room, avoiding society, or even in spending all our time in reading, which is one way of getting out of the present into the past. A habit of reading may indicate strength or weakness. It indicates strength when we read for a purpose; when reading is therefore a study; when we plunge into the past, in order to bring something to the present, as the diver learns to hold his breath, and go down fifty feet deep, in order to bring up pearls. But if we read merely to escape from our present life, duty, and work, into another, then it is no more creditable to read than it is to recreate ourselves in any other way. Of course, we have a right to read as a recreation, just as we may take a walk or amuse ourselves in any other way.

Some people rush from the present into the future on the wings of hope. Some fly back from the present into the past with the trembling steps of fear. These are visionaries; those are anxious and timid souls. Some step aside into Dreamland or into a cloister. People cloister themselves in their parlors or their churches, their studies or their clubs, their cliques, their parties, their sects. So they escape timidly, I may say as cowards, from the battle of the present hour. For the present hour is always the scene of a great battle between right and wrong, truth and falsehood, good and evil; and no one has a right to fly from it into Dreamland or Bookland, or even into meditations on a heaven which God does not deem it well to give us as yet.

The third and highest condition of human culture, therefore, is that in which man lives in the present, but with a life drawn from the past and the future. This is the highest point of development, — to bring past and future into the present. Herein our religion differs from all other religions, and true Christianity differs from all false Christianities. Jesus was most conspicuous for this intense realism, bringing all the past of Judaism and all the future of the kingdom of heaven into the present moment. "Before Abraham was, I am." Thus is the old historic period identified with the present hour. "The hour cometh, and now is," is another favorite formula with the Master. The mind of the Hebrew race was doubly saturated with glorious historic reminiscences and glorious prophetic anticipations, with ancestral pride and Messianic hope. The wonderful thing in the mind of Jesus was, that he could precipitate these religious memories and hopes in one crystal form of present duty, — into a diamond life sparkling at once from every facet with faith, hope, and love. This was the supernatural element in Jesus, to be able to bring down heaven upon earth; to make immortality present; to incarnate the Messianic hope in his own life; and to be, as he said, in heaven and upon earth at the same moment. "No man hath ascended into heaven, save he that came down from heaven; even the Son of man who is in heaven." For as our thought, when we utter it, comes out of our mind, and yet remains *in* our mind; so Jesus came down from heaven into communion with man, while inwardly he remained in heaven in constant communion with God.

The miracle of his life is to make the supernatural, natural; the infinite, finite; the past and future, present; to bring God's kingdom upon earth, and to show his will done here as in heaven. I call it a miracle, because not only no other religion ever accomplished it; but, even after it has been accomplished by Jesus, his Church has never realized it. The Church to-day does not comprehend it. On the one hand, in spite of his own words, a part of the Church refuses to accept a present salvation, and transfers it all to the other world; and, on the other hand, those who do accept it make of it a mere commonplace morality, and make of him only a teacher of ethics.

But "the hour cometh, and now is," when we shall understand Christianity better, and see that now is the day of salvation. In other words, we shall see that the work of the gospel is to show to us God present with us; to show that Christ is "Immanuel," God with us; to show that heaven and hell are here; that Christian salvation is a present salvation; that Christ saves us only as he is a present Saviour; that immortality must begin now; that we must have eternal life abiding in us while in this world.

I think some of our writers make a great mistake in undervaluing the historic and actual life of Jesus. An interesting book has been lately published by a distinguished general officer in the United-States service, which resolves the life of Jesus into symbols.* History disappears in a system of ideas. Now, the ideal, by itself, is no more reality than the

* The book by Major-Gen. Hitchcock, "Christ the Spirit," is the most recent illustration of that habit of mind which has existed in all ages of the Christian Church, and in nearly all religions of men, to idealize history into symbols. This tendency is represented by Philo, as regards Judaism; and in Christianity by a long series of mystical writers, — including such names as Savonarola and Swedenborg, — who remind us of what Kant says of Plato ("Kritik der reinen Vernunft; Einleitung"): "The dove, in his free flight, feeling the resistance of the air, might imagine that it would move more easily in a vacuum. So did Plato leave the world of reality, passing on the wings of ideas into the empty spaces of pure intelligence."

actual by itself. I mean to say, that ideas which never have been incorporated, never have been put in action, are, as yet, not vital. They do not affect the soul of men as seed. They do not tend to progress. But whenever an idea is acted out, whenever a great truth is really lived, it becomes a source of life to multitudes. If the Gospels, therefore, do not give an account of an actual life, they are no more the seeds of life to the world than Spenser's "Fairy Queen," or any other romance containing ideas of truth and beauty. It is not till the great truth becomes a great fact that it really helps us to live it. Suppose that Gen. Washington were a myth or a symbol, the invention of some meditative sage: would his story affect us as it does? I read, in novels and romances, tales of heroism and devotion; but the sight of one heroic deed, the knowledge of one generous action, the coming in contact with one man or woman who is really living nobly, does me more good than a whole library of romantic tales. Suppose one should learn to-day that the story of Savonarola, of Luther, of Joan of Arc, of John Brown, of Theodore Winthrop, were merely symbolic stories; that no such lives had ever actually been lived; that no such sufferings had ever actually been borne: should we not lose something? Therefore it seems to me wonderful that any speculation can so undervalue history as to say, that if the story of Jesus be a symbol only, and not a fact, it can do as much good as now.

Christ, therefore, to be of any use to us, must be a present Christ. The historic Christ of the New Testament, and the ideal Christ of Christian anticipation, must be realized in the present, in order to help us. The hope of glory is Christ within us. The study of the Gospels is necessary to make us acquainted with Jesus as a person; but this person must become our friend in all our daily walk, in order to save us from evil and sin. He foretold that he would come again as a Holy Spirit. We must feel him present, as the Holy Spirit, in society, in history, in providence, in our own heart. We must feel him present in all true reform, in all courageous struggle, in all noble endeavor. We must believe in his resurrection and ascension as well as in his death. He did not die on the cross: he lives, and has risen to that higher spiritual state in which he can be present and active to-day.

Some good people tell us that Christ is to come in 1868, in some outward form; and think that they do us a favor by that information. But, if Christ is not here now, his coming in 1868 will do us little good. And as to his coming in some outward shape, I, for my own part, would say with Paul, that I take less interest in that than in his coming as spirit and power in society, history, and life.* No doubt he will come in 1868, but only as he is coming now in 1861; †

* Paul says, "Though we have known Christ after the flesh, yet now henceforth know we him no more."

† This sermon was preached in the first year of the war.

and those who do not see him now will not see him then. I see Christ visible to-day. I see him plainly, coming in these magnificent events of the present hour. I see him in this coming emancipation of a great people, so long tied down by compromises, and fastened to the dead corpse of corrupt and corrupting institutions. If Christ is not here, where can he be? If he is not in this fine awakening of a nation, in this new crisis of history, in this inspiration which bears all our youth onward to battle for their country, and makes their life poor until it can be given for justice, law, and freedom; if he is not here with us in sympathy, influence, and help, — then he has changed from the Christ whose holy feet walked over the acres of Palestine, bearing sympathy to earth's sorrows, and help to mortal weakness and sin. Do not talk of 1868. Let us see Christ here in the slave whose fetters are breaking; here in the nation which is arising out of selfishness into generosity. Christ is coming in 1868; but he is coming in the form of the hungry, the thirsty, the naked, the stranger, the sick, and the prisoner. Find these, and you find him. For salvation, too, to be of any use to us, must be a present salvation. It is not enough that I passed through some experience, and repented, and was converted and born again last year. I must repent to-day; I must be converted to-day; I must be born again to-day. What I did yesterday answered for yesterday, but does not answer for to-day. Nor can I hope to be saved in the future, except as I am saved now. Immortality must begin here. God is here; Christ is here; his Holy Spirit is here; all good angels are here; all truth is here; and I can be saved now by trusting in God as my Father and my Friend.

We have read the story of a man, who, led by some whim, left his home, and went into another street, and there lived by himself secretly for many years. Every evening he went by his house, and looked into the windows, and saw his family sitting together, but did not go in; till at last, after many years, passing the house as usual, he turned up the steps, opened the door, and entered, and was once again received into the circle of sweet love. We wonder at the folly which can thus throw away years of affection and joy; but we do just so. We pass by, day after day, the home of our soul; we postpone, day after day, entering into the love of God and Christ. So we let years go by: but, at last, we determine to go in; and then, in the peace of forgiven sin, in the sense of God's fatherly love, in the consciousness of living in our true home, we wonder that we postponed it so long; consented so long, in our folly, to live away from God, and so away from heaven.

For, in fine, heaven and hell are both present also: they are both here.

For what is hell, and what is heaven? Hell is absence from God: heaven is the presence of God. To turn away from God in our wilful choice; to separate ourselves from him in our selfishness; to go, like the prodigal, into a far country, — that is hell. It carries with it the famine of the soul, the mortal hunger, the decay and death of all our best nature. We are dead while we live, when we are away from God: there is no real satisfaction in any thing. And what is heaven but to return to God, and so find satisfaction in every thing; to cease from selfish ends; to give ourselves up to noble and true purposes? Those who live pure and generous lives have tasted already "the powers of the world to come."

Thus Christ glorifies the present, throwing over it the ideal glow of the past, and the roseate beauty of the future. He transfigures the present by the great idea of duty, and the inspiration of God's love. As he appeared on the mountain in glory, talking with Moses and Elias of the things belonging to the kingdom of heaven, so he summons the past to talk with him in the present concerning the future. Therefore there is no condition of life so humble, no work of life so common, no sphere of duty so low, as not to grow full of grace and charm as Christ comes to it. Intense light thrown upon a piece of common earth, in a microscope, changes it into a fairyland of beauty: so the intense light of Christian truth beautifies the most insignificant moment of our life. We feel that now is the accepted time, that now is the day of salvation. The present moment becomes infinitely interesting. We cease to meditate on the past, or dream about the future: the NOW is sufficient for us.

"No longer, forward or behind,
I look in hope or fear;
But, grateful, take the good I find,
The best of now and here.

And so the shadows fall apart,
And so the west winds play;
And all the windows of my heart
I open to the day."

XV.

"WHEN HE CAME TO HIMSELF."

Luke xv. 17: "And when he came to himself."

THIS is rather a remarkable expression. How can one come to himself? Are we not always with ourselves? Do we ever go away from ourselves? We may go away from home, friends, and native land; we may go from God and heaven and love and peace; we may go away from truth into falsehood, from innocence into crime: but can we ever go away from ourselves? According to the Horatian verse, never. "Who, by flying his country, can escape himself?" says Horace. And, if we analyze the expression, it grows more difficult to comprehend. "He came to himself." Who was the "he" that came to himself? Was it the soul that came to the body, or the body to the soul, or the personality, the personal will, which came to the spirit? How can the expression be understood or explained by any mental or moral science?

And yet this phrase is one which is quite common, found in many languages; and we all feel it to be singularly appropriate. In this passage, it is exactly the same in Greek as in English; and it is a sort of expression so universal, that there is evidently some reality of human experience lying beneath it. Perhaps we can understand this by seeing under what circumstances the expression is used.

Why do we say that a person "has come to himself" when he recovers his consciousness after having fainted away, after a trance, after being stunned by a blow, after delirium? It is because he has become self-conscious: he has obtained possession of his faculties; ceases to live a merely instinctive life, and lives a conscious moral life. We thus recognize that the true self in man is the power of self-consciousness and self-direction. As long as one has neither self-consciousness nor self-direction, he is out of himself; but, when he has this self-possession, he has come to himself, he has become himself.

I recollect a fact told me once by a friend of mine, who was a sailor, which I have always thought a curious experience, showing what kind of central consciousness in the soul makes the essential self in man. He was one night in a terrible thunder-storm in the Gulf Stream. The bolts of lightning fell all around the vessel; so that, momently expecting it would be struck, the captain told the crew to stay forward and aft, away from the masts. My friend, who was the mate of the vessel, thought he heard a sail beginning to flap; and went to the foot of the mainmast to look up through the solid darkness, if perchance he might see what it was. At that moment, the vessel was struck, and he fell senseless. The effect of the shock on the vessel was to make it, for a moment, lose its way; and the next wave rushed over the deck, washing him to the lee scuppers. Probably the bath saved his life. The men, coming aft to see what had happened, stumbled over him; and he was taken below, and laid in a berth. An hour or two after, the captain came down with a lantern, and, looking at him, spoke to him. He looked at the captain, struggled to collect himself, and at last said, after a great effort of reason, "I am somebody." That was the first sign that he had come to himself. He came out of chaos to individuality. He was conscious that he was a person. Next, after another effort, he took another intellectual step, and said, "I am somewhere." He first individualized himself, then localized himself. First personality, then space. First one's self, then the outward world; or, as I suppose the German metaphysicians would say, first the "I," and then the "Not I."

Something like this happens when we come out of a dream. In sleep, particularly if it be deep and solid, if we have plunged clear down into the depths of a profound sleep, to awake from it is like a resurrection from the dead. We do not, for a moment, know where we are; but I think that we do not go so far out of ourselves in sleep as this young man did who was struck by lightning. We say when we awake, "I am somewhere: where am I?" But we do not say,

"I am some one." In dreams we are still ourselves; but we cease to be localized. Place comes and goes around us. The scene shifts: we are now at home; a moment after, somewhere far off; and we are not surprised. Especially, in sleep, the self-directing will is relieved from duty, the sense of responsibility ceases: we are free from all permanent care, all anxiety about the work of our daily life. The dignity and duty of choice are both temporarily removed. This is what really makes sleep a rest: it rests the body by relaxing the steady tension of the will over the muscles; but it rests the soul more by taking off the steady pressure of purpose and obligation from the mind and heart. We cease to be responsible while we are asleep, — that rests us. Hence, in our dreams, we often do things with very little remorse that would shock our conscience when awake. Gentle persons dream that they commit murder, and do not feel at all unhappy about it. Therefore sleep rests the mind as well as the body, but therefore also it is a lower state; and we *come to ourselves* when we wake, by taking up the duty and dignity of conscientious purpose.

"Coming to one's self," then, is a phrase which very well expresses the collecting of all one's powers and faculties round their true centre of self-consciousness and self-direction. You have seen in water the image of the sun or moon. Something disturbs the surface of the water, and breaks it into waves. Immediately the image is shattered in pieces, and goes apart, the bright fragments oscillating to and fro on the undulating surface; but gradually, as the waves subside, these fragments of the sun's image begin to come together again. They come nearer and nearer, each approaching its proper place, until at last, when the disturbed water has become again smooth, the image of the sun re-appears once more round and distinct as at first. It has come to itself.

So man comes to himself after the distraction of passion, after the stupor of self-indulgence, after the conscience has been disturbed by selfish sophisms. He comes to himself when the broken image of God, reflected in the inward mirror of conscience, has again grown distinct and clear within. He comes to himself when all his faculties gather subserviently around their true centre; when the soul is on its throne, and truth is loved and obeyed; and Christ, who is God's love in the heart, helps us to forget ourselves, and to love others. The soul of man comes to its true self in humility, in obedience, in truthfulness, in generous affection: it is out of itself till then. Thus sin is represented in our text as insanity, as a temporary delirium, and man as only perfectly sane when he is a child of God, and desirous, if he cannot be a son, loving his Father, to be at least a servant obeying him.

Man's true self, accordingly, is good. Man's nature is not bad, but good. When man is himself, as God made him and meant him, he is good. Sin is an unnatural state: it is a derangement. We are all, therefore, when sinners, partially insane. We are in a delirium till we come to truth and love. I think that we all sometimes feel this. If you look back to those hours of life when you were in your best state of mind; when you were most humble, most penitent, most trusting, most loving; when selfishness seemed killed down to its roots; when passion, and love of pleasure, and worldliness, were checked by some great sorrow; when, under the influence of truth and goodness, you looked at life with earnest eyes, — did it not seem as if you were now more sane? as if you were not only better, but also wiser? This, you said, is the true state. I am now really myself. Every other condition is morbid: this is healthy. Every other state is feverish; it is derangement: this is true order, this is self-possession, this is being whole. It is, therefore, not true to say that man by nature is a child of sin. Man by nature is a child of God, and only by disease is a child of sin. Sin is abnormal. Goodness is his proper and healthy condition.

"By our proper motion we ascend
Up to our native height: descent and fall
To us is adverse."

The true life of man is the full activity of all his powers, each in its place and order; but this fulness of manhood comes only when man is self-poised, self-possessed, and self-controlled, according to the divine laws. All disobedience to God's laws re-acts on the soul, and brings famine and want to some part of the nature. It is always derangement, insanity, disease. No one can grow, with a full development of his nature, except according to law. All self-indulgence tends to disease and weakness.

The selfish man of the world, for example, is insane and sick. He thinks, because he devotes himself to his own private ends, that he will achieve success. He says, "Each for himself: no one can succeed in any other way." He thinks that very wise. So he sets aside strict conscience, sets aside generosity, and gives all his energy to his own advancement. Politician, lawyer, merchant, clergyman, writer, whatever he is, he only thinks how he can get fame, position, power, respect, ability, wealth, for himself alone. For a time, he seems to succeed. He rises higher and higher. He attains position. He is distinguished. He has influence. He has fame. But this is all a diseased growth. There is a famine within. He is conscious himself, and others are also conscious, of some fatal and essential deficiency. Perhaps you cannot tell what it is, but you feel that there is something wrong. The real difficulty is, that he is inwardly dying. His life is gradually oozing out of him. The joy of existence ceases. He does not really enjoy even his own success. Those who look at him find something hollow in him. The inevitable law holds him in its relentless grasp. "He who loves his life shall lose it: he who loses his life for others shall find it." Selfishness destroys the true self. For the true self in man, the highest self, is when he looks out, not in; when he thinks of others, not of himself;

when he lives for truth, not for personal success,—lives for right and justice, for humanity and for God.

This successful selfish man is "perishing with hunger." Happy if he finds it out; if he has the honesty to say, "*I perish with hunger.*" Then he comes to himself. In that moment he begins to rise. His true self regains its supremacy. Then he says, "I will go to my Father." All irreligion and all false religion are insanity and derangement. That man only is perfectly healthy in soul whose heart within is a smooth mirror, reflecting evermore the face of God; but it must be the face of the true God, our Father. The face neither of Jupiter nor of Jehovah will suffice: neither that of the cold philosophic God, who is only law; nor of the terrible Calvinistic God, who maintains an eternal hell, into which he casts his children, and on the door of which he writes, "Leave all hope behind, ye who enter here." Such religion as this deranges, dwarfs, stupefies, and cripples the soul. All imperfect and false religions distort man out of himself.

But the religion of Jesus brings us to ourselves by bringing us to our Father. It shows us our God, as the Father, who sees us a great way off as soon as we turn to him, and kisses us with the sweet inward kiss of peace in the heart as soon as we humble ourselves before the truth and right. This image of God in the heart makes us sane, and keeps us so. We know where to go now at all times. We have a friend who knows us better than we know ourselves, loves us better than we love ourselves, helps us when we cannot help ourselves, forgives us when we cannot forgive ourselves, and, in the midst of our mighty despair, breathes round our heart the perfumed breath of a new and divine hope.

When you know God as he is, then you have come to yourself; then you are safe. There is no more danger then: all your faculties then unfold in their true method and order: we see that life is sweet, that duty is attractive, that truth is inspiration, that love is divine, that death —

"Is but a covered way
That opens into light,
Wherein no blinded child can stray
Beyond the Father's sight."

For, with God in the heart, you always feel at home. I do not think we feel at home always with our friends. Some persons you are at home with intellectually: you feel that you have come to yourself intellectually when talking with them; they excite and bring out your best intellectual faculties. With others, you are at home socially: you come to yourself socially in their presence; they are sympathizing, uncritical; they do not censure you; they are a sort of sunny atmosphere, where, in social hours, you expand and blossom out, and rest yourself. Then you are at home with others industrially: you can work with them; they bring out all your practical power; you come to yourself as a worker in their society. Then you are at home politically with others: you sympathize with them, and they with you, in political ideas. With others you come to yourself in religious hours: they and you are in religious sympathy. But he who has come to God as his own Father and Friend, who has that image in his heart, is always at home, and always himself, in that presence. He does not come to God to kneel, to bend, to repent, to say words of prayer and praise: but when he is well and when he is sick; when he is doing right or going wrong; when he is at work or at play, — he looks inward; he feels the strengthening, guiding, helping hand; he hears the loving, tender, warning voice; and he comes to himself. He stands erect in the fulness of his manhood. What can he fear? He has God in his heart.

Look abroad to-day on Nature.* What is this marvellous change which has come over it? Everywhere is life, growth, beauty: the vast forests are stirred in all their awful depths, over the great continent, by this invisible advent of divine life which we call Spring. Every one of their million million buds is stirred, and swells, and shakes out its tender leaves to the warm air. Every prairie covers its ocean-like surface with grass and flowers. Not a weed which creeps but feels it; not an insect beneath the sod but feels it. The great pine-woods of Maine

* This sermon was preached in the spring.

rejoice, and clap their hands; and the majestic mountains, lifting their vast forms into the silent depths of the upper air, — great sentinels, who stand overlooking the continents, from age to age, to watch the progress of human history, — all are softened and vivified by the Spring. What is this mighty change? It is only that the earth has lifted itself toward the sun. The earth has come to itself, — to its true self; for its true self is in making itself the fountain of all this great flood of life.

And so man comes to himself when he turns himself to God: and, when he does this, he, too, will bring forth fruits and flowers; he will become full, all through and through, with productive life; he will be the son of man, because son of God; he will be filled with all the fulness of manhood, because filled with all the fulness of Godhead. The earth comes to itself when it comes to the sun; man comes to himself when he comes to God; society comes to itself when it obeys the divine law, and calls no man common or unclean, but honors the weak, and helps the feeble, and comforts the sad, and cures the sick; the Church comes to itself when it ceases to dogmatize about doctrine, to make proselytes to its party, or to make converts by terror and persuasion, — when it devotes itself to showing God, the Father of Christ, to the heart, intellect, and conscience of man, bringing the world thus to God.

A nation, also, comes to itself, when, instead of devoting itself to mere gain and outward prosperity, it is willing to sacrifice these for the sake of its great ideas; when it renounces peace and prosperity for the sake of justice, right, humanity. Our people, in the midst of this terrible storm of war, are more truly themselves than they ever were before: they have come to self-consciousness. Like my poor friend, the nation says, coming to itself, "I am somebody, and I am somewhere. I am a nation with ideas and duties, and I am here to do them." And that is what it has not said before for the last thirty or forty years. Patriotism is the self-consciousness of a nation; and while we only were individuals, struggling for our own selfish good, we had no patriotism, and could have none.

When men wish to try the force of a cannon, and the momentum of its ball, there are two methods by which they do it. They suspend a heavy pendulum of iron and wood weighing several tons, and shoot the ball against it; then they determine the force of the ball by seeing how far the pendulum swings out of the perpendicular by the impact of the shot. Or else they suspend the gun itself in a pendulum; and, when it is fired, see how far the recoil causes the pendulum in which it hangs to swing back out of the perpendicular. Now, it is found that the result is almost exactly the same in the two cases. The gun-pendulum gives precisely the same result as the ballistic pendulum; that is to say, the recoil of the gun is exactly equal to the force with which it projects the ball. So also it is with man's every action. Action and re-action are equal in our life. "Draw nigh to God, and he draws nigh to you." "Arise, and go to your Father," and your Father comes to you. "Give, and it shall be given." Do good to others, and love comes back to fill your own heart with joy. But seek a selfish good, and you lose yourself. Try to live for yourself alone, and you go out of yourself; you lose your self-poise, your self-consciousness, your self-control.

Let us, then, *come to ourselves* by coming to God; by obeying him; by living for his truth; by giving ourselves to true and just ends; by filling life with nobleness, truth, purity, and love.

XVI.

THE CHEERFUL GIVER.

2 Cor. ix. 7: "God loveth a cheerful giver."

"ALMSGIVING and prayer," says the Koran, "are the two wings of the soul, by means of which it flies to heaven. The soul cannot mount with either by itself, any more than the bird can fly with one wing." This is a very good saying, if it means that faith and works must go together, — faith without works being dead, and works without faith being machinery which has never been alive.

The Jewish Scriptures also lay great stress on almsgiving. "He who hath pity on the poor lendeth to the Lord," says the proverb.

But, according to Christianity, it is not enough to give: the question is *how* to give. The spirit in which one gives is the important thing. A man may give as the Pharisee, who sounded a trumpet before him; or he may give, not letting his left hand know what his right hand doeth. Men may give because they think they ought, though they had rather not; or because they are expected to give, and will be considered mean if they do not; or because everybody else is giving, and they don't like to be singular. They may give grudgingly, and scold about it, and say "they have to give, all the time;" or they may give cheerfully, promptly, joyfully, lovingly, just as if it was the pleasantest thing in the world to do, as indeed it is.

However, giving money is not the only thing I am to speak of this morning. I shall say a word of that, and then speak of other ways of giving. But, in all our giving, we must give, "not grudgingly, nor of necessity; for God loves a cheerful giver."

Christianity did not invent giving. Giving is a luxury which has been enjoyed in all ages, religions, and countries. The Humane Society in Massachusetts has built huts on the south side of Cape Cod, where ships often go ashore in winter; and have put straw and firewood in them, and other comforts for the poor people who have need. But the Brahmin Gangooly tells us that the Hindoos, too, practise a wayside hospitality. Private persons build cottages by the side of the roads where the tired passengers refresh themselves. Every cottage has a man hired to keep it, and to ask the passer-by to walk in, and be rested. The Brahmins do not often go there, for they do not think it quite respectable to go to such places; but low-caste travellers go in, and are entertained with sugar, pease, and cold water; and even large tubs of water are put outside for the cattle to drink.

So you see that humanity and hospitality are not Christian inventions. They were invented when God Almighty invented man, and put into him such a complex host of tendencies, reaching out in all directions, some downward to the earth, some upward to the skies, some abroad toward his fellow-man. Self-love was put into him, but sympathy to balance it; freedom was given him, but something fatal to balance it; the love of getting, but the love of giving too; the love of keeping to himself, and the love of helping others.

What, then, is specially Christian in giving? I think it is love,—love to God and man, blending in one in every gift; and love is always a cheerful giver. Love does not grumble at being called on ever so often. Love does not merely give what is necessary or expected: it chooses to surprise by some unexpected present,—something entirely uncalled for. Suppose you should meet a lover going with a magnificent bunch of roses to give to the lady to whom he was engaged yesterday, and should say, "It is not necessary to give so many; you have a dozen roses there,—three or four would have been enough;" or, "Why do you give her that handsomely bound book? one in cloth would answer,"—I do not think he would thank you for your economical suggestion. He does not give grudgingly, or of necessity. But Mr. Beecher tells us that there are "many professing Christians who are secretly vexed on account of the charity they have to bestow, and the self-denial they have to use. If, instead of the smooth prayers they do pray, they would speak out the things they really feel, they would say, when they go home at night, 'O Lord! I met a poor wretch of yours to-day, a miserable unwashed brat, and I gave him sixpence, and I have been sorry for it ever since;' or, 'O Lord! if I had not signed those articles of faith, I might have gone to the theatre this evening. Your religion deprives me of a great deal of enjoyment; but I mean to stick to it. There is no other way of getting into heaven, I suppose.'"

A gift which expresses love carries gladness with it, and leaves gladness behind it; blessing him who gives, and him who takes. Gifts among friends are pleasant: but I do not know that there is any thing particularly Christian about them; and, unless you take great care, they will suddenly become uncomfortable, and lose their first freedom. They should never come to be expected. Better to remember what Jesus said: "Thou, when thou givest a feast, call not thy rich friends and neighbors, who can give to thee again; but call in the poor, the maimed, the halt, and the blind." On the whole, people who love each other had better not give a great deal to each other. They have already given the best thing in loving each other.

Suppose, then, we give only to strangers and to the poor. There is great delight in giving when the gift comes unexpectedly, and when it goes a great way. But there are rocks on all sides; and here, too, we risk becoming self-satisfied and ostentatious in our charities, as though we had done some great thing in giving a little of our superfluity: so that what Jesus says, of not letting the left hand know what the right hand does, may come in well as a wholesome safeguard against such dangers.

The Church, in its anxiety to do all the good it can, sometimes forgets its Master's rule. All the missionary and Bible societies, and all philanthropic societies, appeal to very mixed motives, — to the motive of ostentation, by publishing lists of donors in all annual reports; to the motive of necessity, by showing to every man how much is expected of him; to the motive of conscience, by making it seem to be an absolute and commanding duty, which it would be a sin to shirk; to the motive of fear, teaching that God may punish our unwise and unrighteous economy by some sudden retribution; and even to the motive of worldly gain, hinting that those who give freely for religious objects are apt to be largely rewarded in this world. In this way, Christians are induced to give much to all these great charities; but they cease to give freely and joyfully. They are *educated* to give grudgingly, and as of necessity, by the very process which is taken to induce them to give.

Now, it seems to me that so much pleasure comes from giving in a right way and for right purposes, that the Christian Church, by this time, ought to have been educated to a large, systematic, and cheerful benevolence.

But there are other kinds of giving besides giving money. And the second kind of giving I have to mention is *giving up*. It is making sacrifices of what we like; giving up to conscience and right and truth our desires, ease, and comfort. We are all called on to do this. No one can have his way, or do what he would like to do. But, when we give up, it is Christian to give up "not grudgingly nor of necessity." God loves a cheerful giver also here.

Many people parade their sacrifices, exaggerate what they endure for conscience' sake, and make loud lamentation over their hard fate. Jesus says, "Thou, when thou fastest, anoint thy head, and wash thy face, that thou appear not unto men to fast." Haydon spent his life in painting historical pictures, in quarrelling with those who did not like them, and in scolding because they were not better liked; crying out against the false taste of the age, that would give a ballet-dancer a hundred pounds an evening, and would not pay him for his pictures. But I think such complaints show that a man has not a pure love for his art. What he chiefly wanted were fame and money, not success in his art. I do not think that Fra Angelico and Andrea del Sarto, when painting, for a few dollars, pictures which cannot be bought now for as many thousands, complained that they made too great sacrifices for their art. Their art was reward in itself. It was reward enough to see the gradual realization of their dream; to see the face of saint or holy martyr or tender angelic child come beaming out on their canvas,

— their heaven-sent inspiration fixed in glory and beauty to elevate and sweeten life for generations unborn. Whenever a man makes a sacrifice for any great cause or noble end, he is repaid, and more than repaid, at the time, if his motive be pure. "He has a hundred-fold more now in the present time." Therefore, how cheerful and happy are most artists in their poverty! How cheerful and happy are the men and women who work in any great humane cause, or contend for any unpopular truth! They are amply compensated for popular neglect or odium by the ardent love of a few, by their own secure sense of strength, by the consciousness of being right, by the foresight of an ultimate triumph of their cause, by the knowledge that it is even now triumphant. Only let love be the motive, not vanity or pride, and you do not know that you are giving up any thing. All great discoverers, like Columbus, Kane, Parry; all great inventors, like those who invented printing, cotton machinery, the steam-engine, the steamboat, the locomotive, — live in poverty and neglect, and, all their lives, are usually called dreamers and visionaries; but they are very cheerful, for they are in love with their ideas.

If you look over the Harvard-College catalogue, you will see that there are some families in New England which are always represented. In almost every class there is one of them, — an Allen or a Stearns or an Abbot or a Parker or a Williams; and many of these names are in Italics, indicating that they became clergymen. The same names are also in all the other New-England colleges. Each one of these country clergymen, on a salary of six or eight hundred dollars, sends all his sons to college, just as he was sent; and they go through the Union as ministers, physicians, lawyers, merchants, members of Congress, useful men, leading men everywhere. How do these clergymen contrive, with their small salaries, to send all their sons to college? Why, the whole family unite in glad sacrifices and self-denials. When the time comes for another son to go, the father sells his horse, and gives up his newspaper, with his annual journey to the May anniversaries; the mother makes butter, and sells both it and her eggs; the daughters teach in the primary schools in the neighboring towns. All earn a little, and save a little. The boy himself teaches school in the vacation, and perhaps earns something more by teaching the idle son of a rich man; and so he gets through college. Do they do this grudgingly? No: they enjoy their sacrifices, and do not appear unto their neighbors to fast. Very often they go without meat for dinner, or without sugar in their tea; and that, I think, is a better fast in the sight of God than eating fish instead of meat because it is Friday, and telling all your neighbors that you have been fasting. I do not refer now to honest Catholics, who fast in Lent and on Friday because they have been taught so, and know no better; but to those modern Catholics, who *play* being Catholic, and have a sort of æsthetic and sentimental religion, made up of poor imitations of a worn-out ritual.

The third kind of giving is *giving ourselves,* — giving ourselves up to God by the submission and surrender of our wills; or what we call conversion.

Nothing shows more strikingly how low are the motives in much of our religion than the gloomy way in which men become religious. Too many are driven to God by fear of his anger or of an outward hell. They had rather stay away from him if they could, and usually do stay away as long as they can. They postpone religion till they are too old for any thing else, and then lead a religious life, looking discontented and gloomy, as if to love God and be loved by him was the most disagreeable, though the most necessary, of all duties.

But what is being religious, but always seeing God's infinite love in every thing, and loving him all the time? It is seeing his mercy in the sun and sky; in the hills and plains; in daily life, with its discipline and education; in the friendship of our friends; in our insight into new truths; in the grand opportunities of daily service of the human race which he affords us. It is hearing and answering his invitation to come to him to be inspired, to be filled with light, to be filled with love, to be filled with power.

Suppose all the little buds and seeds should say, "Oh, dear! April has come; and now we shall have to unpack ourselves, and go out of these snug little chambers where we have been sleeping all winter, with nothing to do but rest. It is getting warmer and warmer every day. Strange thrills pass through us, 'the blind motions of the Spring.' But do let us stay as long as we can, shut up here; for it will be a very gloomy thing to go out into the soft summer air, and unfold ourselves in the sunlight into tremulous leaves, bending stalks, and fragrant flowers." But Nature does not look unhappy in unfolding. "It is my faith that every flower enjoys the life it breathes." And why, if seeds and buds enjoy unfolding in the sun, should not our souls enjoy unfolding in the sunlight of our Father's infinite tenderness and perfect love?

Here are two young folks that have just agreed that life would be misery, except they can live for each other, and give themselves up for each other. Now, suppose that these young people, just falling in love, should say, "What a very solemn thing it is to have to love each other!" Suppose they should go about with long faces, and put off the marriage-day for as many years as they could, saying they were afraid they did not love each other well enough to be married, and finally, on their wedding-day, feel as if they had made some great sacrifice for each other, and given up a great deal. That would not be love, would it?

All human love is typical of divine love. Love is love, whether its object be God or man. It is that miracle by which we are able to live out of ourselves in another life,—absolutely escaping from ourselves. Man is selfish, say the wise sceptical philosophers; but what they do not see is, that this centripetal force of self-preservation is balanced by a centrifugal force of enthusiastic interest in that which is least ourselves. There is native to man a joy in finding something other than himself, — a joy in giving himself up to the life of another, and thinking only what that other is and does and wishes. This is just as natural to man as self-love; and, while self-love is necessary, self-surrender is joyful.

Then why should we give ourselves grudgingly, and as of necessity, to the love of God? Why hesitate and tremble, and think we are not good enough to love him, or to be loved by him; and that it is some great sacrifice we are making, when we enter into the sweet peace of our heavenly Father's tenderness and grace?

I understand thus why Jesus, when he called a disciple, wished him to come at once. It was the test of the motive. Love does not hesitate. Love leaves all, and follows. Love does not say, "Suffer me first to go and bury my father." Those disciples who dropped their nets in the boat, and followed Jesus, did not hesitate, calculate, grieve, or look gloomy, but were attracted by the words and character of Jesus. They did not wish to leave him: they wished to hear all he had to say; and so they went with him, though they knew not that, in thus going, they were to become the great apostles and leaders of the human race.

But there is still another kind of giving which it is hard to do cheerfully; and that is the *giving-up of those we love*, when we are invited to let them go to be with God and his angels in a higher world.

Yet love can conquer this reluctance too, — love which sets aside private needs, dependence, necessity, for the good of the one loved. Affection, purified in the fire of religion, can understand Christ when he says, "If ye loved me, ye would rejoice, because I go to my Father; for my Father is greater than I."

This joy comes in the midst of grief to all who have any pure love for their friends, — grief with joy inside of it, tears with deeper smiles, like the sun breaking through the driving rain. It is joy that they are safe; that their life cannot cease to be bright; that they are above desire and fear; that they have outsoared the shadow of our night; that they are free from the contagion of the world's slow stain; that they have arisen with Jesus, and are with his Father and our Father. So that it is not strange or morbid to have with our natural grief also a profound joy when those we love best ascend by God's invitation to him. Suppose you should meet a friend, and, seeing him very happy, should ask the reason, and he should say, "It is because my son is to leave me, to go where I shall not see him for the next three years." — "Well," you would say, "that is strange, and a little unnatural, I think, and not quite parental, that you should be so glad to lose your son." — "Ah! but understand me," he replies. "I am not glad to lose my son: but I have been wishing and making exertions to get him a situation; which is just what he desires and needs; which is exactly suited to him; which will give him present comfort, together with education, and opportunity of progress. It is the very thing of all things for him; and I have just heard that it is given to him. This is what I am glad of." — "Ah!" say you: "that is not so unnatural, then, after all."

Gladly, cheerfully, the young men of our land have given themselves to their country in its hour of peril. Gladly, earnestly, they have gone out to live or to die, as God might determine. Gladly, yet with tears, have their mothers, sisters, wives, friends, bidden them farewell, not wishing to hold them back from the heroic and noble work; and so they go, and fall, and rise, — rise into a higher life with God, rise into the great historic figures of our history. They stand for ever as illustrious teachers of the old classic truth, that it is sweet and honorable to die for one's country, — sweet and honorable to die for any truly great cause. They shall teach coming generations, if perchance we tend once more in times of peace and prosperity to forget it, that there is in us all something higher than self-love, something stronger than the love of ease; that God has made us all with power to go joyfully to suffer in a good cause; and that, in all such suffering, there is more joy than pain.

But it is not necessary to be a soldier in order to give up our life cheerfully to God, truth, and humanity. I stood this week by the remains of a young woman, who was a cheerful giver of all she had to the cause of God and man. She was a teacher for many years in a primary school in this city; and she did not teach, as many do, "grudgingly and of necessity," but put her whole heart into this work, and so ennobled it to a sacred mission. The poor little Irish children were, to her, Christ's little ones, and each of them was precious to her; so that, systematizing her life, she had time every day after school to visit them in order at their homes, taking the last first, and sweetly emphasizing with special tenderness those whose homes were most forlorn and whose surroundings least favorable. If they needed clothes or shoes, she always provided them, — going to generous people, and telling each case: and, as she knew all about it, she never failed; or, if she failed, she took it from her own small salary, with which she had other things to do besides taking care of herself. So she was a providence to so many little children, who never knew any Christian love till they knew hers; and so she made her schoolhouse a divine temple, and her work a holy mission; and when she went, last week, into the world, "so far, so near," her works preceded, attended, and followed her, because she was a cheerful giver.

God has never left himself without a witness anywhere in the world. I was reading the other day an account of a Roman funeral. When the head of one of the Roman families died, all his ancestors, whose statues stood in his hall, represented by their descendants, went with him to the tomb. But first the procession went to the forum; and then the representatives of all his great ancestors, each in his appropriate dress, with consular robes, or senatorial toga, as worn in life, seated themselves by the rostra, in the curule-chairs, while the nearest descendant recounted the deeds of the departed warrior or statesman. Was it not some word of God in the hearts of those old Romans which taught them thus to make life triumphant over death, and to carry the body to the tomb, not talking of what was lost, but of what was won and saved? God sends his consolations and his intuitions of truth into every race; and the human hearts of his children cry aloud to him, for comfort in their sorrow, from all countries and lands, and are fed.

The rules of Christian bounty are therefore simple. First, it should be generous. Jesus says, "Give, hoping for nothing again." Secondly, it should be modest. Jesus says, "When thou doest alms, let not thy left hand know what thy right hand doeth." Thirdly, it should be spontaneous, not waiting to be sought for, or following routine. Many persons give only where they are expected to give; not taking the initiative, but always waiting till they are asked. But true bounty is like the man in the Gospel who went out into the highway, and called those in to his feast who expected no such invitation, and were no doubt much surprised at it. And, fourthly, all true bounty proceeds from love to God and man. For "though I bestow all my goods to feed the poor, and have not love, it profiteth me nothing." Such are the rules of Christian bounty. And all such bounty resembles the divine bounty; for God gives cheerfully and generously. He gives, hoping for nothing again; for he gives to the bad man, who makes no return, as well as to the good. His sun shines on the unthankful as well as upon the grateful. God gives cheerfully. All nature is full of cheer. The gifts of God fall freely and willingly from the skies. He also gives a thousand things secretly, as well as openly, not letting his left hand know what his right hand doeth. He hides his mercies, so that we do not know them till long after. He conceals his blessings under the form of evils. Again: the gifts of God are spontaneous. He gives without waiting to be asked. He not only answers our prayer, but teaches us how to pray. And, finally, he gives all from love: for love is his essence; and the explanation of all existence, of all history, of all life, is to be found in the necessary activity of infinite love. If we would be the children of our Father in heaven, let us give as he does. Let us give like him in these particulars, and we shall give well, whether we give our means, ourselves, or that which is most dear to us. Give cheerfully, not grudgingly; give modestly, not ostentatiously; give generously, not selfishly; give spontaneously, and not as of necessity; and, in all these, give lovingly.

Jesus was a man of sorrows. But the greatest artists, in painting his features, have recognized that beneath all sorrow was a perfect peace. The mediæval and monkish artists gave him an expression of dejection, and of passive submission to inevitable ill; but the greater painters who succeeded joined in the Master's face the perfect harmony of sorrow and joy, blended and made at one in a divine peace. Sorrow is there: for he had always before him human woe and sin; the imperfect present; the degraded and unworthy condition of man; the soul enchained, and held down from its great ideal. But a deeper joy is also there, — joy in the sense that God was with and in every struggling soul, every aspiration for good, every hunger and thirst after righteousness. These artists are right; for Jesus began his first sermon, not by saying, "Cursed are the heretics," but by saying, "Blessed are the pure in spirit;" not by saying, "Cursed are the sinners," but "Blessed are those who mourn over their sin." They are blessed while they mourn. Like their Master, they are happier in their grief than others in their gladness.

"That high suffering which we dread
A higher joy discloses:
Men saw the thorns on Jesus' brow;
But angels saw the roses."

"God loves a cheerful giver." Jesus was his well-beloved Son, giving himself cheerfully for man, giving his life a ransom for many. God loves us when we follow Jesus, — when we are cheerful in our submission; cheerful in our sacrifice; cheerful in our trial; cheerful in our loneliness, our bereavement, our sorrow; cheerful even in our struggle with sin, — knowing that we shall come off conquerors, and more than conquerors, through him who loved us; and that nothing can separate us from the love of God.

XVII.

THE GRACE OF GOD.

Eph. ii. 8: "BY GRACE YE ARE SAVED, THROUGH FAITH; AND THAT NOT OF YOURSELVES: IT IS THE GIFT OF GOD."

EVERY THING which we have in this world — all our joy, our culture, our powers of body and mind, our outward and inward wealth — comes to us in one of two ways: it comes with or without our own efforts; it comes as a consequence of what we do, or without any reference to what we do; it comes as retribution, in the form of reward and punishment; or it comes as free gift or grace. When good comes to us in consequence of what we have done, we call it reward; when evil comes in consequence of what we have done, we call it punishment; when good comes, not in consequence of any thing we have done, we call it grace, a free gift, or mercy; when evil comes, not in consequence of what we have done, we do not call it punishment, but trial, discipline, education.

These are the two sides of life; these are the two laws which govern us all. Gift and payment, — these are the positive and negative poles of human life.

Now, moralists lay the greatest stress on the law of retribution, while religious people lay the greatest stress on the law of grace. When the question is raised, "How is one to be saved?" moralists reply, "By works, by doing one's duty, by trying to obey God, by being faithful in all relations of life." Religious people, on the contrary, — all Orthodox theologians especially, — say, "Not at all. We are not saved by works, but by grace, through faith. It is the pure work of God, no work of ours, which saves us, if we are saved."

Now, I shall try to show that the theologians are nearer right than the moralists on this point. Herein I shall, no doubt, depart from the traditions of the Unitarians; for Unitarians have, on this subject, usually sided with the moralists, and not with the theologians. I shall, however, also depart in this discussion somewhat from the theologians, because I shall translate the whole matter out of the language of theology into that of common life and daily experience. Instead of saying, "By grace we are saved, through faith; and that not of ourselves: it is the gift of God," I would put it in this form, as being more intelligible: —

"Every one, in his heart, desires to be better than he is. Every one would like to be, not a bad, but a good man. No one desires to be mean, false, cowardly; but each wishes to be noble, generous, pure, true, loving, and beloved. We all would like to lead a higher, nobler, better life than we do. Now, this better life is what we mean by being saved. It is going up, not down; toward God, not toward Satan; toward the heaven which is the home of all angelic, loving souls, not to the hell which is the home of all mean, selfish, cruel, hateful, and demoniacal beings."

Now, the question is, "How are we to go upward? how are we to grow better? how are we, in short, to be saved?"

In passing down the street a day or two since, I saw a placard announcing a convention of "all persons who believe in the speedy personal coming of Christ; and who also believe in the immortality of the righteous, and destruction of the wicked." As I walked on, I said to myself, But who are the righteous, and who are the wicked?

I suppose the righteous are those who do right, and the wicked those who do wrong. But who will claim to be righteous in this sense? How much better is one man than another? The differences between good men and bad men are, no doubt, very important as regards our relations to each other here. A man who steals and lies and misbehaves himself is a very inconvenient neighbor, a very uncomfortable companion; but when we come to talk of guilt and of merit in the sight of God, and in view of eternal judgment, how insignificant the differences between men appear! Those who believe in the final destruction of the wicked must have little hope for themselves or any one else: for who is not wicked? who can claim to be good? who can pretend to have led a perfectly pure, true, generous life? who has been good for a year at a time, a month, a day? Good heavens! who can say that he has been, even for an hour, good, in any great and noble sense of the word?

We may judge, then, that we are not likely to be saved by our works. If we go up toward heaven, escape from evil, and become pure, true, fit companions for angels, and fit to be near God, we shall not have made ourselves so. I think we shall have to be made so by God.

By this is not meant that we have nothing to do ourselves in order to be saved. I believe that *work* is an important element of salvation itself. Only I do not think that we work in order to make God love us; but, on the contrary, it is his love that makes us work. It is the Divine Grace — that is, the love and mercy of our Father in heaven — which makes us faithful and obedient, inspires us with ardor, and helps us to serve him. The grace of God, which brings salvation, has appeared to men; teaching us, that, denying ungodliness and worldly lusts, we should live soberly, righteously, and godly in this world. That is, our temperance, our self-control, is a pure gift of God; our righteousness, or just behavior to men, is a pure gift of God; and our religion is a pure gift. All our work has a gift at the root of it. God sows his love in our heart as a seed, out of which, after a while, our work grows.

Nearly every thing which comes to us in this world comes by grace. The doctrine of salvation by God's love was first uttered by Jesus, when he said, "Be the children of your Father in heaven; for his sun shines on the evil and the good, and he sends his rain on the just and unjust." He uttered it again in the parable of the laborer in the vineyard, who wrought one hour, but whom God made equal with those "who had borne the burden and heat of the day."

There was a book written by Dr. Combe, called the "Constitution of Man," — a very popular work, — the immense success of which is due to the fact, that it sets forth in the fullest form the opposite doctrine of works. "Salvation by works" is the doctrine of that excellent book. "As a man sows, so shall he reap." He who has earned five talents shall be over five cities; he who has earned two talents, over two cities; he who has earned one, over one city: strict justice, impartial retribution, unerring law, a certain retaliation. This is all perfectly true. It is also taught by Jesus; it was taught by Moses; it is taught by Nature. He who does not work shall not eat; he who puts his finger in the fire shall be burned. Jesus did not come to destroy these laws, but to fulfil them.

In the other world, as in this world, these laws apply. There, as here, there will be a perfect retribution. There will be rewards and punishments in the other life, just as there are here. Those who have done much shall stand high; those who have been faithful in few things shall be rulers over many things. Jesus does not set aside any of these laws. Combe's book on the Constitution of Man is as true in heaven as on earth.

But, though Christ does not come to destroy the law of recompense, he does come to fulfil it. We must work out our salvation with fear and trembling; but we *can* work it out because God works in us to will and to do of his good pleasure. That is, God is in our hearts, just as he is in Nature; his sun shines in the hearts of bad men, as in the hearts of good men, to make daylight and warmth come in. He does not wait till they have begun to be good: he works in them to will. He does not leave them to do all the work by themselves: he works in them to do.

What a terrible task, what an impossible duty, we should have to perform, if we had to work out our salvation from evil, our salvation into good, all by ourselves and from ourselves! What utter discouragement and despair, if we had not these promises!

But see how everywhere the law of grace pours out its unceasing blessings within and around the law of works! God pays us our wages with strict accuracy every evening; but he gives us a thousand times as much as he pays us. So I have seen a father agreeing with his little son to pay him so many cents a day for doing such and such little pieces of work. The child's mind is full of what he is earning; and he is thus encouraged to form habits of diligence, punctuality, self-denial, and perseverance: but, while the father pays the child his few cents a day, he is giving the child home, clothing, food, school, and all sorts of comforts and blessings. He is working for his child's present and future good all day long. So it is with us: we are such little children. God pays us regularly, with reward and punishment, our three cents a day; but he gives us all the perfect beauty and blessing, which is new every morning in the divine providence of this world.

Now see how the grace of God, which brings salvation, has appeared to us in Nature and Providence, and how it has taught us to deny ungodliness and worldly lusts, and to live soberly, righteously, and godly in this world.

Part of the goodness there is in this world comes naturally. It is in the organization of soul and body. The sense of right and wrong, the delicacy of conscience, the feeling of moral obligation, which is in us, we did not make ourselves. God gives this to us: he gives it new all the time. It is a light from him, shining into our hearts. It is his Holy Spirit dwelling in us, warning, advising, restraining, impelling us. It is in every human soul. His sun shines on the evil and on the good. This holy monitor, this careful inspector, this sacred, solemn voice, is from grace, from love. It is the Father's arm, held round every child to keep him safe from evil.

Some have more of this, some less. Some persons seem to have a great instinct of conscience, a good genius for virtue. But they do not deserve the credit of it. They do not make themselves so: God makes them so. Others have less. That is no fault of theirs. So in an army, on a field-day, some stand nearer to the commander, and hear his voice more plainly; and others far off, where they have to listen sharply to hear the command. It is not a merit to be placed near, nor a fault to be placed far away: but it is a fault if we do not try hard to hear the command; a fault if we do not listen.

So the grace of God puts into our organization sympathy, good-nature, kindliness; giving more to some, and less to others, but giving to all their share. Some are, by their very nature, sweet and gentle, kind and self-forgetting, and ready to sympathize. They cannot help being sweet and sunny. It is like a perpetual Sunday when they are near us. But that is no merit of theirs: it is the gift of God.

And so some persons have, by nature, a certain sagacity, and a justness of perception, which keep them from going wrong. Good sense is an important element in good behavior. And some persons are full of hope, and see the great things which may be done; and so inspire others to labor, and labor themselves, in the light of a noble expectation. But that is of grace. God made them so: they did not make themselves so.

We have no right to blame people for not being

born with all these delicate and charming qualities. Thank God for those who have them, and be willing to rejoice in their light; but do not blame those to whom God has not given the great torches and majestic blazing candelabra, but only penny candles, in this illumination of Nature.

The religious instinct in man is also, to a great extent, organic. What most men call religion, — the tendency to adore, the joy of piety, the feeling which carries one to worship, the satisfaction in religious ceremonies and forms, in liturgies and sacred occasions, — this is a constitutional thing. Some races have more, some less. The ancient Egyptians had the most of any races ever yet known. They lived to worship. Their national life was in worship. Their political constitution was a hierarchy. It was a government of priests. So some persons now are made very prone to worship: others have little of this tendency. It is a deep and beautiful element in the soul; but it is no merit to have it, no sin to be without it.

Part of our human goodness comes from these natural sources; but another part comes from education, from outward influence. This also is of grace, not of works.

Look back on your life, and see what blessed influences have come to you to form your character, to ennoble your aims, to inspire you with a true spirit, — from the home of your childhood, from your father and mother and the dear friends of your youth, from the revered and holy men and women whose mature virtues rose around you, like solid walls of marble, to keep out evil influence. You heard, in your childhood, good and just sentiments. It was taken for granted, in all the conversation, that men were to be true and pure, upright and firm; that life was a trust, not given for selfish ends, but to be used for good. It was not the direct moral teaching you heard at home which did you the most good, but the indirect, spontaneous, automatic teaching, — that which came from the character of others, not from their thoughts. We, my dear friends, have been born in a community saturated by the teachings of the New Testament. The conscience of society has been educated by the Sermon on the Mount. In every New-England village, when the Sunday bells send their mellow invitations to praise and prayer over the sleeping hills and valleys, on each returning day of Jesus Christ, the little children are taken into his arms, and pressed to his loving heart. The sun of Christianity shines on the evil and the good. Not a reckless boy, the torment of his home; not a hard, grasping, selfish, sharp-featured country trader or lawyer, — but has, in the depth of his soul, some sweet and holy influence which came to him as a divine gift when he was a little child; and there it is down in the depth of his heart to-day.

Who is there that has not loved, and has not been loved? What did we do to merit that tender love of parent and child, of grandfather and grandmother, of husband and wife, — that generous, self-forgetting devotion of friend, of brother and sister? What did we ever do to be so loved? Who ever deserved half the love he has received? Of the good in our hearts, how large a part has flowed from this grace of God, which made others come to us with their noble, frank, true-hearted affection! All love is of grace. It is never deserved. Nobody ever deserved to be loved; but being loved makes us more deserving than any thing else can.

> "Love is too young to know what conscience is;
> But who knows not conscience is born of love?"

Then more of our goodness than we think comes from the divine presence of God in Nature. The calm succession of day and night, of spring and summer, teaches us the dignity of order and law. The serene beauty of the sky and the fields; the widespread joy coming from the clouds, the forest, the grassy meadows, the flowing streams, — take us out of our own little projects and plans, and teach us that what God has made common to all men is the best thing he has given us. Nature, enlarging our conceptions, unites us with our fellow-men, and teaches us humanity. And who ever did any thing to earn this? God gives all this lavish beauty and abundant glory to every creature who has eyes to see it and a heart to feel it.

So, too, the grace of God has given us Jesus Christ. We, who have heard, learned, and been taught of him, did nothing ourselves to obtain that privilege.

It is God's free love which caused us to be born in this Christendom, not in China; in Protestantism, not in Italy or Spain; and under the most liberal form of Protestantism, where God is seen as a father, loving all his children, and not as a stern judge or an awful angry king.

Thus we see how the grace of God has been the source of nearly all the good there is in us. Some of it has come to us in our original organization, some has been given us through education, some through Christianity. And now the gospel says to us, that all this is only the preparation for a deeper and fuller life of love which God means to give to all of us on the condition of faith. That is, trust him. Do not doubt his nearness, his influence, his good-will. Believe that, what he has begun, he means to carry on and finish. Trust in your Father, and each day accept, as from him, the gift of life, the inflowing light of conscience and of reason; the inflowing love which draws out your heart to those around you, the inflowing aspiration which longs for some better and higher goodness. It is always ready to come into your soul. Only open your heart to receive this new life, each day, in faith. This faith in God and ourselves will make us do more, make us more faithful, conscientious, obedient. We shall work more when we do not work to gain a reward or to escape a punishment, but because God is our Father, and we know it, and so feel perfectly safe.

This is the true doctrine of salvation by grace.

We are safe because God is our Father. And the true doctrine of work is, that we will work, because, since God is on our side, it is worth while to work: our work is sure to be effectual, and come to something.

The Christian Church rests entirely on this doctrine. Reward and punishment separate men: the doctrine of God as a judge puts each man alone with his conscience. When men are striving for a prize, each man strives alone for himself; but, as soon as God is seen as a Father, the Church becomes a family. Then it is not the good alone who belong to the family, but all men, because all are God's children.

The only condition of membership in the true Church is to believe that God is your Father; then you at once see that all who believe it with you are your brothers, and know it. You look on them as brothers, not because of any goodness in them; they look on you as their brother, not because of any goodness in you, but because you are God's child just as much as they are.

The Church is founded on this doctrine. We believe that God is our Father, not our Judge or King. We believe that we are to be saved by his grace, not by our own peculiar or special goodness. Therefore we recognize all as brothers who recognize God as their Father. Christ is our Master, because he teaches us this. We wish to learn it more fully: therefore we come together. We invite all to join us, and become members of the Church, if they believe God to be their Father; if they can trust in him as able and willing to save their souls. If they feel safe because they see God as a Father, they can take each other as brethren and sisters, and try to work out this salvation together.

Therefore, my friends, in conclusion of our meditations, let me give you, as the sum and substance of the Christian doctrine of grace, these statements:—

1. God's free, fatherly love has made all men to become his spiritual children. His grace has predestined us, before the foundation of the world, to become wholly his, free from sin, and full of truth and holiness.

2. We become his children as soon as we see that he is our Father; and our salvation is this,—we are safe as long as we believe that we are God's children, because then we shall always go to him in any temptation and danger. We are therefore saved through faith by grace.

3. We work out this salvation by obedience; correcting all our faults, learning to do all we ought, not in any strength of our own, but by means of the inflowing life and love of God, which he pours into our hearts so long as they are open to him.

This is the gospel. It is not the law of Moses. It is not the law of morality. It is not the law of prudence. But it fulfils all these laws by making us do, from gratitude, love, hope, and faith, what these laws make us do from fear, from conscience, from good sense, and a refined, virtuous prudence; and so we may say always as Paul said, "By the grace of God, I am what I am."

XVIII.

"NO MAN CARED FOR MY SOUL."

Ps. cxlii. 4: "No man cared for my soul."

WHAT an amount of pathos is contained in this expression! How sad that any human being should ever have occasion to utter it! As long as any Christianity is left in the world, as long as common humanity even has not wholly deserted it, no one, we should think, would be so utterly forlorn, so wholly desolate, as to be obliged to say, "No man cared for my soul."

Several winters since, a fleet of fishing schooners came to anchor in one of the harbors of Massachusetts Bay, just at evening, in anticipation of a storm which seemed to be coming on. It came that night, one of the most terrible tempests known for many years; and the wind blew so directly into the harbor, that the place where they were riding at anchor, usually quite safe, soon became very dangerous. One after another of the vessels was blown from its moorings, across the harbor, upon the rocks, close to the shore, but where it was impossible to render them any assistance. The inhabitants of the town, crowded together on the bank, saw the faces of their neighbors and friends on board, saw the vessels go to pieces, and could do nothing to help them. Yet what a terrible night it was to those who stood in safety on the land, no less than to those whose lives were in peril! And when, on the morrow, they carried to the church the bodies of twenty or thirty persons, many of them strangers, the town was filled with gloom, and sadness rested on all minds long after. If it had been otherwise, they would have been barbarians. Common humanity dictated this sympathy and interest in the distress and peril of their fellow-creatures.

Why, then, should there not be equal sympathy, equal interest, manifested when *souls* are in danger, — when souls are shipwrecked on the rocks of sin? The danger is as great, the consequences more terrible. Even if we could do nothing to help each other's souls, we might show an interest in their condition, and grief for their destruction.

When an alarm of fire is given in the night-time, the whole city rouses itself from its slumbers, and multitudes hasten to preserve the property of a fellow-citizen from danger. Why should not church-bells be rung when his soul is on fire with bad passions and hot desires, and Christians run to snatch him like a brand from the burning? How often, when a child falls into the water, and is likely to be drowned, does the impulse of humanity cause a stranger to leap in, and risk his own life to save it? If the child's soul is likely to be drowned beneath the accumulating waves of worldliness and worldly prosperity, ought we not to hasten as suddenly to rescue it? I read the other day of a child who was lost in the woods, and how the whole population turned out, and spent days in looking for him, and was filled with joy when he was found. But if he had become lost to God and lost to himself, if he had wandered from his Father's house, if he had become entangled and bewildered in the mazes of sophistry and falsehood, how much greater might have been his real peril, and how much more ought a Christian community to have exerted themselves to save him!

If death enters a home, and a fair child, a dear wife, an aged and honored parent, is taken, all come to mourn with the mourner; all come with softened and humbled minds, deeply impressed with the solemnity of the presence of death. But, if *souls* die, ought we not to show a deeper sympathy? Ought we not to go and mourn over the morally dead? Ought we not to attend the funeral of innocence, of purity, of peace? Ought we not to console, if we can, those who are bereaved of the *living*, and to sympathize with the exceeding grief of the mother in whose child's heart affection has died, obedience and gratitude lie in their coffin? Ought we not to sympathize with the father whose son has become polluted with sin, stained with guilt?

"They are the dead, the buried,
They who do still survive;
In sin and sense interrèd,
The *dead*, they are alive."

That the sensual and the worldly should not care for the souls of their brethren, might not indeed surprise us; but that Christians should not, is truly wonderful. If we feel it a duty to feed the hunger and clothe the nakedness of the body; to visit the friend who suffers from physical disease, and constantly inquire after his bodily health; to congratulate him on his outward prosperity, and mourn with him over his temporal losses, — much more should we endeavor to feed *moral* hunger; to clothe *moral* nakedness; to visit those whose souls are diseased; to congratulate them when they have performed an act of integrity, of self-denial; to weep with them when they have gained the whole world by means of a baseness. Is it not strange that there should be any in Christian lands destitute of this *Christian* sympathy? any who can truly say, "*No man* cared for my soul"?

Yet, if we may anticipate the scenes of the judgment, how many there may be from our own community who shall stand up there, and say to us Christians, "None of you cared for my soul"!

One will perhaps speak thus: "I was the child of ignorance and poverty. I grew up in your city in the midst of schools; but there was no one to take me to school. I was in the midst of your churches; but none of you ever asked me to enter their doors. I was in a home of profanity and intemperance, and iniquity ran like water into my ears and eyes every day; but no one came to take me by the hand and carry me to Sunday school, or to teach me any lessons of virtue. I grew up lawless in will, violent in passions, coarse in mind; I fell into petty vice; I plunged into deeper crime; I was sent from prison to prison; but no man once asked what moral influences I was under while there, or what became of me when I left it. 'No man cared for my soul.'"

And another may say, "I was the daughter of pious and good parents; but I was obliged to leave my home to earn a support. I lived in your homes, and served you; but you never cared for my soul. You never asked what was the state of my mind or heart. Seeds of vanity took root in them. I became a lover of pleasure. I went down, step by step, from follies to faults, from faults to sins; but no one ever cared to ask what I was thinking of, what were my aims. And so at last I became profligate and vicious, and then you called me an *abandoned* woman; as though my being *abandoned* by you was my fault more than yours."

So, too, may the children of the wealthy, the cultivated, and the refined, stand up in that day, and say to their parents, "Why did you care so little for our souls? You cared for our body; you devoted yourselves with anxious thought to our outward health, comfort, ease; you provided us with all luxuries; you shielded us from all temporal dangers; you labored, day and night, to build up a fortune for us; you sought to establish us in good connections; you spared no expense to provide us with accomplishments: but you allowed the canker of vanity, the black spot of selfishness, to corrode our hearts. You taught us proprieties before man, not responsibilities toward God; you taught us not to violate the laws of society, not to disobey the commands of fashion; to submit to public opinion: but you never taught us to make it our meat and drink to do the will of God. You incited us to no heroic devotion, no generous emulation; you awakened within us no spiritual aspirations or hopes. Your lives were consumed with anxiety for our outward success; but you never cared for our souls." What terrible words will these be for parents to hear from their children in the day of account!

And how many on that day will complain of the Christian Church, whose especial duty it is to care for souls, that it neglected that duty! The slaves will rise up, and say, "You sent Bibles to the heathen in foreign lands: but you did not teach us, at your own doors, to read the gospel; you did not send missionaries to the heathen in your own land; no man among you told us of the sins which we were committing; no man rebuked our masters for keeping us in a condition which made falsehood, cruelty, theft, sensuality, almost a matter of necessity. No; but you justified the system, and defended it out of the word of God."

And will not the slaveholder have cause to say, "You did not care for my soul. You did not warn me of the unrighteousness of my conduct. You said it was wrong in the abstract, but very allowable in the concrete; wrong as an idea, but right enough as a fact. You were watchmen, put to blow the trumpet, and to say to the wicked, 'Thou shalt surely die;' yet you acted, instead, the part of the serpent, and said, 'Ye shall *not* surely die, but shall be as gods.' My blood shall be required at your hands"?

Not only the Church generally, but the ministry in particular, will have to hear from many in that day the terrible words, "You did not care for our souls." How dreadful a thing will it be to the unfaithful minister to hear from those souls whom it was his especial business to watch for, as one who should give account, "You did not care for our spiritual condition. You had no love for our souls. You loved to fill your church full of hearers, to make proselytes to your party, to get the reputation of a powerful and eloquent preacher, to acquire influence in the church; but you did not love our souls. You preached against scribes and Pharisees among the Jews, not against the heart of Phariseeism among ourselves: you preached against heretics and sinners in other places, not those in the pews before you: you advocated reforms after they became popular; but you fled, because you were a hireling, from —

> 'The grim wolf, who, with privy paw,
> Daily devours apace, and nothing said!'"

But there will be other voices heard on that day uttering expressions of gratitude to those who *have* cared for their souls; for the word spoken in season which determined the undecided will in favor of right; for the wise counsel, the pure precepts of love, the faithful rebuke, the cordial sympathy, the kind encouragement, which have turned many to righteousness. They will say, "We were without hope, and you gave it to us. We were living in godlessness and sin, and your affectionate warnings opened our eyes to the perils of our condition. You came to us in our doubts with cheerful encouragement, in our despair to lead us to look to God. You have taught us the true value of life; you have set us in the right way. Others have done much for our outward prosperity, and we thank them; but you have made our *souls* alive, and you are the greatest of our benefactors."

My friends, how easy it is to earn the sweetness which belongs to those who have turned many to righteousness! It is not necessary that one should be a minister, that he should be learned in theology or possess worldly treasures, to do good in this way. Silver and gold we may not have; but such as we have we may give in a spiritual influence which will be far better than any earthly treasure. Oh that we might feel that love of souls which filled the heart of the Saviour and of his apostles; which led Jesus to rejoice in the opportunity of teaching the Samaritan woman; which caused Paul to feel that he would gladly spend and be spent for the Corinthian converts, for that he sought not theirs, but them; and to say to the Thessalonians, "Ye are my glory and my joy, my hope, and crown of rejoicing. Yourselves know, brethren, that, being affectionately desirous of you, we were willing to have imparted unto you, not the gospel of God only, but also our own souls, because ye were dear to us; as ye know how we exhorted and comforted and charged every one of you, as a father doth his children, that ye should walk worthy of God"!

How infinitely greater, deeper, more permanent, is the good which we do to others, when we do good to their souls, than that which we can do for them in any other way! If we can bring any one to live in reliance on God, in submission to his will, in the discharge of duty, in the love and service of his neighbor, we may be sure that we have done them real good,—good which may outlast the Pyramids; which may fill heaven with joy in the most distant ages, and materially advance the cause of Christ in the world. I remember a distinguished man in the Church, a man whose influence was wide and profound, who said that his earliest religious impressions came from a humble and ignorant woman, who used to exhort him earnestly when he was a child, and whose deep faith he felt and acknowledged. Through him and his writings, this poor woman is now moving the world.

Why, then, do we not have more care for souls? It is partly because the God of this world has blinded our hearts; because, not being spiritual, we do not feel the reality of spiritual things; because we do not feel the infinite value of souls, the terrible evil of sin;

because we have not faith in ourselves, in our own power of doing good by any thing we can say; because we have not faith that God will help us to say what we ought; and because, moreover, we sometimes say as Cain did, "Am I my brother's keeper?" though in a different spirit from that in which he said it. We doubt whether we have a right to do any thing for the spiritual good of our neighbor; we think that religion is a matter between him and God, which we cannot interfere with; we think that he must bear his own burden, and we forget that we must help him to bear it. We carry independence in religion too far, till it becomes mere individualism; and we neglect the great law of love, which binds soul to soul, and ordains that no man liveth to himself, and no man dieth to himself.

There is still another feeling which prevents us from direct attempts to help each other's soul,— the feeling that more can be done *indirectly* than *directly;* that we can do more for others by the influence of a good life and good example than by direct exhortation or advice. There is, indeed, great weight in this consideration. Certainly, one way, and perhaps the most important way, in which we can help the souls of others, is by manifesting good principles, living convictions, faithfulness to right, a tender and loving humanity in our own lives. I have known men, who were never in the habit of giving any direct spiritual advice or counsel at all, who would never say a word to those about them concerning duty, but who exercised the profoundest moral influence on all that came near them. They rayed moral light on them like the sun, and the warm influence of their virtues opened the hearts and elevated the souls of all near. One of our poets says well,—

> "Nor knowest thou what argument
> Thy *life* to thy neighbor's *creed* hath lent."

Yet I cannot but think that direct influence might often with advantage be added to indirect; and that, without urging upon reluctant minds spiritual considerations, without prematurely pulling open the folded bud of the spiritual life, without violating the sacred retirement and holy privacy of the interior soul, we may yet, if we are watchful, find many opportunities of saying words of direct counsel, which shall come at the right time, shall fall into the right place, and be like seed, to bear thirty, fifty, and a hundred fold. There are many, more than I suppose we think of, who are waiting and wishing to be spoken to upon such themes as these. There are many more, who, though now immersed in worldliness, feel no satisfaction therein, and would gladly be called up to a higher mode of life by the tender, friendly, and elevating voice which should speak to the deepest places of the heart and mind.

There are, then, these ways in which we can manifest our care of souls: By shedding a good influence upon them from our own life; by studying their state, and trying to find fit opportunities of uttering words of caution or encouragement, or of—

> "Soft rebuke in blessings ended;"

and finally by prayer. For we can never approach God more acceptably, or with a greater certainty of having our prayers answered, than when we are praying for the soul's good of our brethren. We must be praying then in the spirit of Christ. We may then lean on the promise, "If ye abide in me, and my words abide in you, ye shall ask what ye will, and it shall be done for you." No prayer can go up more acceptable to God from any human heart than that which asks that the loved one may be preserved from some insnaring temptation, from the bewildering sophistry of worldliness, from the snares of error; which asks not outward good, but inward life, for those most dear; which prays that they may hold fast their integrity, and enter into the blessed rest of the children of God. When Augustine was about to go to Italy, his mother Monica, a pious Christian, prayed that he might be prevented, as she feared the temptations of Rome. But he went, and was converted to Christianity at Milan by Ambrose. "Thou, O my God!" says he, "didst give her not what she asked then, but, by refusing that, didst give what she was *always* asking." The prayer of the righteous for the souls of others must be at last effectual.

But though Christians are not faithful to this duty, though their love grows cold, and though many are obliged to say, "No man cares for my soul," yet there is One who always cares for the souls of all his children. *God* cares for souls evermore. All souls are his, and he will not let them go without many an effort to draw them up to himself. He sends many blessed influences, he sends many holy providences, ever to those who are neglected and forsaken by man. He does not leave himself without a witness in the most abandoned heart. Multitudes are abandoned of man, but none abandoned of God. If they do not like to retain him in their thoughts, he leaves them to themselves; but he does not forget nor forsake them. His love pursues, surrounds, and calls after them. He sees the first dawning light in their heart; he sees them when yet a great way off. If we are God's children, if we are Christ's disciples, we also should love the souls of all; for to God and to Christ all souls are dear.

XIX.

LIFE AND THE RESURRECTION.

(An Easter Sermon.)

John xi. 25, 26: "I am the resurrection and the life. He that believeth in me, though he were dead, yet shall he live; and whosoever liveth and believeth in me shall never die."

1 Pet. i. 3: "Blessed be the God and Father of our Lord Jesus Christ, which, according to his abundant mercy, hath begotten us again unto a living hope by the resurrection of Jesus Christ from the dead."

Phil. iii. 10–12: "That I may know him, and the power of his resurrection, and the fellowship of his sufferings, being made conformable unto his death; if by any means I might attain unto the resurrection of the dead; not as though I had already attained, either were already perfect."

Rom. vi. 3–8: "Know ye not that so many of us as were baptized into Jesus Christ were baptized into his death? Therefore we are buried with him by baptism into death; that like as Christ was raised up from the dead by the glory of the Father, even so we also should walk in newness of life. For, if we have been planted together in the likeness of his death, we shall be also in the likeness of his resurrection. . . . Now, if we be dead with Christ, we believe that we shall also live with him."

1 Cor. xv. 49: "As we have borne the image of the earthy, we shall also bear the image of the heavenly."

THAT God has placed in man an instinctive consciousness of his immortality, is, I think, very evident. We call it an *instinct*, because we can find no better word for it; but man's instincts differ from those of the animals in several ways. The instincts of animals are invariable, universal, and unchangeable, or nearly so. Those of men are different in degree in different persons; are modified and changed by circumstances in each man; and are susceptible of modification, growth, and improvement.

The instincts of dogs, foxes, and vipers, were the same in the days of Æsop that they are now; the eagle fed its young in the time of Isaiah very much as at the present day; the community of bees, of beavers, and of ants, was governed and arranged according to the same constitution and code of laws in the nineteenth century before Christ as in the nineteenth century after him. Man, too, has a social instinct, which causes him always to organize a society, and to come into some kind of community. He does this instinctively and necessarily; but how different are his societies, and modes of organizing them! They were patriarchal among the Jews, arranged in families; hierarchal among the Egyptians, formed according to priestly arrangements and religious laws. Society took the form of clans in Scotland; of tribes among the Indians; of feudal societies, or a military system, in the middle ages; of castes and fixed occupations in India; and, in modern Europe and America, of perfect liberty, or the absence of all organization. Yet through all this variety remains the same instinct of society; the disposition to come together and work together in clans, families, castes, towns, corporations, armies, or churches. If men wish to fight, they unite in an army; if they wish to make cotton, they unite in a corporation; if they wish to pray, they unite in a church; if they wish to amuse themselves, they unite in a club or picnic or ball-room; if they wish to study, they unite in a school or a college. Who does not see here an irresistible instinct of society existing in man, yet modified in a thousand ways by circumstances, by choice, or by reason?

We call that tendency, then, *an instinct* in mankind, which causes it continually to think, feel, and act in certain ways. These instincts are very numerous. There are religious instincts, moral instincts, social instincts, warlike instincts; the instinct of construction, of art, of science, of commerce, of accumulation. An instinctive tendency is that which is to be found more or less developed in every one, and which acts in every one at first independently of reason and choice.

Now, there is in man an instinctive feeling of immortality. This shows itself exactly as all the other instincts show themselves. Men, in all ages, countries, nations, races, have believed in a future life; but they have had very different notions about the future life. The Egyptians, long before Moses, believed fully in a future life, into which men were admitted after a judgment by Osiris. Pythagoras, and many ancient religions, taught transmigration; the Greeks held to the Elysian Fields and Tartarus.

The Chinese, Hindoos, Buddhists, ancient Persians, Scandinavians, North-American Indians, Mexicans, Peruvians, all had an instinctive belief in immortality, though they took a hundred different views as to its nature. This, I think, proves the existence, in man, of an instinct of immortality; for it has all the attributes of an instinct. It is universal, — appearing in all races and times. It is involuntary, — coming up of itself before any instruction. It is constant, — never disappearing from human consciousness, however much it may be modified therein. It is active and operative, — showing itself as a feeling, a longing after immortality; as a belief in some kind of immortality; and an action leading to certain religious practices in relation to immortality.

Moreover, every one is conscious of this instinct in himself. We all, in our desire and thought, reach forward beyond death; we imagine ourselves as present in this world after we die, and as always existing somewhere. It is almost impossible to realize the end of our own consciousness. If we try to imagine ourselves as annihilated, we also imagine ourselves as looking on, and seeing ourselves annihilated.

This instinct of immortality may, indeed, be dormant in man. It is so as long as the lower nature is supreme. While we live from the body, we die, and have no sense of immortal life: when we live from the spirit, we are full of immortality, and death is abolished. Hence Paul says, "In Adam we die, in

Christ we are made alive;" because Christ rouses the immortal part of our nature. The Adam within us has no faith in immortality, no sense of a higher life. It is not until it is quickened by the spirit, not till the spirit is alive, that it believes in life. One part of our nature has no instinct of immortality; and those in whom that part is supreme know nothing in their consciousness of any permanent and advancing life: their life holds by the body, not by the spirit. But those in whom spirit is supreme have an instinctive sense of permanent being: their life is the guaranty of its own perpetuity. They need no argument to convince them of immortality: the law of life within them is its own argument.

This instinct of immortality in man has been made, by all thinkers from the time of Plato, an argument for a *belief* in immortality.*

---

* In a recent number, however, of the "Atlantic Magazine," a writer has denied the force of this argument, in a somewhat flippant way. This is the writer known by the title of the "Country Parson;" and he understands the argument to be, that man wishes for immortality, and consequently is immortal. This argument he easily refutes, and calls it rubbish. Now, when all great thinkers, from Plato to Addison inclusive, have considered an argument sound which this writer calls rubbish, saying that he "cannot understand how any one ever regarded it as having the smallest force," it is well to recall the maxim of Coleridge: "Until I can understand the *ignorance* of Plato, I will conclude myself ignorant of his understanding." This writer does not understand the argument. The argument is not, that, because we wish for a thing, we shall certainly have it; but it is this: "Whenever God places an instinctive tendency in his creatures, universal, constant, permanent, he provides something which corresponds, in reality and fact, to that tendency." For example: He gives to certain

I do not think it does much good to argue with those in whom the instinct of immortality has not been awakened. Two men were once arguing about immortality; Mr. A trying to convince Mr. B that there was such a thing, and Mr. B not being able to believe it. At last, after a long conversation, Mr. B took his hat, and departed. Mr. A sat in his chair,

---

birds the instinct of migration. Some of the duck and geese family go north as far as the shores of Hudson's Bay, and to the fifty-third degree of north latitude, every autumn, and return to the Middle and Southern States every spring. Accordingly, the particular grasses and berries needed by these birds grow in that region. The horse has an instinct for grass, and God makes grass for him to eat. Animals, as soon as they are born, begin to exercise these instincts, and find always provision made for them. So man, having a social instinct, finds opportunities for society; having an instinct for construction, finds himself provided with that most wonderful and comprehensive chest of tools, — *a hand;* having an instinct of observation, has the portable telescope and microscope called *an eye.* The argument, therefore, is, that, an instinctive longing for immortality having been given, immortality is provided. This, it may be observed, is quite a different argument from what the modern critic imagines it to be. Suppose, when the flock of geese is preparing itself to quit its winter residence in North Carolina, and collects in the swamps to make its arrangements for moving to its summer villa on Hudson's Bay, a young goose, who had never yet made the journey, should fly up on a stump, and make a speech to show that they had no reason for believing there was any such place as the North, with its grass and berries; and suppose the geese should reply, that, since an instinct to migrate North had been given them by God, they might assume that God had provided a North for them to go to. *That* would be Plato's argument, as Plato made it. And if the young goose should reply, that, because they *wished* for a thing, it was no reason for believing it, since he had often wished for a berry, and had not found it, *that* would be the argument of the "Country Parson," — unable to distinguish between a transient wish for a particular fact, and a permanent instinct tending toward a distant state or condition.

thinking, and at last fell asleep. He dreamed he was walking in the Mammoth Cave, stumbling along through its many avenues and intricate recesses, till he came to the river. Here two little fishes put up their heads, and said, "Mr. A, Mr. A, do you really believe there is such a thing as sunlight? We hear those who go through this cave talking about sunlight; but we do not believe in it." So he stopped, and argued with them, quoted all authorities on optics, expounded to them the doctrines of refraction and reflection, referred to Sir Isaac Newton, and even pulled a prism from his pocket to explain the prismatic rays. "Why," said he, "without light, how could we do any thing? how read, how work, how play, how distinguish the colors and forms of flowers? and of what use would our eyes be?"—"We have not got any eyes," said the two little fishes; and so, to be sure, it was. They had no eyes! No use arguing with them about light, so long as they had no eyes. There are many things which we believe, not because of any argument, but by the exercise of the faculty appropriate to the thing. The affectionate man believes in love, the generous man in generosity, the religious man in God, the musician in music. The man with a large organ of marvellousness easily believes in spirits and in miracles. The man with a large organ of hope easily believes in the future life. Cultivate the musical organ, and you become convinced of the reality of music. Cultivate the organs of faith and hope and you see the reality of a future life. It becomes a part of your own existence; something that no sceptical argument can touch.

So much for immortality; but what is the *resurrection?* It is the human being rising up, at death, into a higher state. The doctrine of the resurrection teaches that the state after death is higher than the present state; that it is a rising-up of all souls into a higher life than this. It is the rising of all, good and bad, — the good rising into life; the bad rising into judgment, or to the sight of truth. That all rise, appears from the passage which makes life in Christ exactly equal in extent to death in Adam. "As in Adam all die, even so in Christ shall all be made alive." That the resurrection is of the wicked as well as of the good, appears from the passage which declares that "the hour cometh in which all that are in their graves shall hear the voice of the Son of man, and come forth, — they that have done good, to the resurrection of life; and they that have done evil, to the resurrection of damnation." That is, speaking strictly, to the resurrection of *judgment.** Though

* "Resurrection of damnation" (John v. 29), ἀνάστασιν κρίσεως, — *the rising-up for judgment.* The word κρίσις, translated "damnation" here in our Bible, occurs forty-eight times in the New Testament.

It is translated by "damnation" three times, by "condemnation" twice, by "accusation" twice, by "judgment" *forty-one times.* Wherever the word is translated "damnation," it might be rendered "judgment," and the sense would be good; but where it is translated "judgment," if we should change it to "damnation," it would make nonsense.

For example: In the passage, "He hath committed all *judgment* unto the Son," we could hardly say, "He hath committed all *damnation*

17

this judgment on the soul, which shows to it its sin, is a source of suffering, it is nevertheless an ascent to a higher state, a rising-up of the soul. This is the resurrection. It is not merely rising again, but it is rising up. It is not simply a return to life, but it is an ascent to a higher life. Christ himself is the resurrection, because he is this higher life of the soul. He is the life-giving Spirit. It is because all have affinity with him that all rise. In every man there is spirit as well as soul; and the spirit is the buoyant principle which carries us up to a higher state.

It will be seen that I by no means accept the common idea of the resurrection. I by no means regard it as merely a return to life. It is not rising again: it is rising up. The doctrine of the resurrection is, that the future life is an advance upon the present, — a higher state.

With this view of the resurrection, and omitting, for the present, all reference to the resurrection of the body, let us look at one particular passage to see if we can understand its statements. This passage is 1 Cor. xv. 12–23, and contains the famous discussion of the resurrection.

---

unto the Son." In the passage, — "the weightier matters of the law, *judgment*, mercy, and faith," — it would not do to say, "Ye have omitted *damnation*, mercy, and faith." But where it is declared, that he who blasphemes the Holy Ghost "is in danger of eternal damnation," it would do perfectly well to say, "Is in danger of eternal judgment."

The radical meaning of the word is unquestionably "judgment;" and this meaning we may give wherever it makes good sense.

Some persons among the Corinthians said that there was no resurrection of the dead. Who were they? and what did they deny? Did they deny a future life altogether? This is impossible. It is impossible to suppose that any members of the Christian Church in that age could have held such a doctrine as this. With what motive could any have joined the Church of Christ, in the face of persecution, if they did not believe in a future life? They were not materialists, but idealists. They maintained, probably, like Hymeneus and Philetus, that the resurrection is past already. They believed in a future life, but in no future universal rising-up into a higher state. Perhaps they held that ideal opinion common to so many countries, and in so many ages, of the absorption of the soul in God. They believed in an immortality of the soul; for that was a common belief in Greece: but they did not believe in the rising-up of the whole man, soul and body, into a higher life.

Paul maintains, in opposition to this doubt, that there is a resurrection of all the dead; and, first, from the consequences of the opposite opinion.

If there be no resurrection, the first consequence is, that Christ has not risen. Christ has not gone up to a higher degree of power, into a higher state of life, nearer to God. Christ is living somewhere in the realm of departed souls; but we know not where, nor how. He is not near to us; he has no power to help us; and, if this is so, our faith is vain. It is empty of all substance. It is as true as ever; but it has no power, no life, no conquering energy. The gospel was as true as ever when Christ hung on the cross; it was as true as ever when he lay in the tomb. If Christ were no more, the Sermon on the Mount would still be true. It would still be our duty to love our neighbor as ourselves. The parable of the Prodigal Son would be for ever true; but it would be truth like that of Plato or Seneca, — abstract truth. When Christ rose, he added power to truth. It was triumphant truth. He had conquered his foes. He was still present with his disciples, seen by them in his risen state. He was with them, ready to help them from that higher state. Now their faith is not empty, but filled with living courage and hope. They can do all things now; for Christ strengthens them. If they die, they rise up to be with him. But if this is all a mistake, and there be no such law of progress at all, then there is no hope for us to conquer our sins; then those who have fallen asleep in Christ have not gone up to be with him, living and advancing souls, but have disappeared into the inane realm of Hades. Then our great hope for ourselves and for humanity is idle. Our preaching of the gospel, and our labors in its behalf, are a dream. Our expectations are an illusion; and, if we are thus disappointed, we are, of all men, the most miserable.

You may say, "Oh, no! Paul was not the most miserable of all men; for he had the satisfaction of doing his duty. Virtue is its own reward. He had the peace which passes understanding. He was happy in himself. He had received a hundred-fold more in the present time. He himself said, that 'godliness has the promise of the life which now is, as well as that which is to come.' Why then say, 'If in this life only we have hope in Christ, we are of all men most miserable?'"

Well; some men may support themselves in this way, and take this comfort; but Paul could not. His object was not self-culture, not to save his own soul, not to be the stoical wise man, satisfied in his own virtue. Paul wished to save the world; to do all things through Christ, who strengthened him. He was by no means satisfied with any thing less than helping Christ to redeem the world. He did not wish to be happy, or to save his own soul; but he was willing even to be banished from the presence of Christ, if he could thereby save the souls of his brethren. Therefore he would be, of all men, the most miserable, if that great hope for the world was disappointed.

"But now is Christ risen from the dead, and become the first-fruits of them that slept."

The first-fruits, says Robertson, were offered to God, as a sign that the whole harvest belonged to him. Christ therefore, in rising, shows that all are to rise, that all are to ascend into a higher state of being. It will be a state in which all move forward. All may not be happier or better, but all will be higher. All rise, — some to life, some to judgment. Then Paul goes on to say why they rise, by what law, and by what power. "As in Adam all die, even so in Christ shall all be made alive." In every man, according to Paul's view, is the natural soul, or the Adam, subject to death; and in every man there is also spirit, often dormant, but capable of being quickened into life by the power of divine truth. This living spirit in us is Christ within us. When the truth is accepted by the soul, the soul is rescued from death, and made alive. All die in Adam. That is, the natural man, or the man in whom the finite soul is supreme, does not see spiritual things; has, therefore, no sense of immortality; sees only this life. This Adam is in all of us, this first Adam, which was only made a living soul; made natural, not spiritual; made for space and time. When this part of our nature is supreme, we may believe in immortality, but we do not realize it; we are dead while we live. But when the spirit is roused by the divine truth which is in Christ, whether we believe in immortality or not, we have a foretaste of it. Immortality has begun within us. The spirit being alive, the life descends into the soul, and that is full of life. We walk in newness of life. We are planted together in the likeness of Christ's resurrection. We are dead to sin, but alive to God. The law of the spirit of life in Christ Jesus has made us free from the law of sin and death: for to be spiritually-minded is life; and the spirit is life, because of righteousness. So Christ says that he is Resurrection and Life, — not meaning, certainly, that he brings dead people to life again, or that he makes new bodies for them; but that he is a life-giving spirit to the soul.

This passage, therefore, declares, that, in the Adam part of our nature, we die; but, in the Christ part of our nature, we have life. Now, this life is not mere existence: it is activity and progress. The signs of life are sensibility, activity, growth, intelligent consciousness, rational will. A stone does not live: but a plant lives; for the plant acts and re-acts on Nature, can grow, can bear fruit. The dog has more of life: he can feel, think, and will. But the man has more: for he can rise out of soul into spirit; can see ideal truth; can devote himself to a rational purpose; can have, not merely attachment, but affection; can be tormented with his sins; can feel the pardoning love of God; can love abstract truth and infinite beauty; is capable of endless progress; can worship the invisible. Now, this, and this only, is real life; and this life excludes the thought of death, and the fear of it.

We see in this passage the truth that there is in the doctrine of universal salvation.

Universalism is not true if it teaches that there is no distinction after death between good men and bad; if it says that all after death go into a state of happiness, or asserts that all judgment and retribution take place in the present life. For the mere act of dying does not change a bad man into a good one; nor will any one be compelled to be happy or to be good hereafter, against his will. A future judgment is necessary, because, in this life, men deceive themselves, resist the truth, and refuse to see it; and, wherever there is judgment, there is suffering. In these points, therefore, some forms of Universalism are not true.

But I think that the Apostle Paul here plainly asserts that the life in Christ is co-extensive with the death in Adam. Now, as all men, without exception, die in Adam; so all men, without exception, must be made alive in Christ. It makes no difference whether death be understood here as physical death or as spiritual death. In either case, it includes all human beings; for all human beings are mortal, and all human beings commit sin. It therefore follows that all human beings shall be made alive; and not only that, but that they shall be alive in Christ. But life in Christ is salvation from sin and all evil. When Christ, who is our life, shall appear, we shall appear with him in glory. The spirit of life in Christ Jesus makes us free from the law of sin and death. To live in Christ is necessarily salvation. Therefore the apostle asserts here, that all human beings shall ultimately be saved. Ultimately; for he takes care immediately to say, that every man is to be made alive "in his own order." Christ rises first into a higher state, as the first-fruits; then those who belong to him "at his coming;" that is, those who, when he is manifested to them, accept him, showing that their hearts are right, and that they can receive the immortal Word, which shall fill them with the higher life of God. Paul then goes on to speak of the end, of the great consummation, the fulfilment of the Messianic reign and work, when all souls shall be brought to God; when no more mediation shall be necessary; when all shall believe and accept the truth, and God be all in all.

The main point in the Christian doctrine of the resurrection is, that it is a higher life for all. All who have borne the image of the earthy are to bear the image of the heavenly. All who die in Adam are to be made alive in Christ. The next life is higher than this in all ways,—physically, mentally, morally, spiritually. There will be more of thought, love, and action; more of inward life, more of outward activity. It is true that there may be many lower down in the scale of being after they get there than some are in this world. Some attain to a better resurrection in this life than others do in the next. Still, Christianity teaches that the human race moves up, after death, to a higher level. So, in this world, we are no doubt on a higher level than animals; but I know some horses and dogs which are much better behaved, more intelligent, refined, and moral beings, than some men. Still, the man is the higher animal. The Apostle Paul, though he did not think he had attained to the resurrection of the dead or was perfect, had attained to it far more than most of us will, long after we have entered the higher state.

The doctrine of the resurrection, therefore, is not

merely that we continue to exist after death: it is that we ascend to a higher condition of being. This is the faith of Christianity; this is what Christianity has always taught, and induced men to believe. The teaching of the Church has been partial, not universal; dogmatic, not scientific; and so has repelled a great many. To many, the resurrection is as repulsive an idea now as it was to the Athenians and Corinthians, because it seems not a grand rational conviction, but a narrow theological dogma. It was a stumbling-block to the Athenians. "When they heard of the resurrection of the dead, some mocked." It was a stumbling-block to the Corinthians; for, even in the Christian Church at Corinth, there were some who said there was "no resurrection of the dead." They did not deny immortality; they were not materialists, — they were idealists: but they denied the resurrection.

But the highest power of the resurrection of Jesus is, that it destroys the sense of weakness, doubt, unworthiness, sinfulness, which belongs to us all, and gives us instead courage and hope. It does for us what it did for the apostles: it brings us near to God, and so gives us power in our own souls. Therefore it is said that Christ was "raised for our justification." The theologian is astonished at this saying. He thinks that we are justified by Christ's death. So we are, but by his resurrection too. Scripture is more liberal in its theology than we are. It is like Nature: it can reach the same end by different methods. If Nature sees the air full of miasma, it can purify it by electricity, — sending lightning and thunder to shake it through and through, and rain to wash it clean: or it can do the same thing by freezing cold; one sharp frost will drive away all seeds of disease and death.

So we are justified by Christ's death. For in that holy hour of ineffable, unspeakable sorrow, in that shame to which he came down for us, he touches all hearts. We are drawn to him by his patient love, and our sins pass away. The ice which covered our hearts like a thick breastplate melts under these continuous showers of sorrow, and we feel ourselves drawn to God by the death of his Son. But also we are drawn to God by the ascended Christ; Christ living now above; Christ working now for the world; Christ glorified, and surrounded by a great company of loving, laboring men and angels. This also fills us with a desire to leave our sins, and join the great and holy company whose names are written in his book. Dark, driving rains melt the ice; warm, glorious, sunny days melt it also.

Persons sometimes have a fear lest the friends who have gone before them may have gone on away from them; that progress may have removed them too far; that they will never be able to rise to their communion. But this is to forget, that, while progress tends to separate, *love* tends to unite again. The balance of the spiritual universe is maintained by these two antagonistic forces, just as the balance of the material universe is preserved by attraction on the one side, and the centrifugal force on the other. Does not a parent love a child, though the parent knows more, and is higher? Did not Christ love his disciples? When he went away, did not he say that he went to return again? It is the work of the highest angels to help the lowliest sinners; and love always tends to bring together extremes and opposites, in order that progress may not pull the universe of souls apart. Our angels do not love us less because they have gone into heaven: they love us more. They do not forget us because they have ascended to God: they remember us more. The higher they go up, the lowlier they lean down; for every acquisition, attainment, and elevation in God's heaven is used for the good of those who most need help, light, and deliverance.

In thinking of the other world, we sometimes seem to consider it impossible that the myriads of human beings who pass into it from all lands, races, nations; of all habits, tastes, characters, opinions, ages; infants and old men, saints and pirates; thousands going at once from a field of battle, — should be provided, each with his own home, sphere, surroundings; that a suitable place should be got ready beforehand to receive every one of them. But why should that be more strange than that the same provision has been made in this world; that the tens of thousands who are born daily are born each into a home, on the bosom of a mother, with fostering care and patient love around him? Each comes wholly helpless; each is helped, fed, clothed, taught, by provided love. Not only so, but of the millions of insects, reptiles, animals, fishes, daily arriving, each one comes to find its blade of grass, its leaf, made ready for it; each with the climate, the home, the food it needs. "In my Father's house are many mansions: if it were not so, I would have told you. I go to prepare a place for you." It may be part of the occupation of angels and higher spirits to prepare suitable circumstances for those who are to come after.

We must not think of the other world as lonely, empty, or monotonous. It is more full, rich, varied, than this; it has a richer nature, more divine scenery, more precious society, more life, growth, thought, action, love, than this world. If it is a higher world, it *must* be more full, rich, and beautiful.

The resurrection of Christ also teaches us that those who ascend to God continue the same persons they were before, — that they have the same character, only elevated; the same individual essence, only purified; the same sweetness which we loved, only sweeter; the same beauty which seemed to us so enchanting, only more beautiful still. They are, as Bryant says, —

> "Lovelier in heaven's sweet climate, yet the same."

For the *poets* are the prophets still, and often tell us the truth by an inspiration more orthodox than that of the theologians. No true poet ever for a moment doubted that he should know his friend hereafter, though theologians may sometimes doubt it; for the heart which is illuminated by inspired thought can read beforehand the immortal and infinite quality in the soul, — that which is to make the future angel. When poets describe their friend, it seems extravagance to a prosaic nature; but it is the ideal nature of their friend they see and know, — the future angel in the present mortal.

When Whittier describes the young girl who is gone, he describes her as she inwardly was before she went, as she radiantly is now: —

"As pure and sweet her fair brow seemed,
Eternal as the sky;
And like the brook's low song her voice, —
A sound which could not die.

And half we deemed she needed not
The changing of her sphere
To give to heaven a shining one
Who walked an angel here.

The blessing of her quiet life
Fell on us like the dew;
And good thoughts, where her footsteps pressed,
Like fairy blossoms grew.

The measure of a blessed hymn,
To which our hearts could move;
The breathing of an inward psalm,
A canticle of love."

Jesus rose, and continued the same Jesus as before. He continues the same Jesus still. Our hearts burn within us as he talks to us on this Easter morning, as on that first Easter when the two disciples walked over the bare hills of Judæa on their way to Emmaus. Jesus has ascended up higher and higher; but he is the same tender friend, the same forgiving and merciful master, the same perfect harmony of awful truth and sweetest affection, before whom the Pharisee trembled, and to whom the little children crept. He is still the same who said to the hard bigots, "Ye serpents, ye generation of vipers!" and to the poor, trembling, sinful woman, "Neither do I condemn thee: go, and sin no more."

And because Jesus in the resurrection is the same, therefore all those who surround him are the same as they were before. "We shall be like him; for we shall see him as he is." *He* was not unclothed, but clothed upon, — his mortality swallowed up of life. So shall it be with our friends; so, too, with ourselves.

Christ makes the soul alive; but it is not a belief in the *historical* Christ which makes the soul alive, but in the Christ formed within us. I can conceive of one full of doubts, scepticism, and unbelief in regard to the historic Christ, but with a soul full of spiritual life. If a man loves God, and trusts in him; if he believes in spirit more than in matter; if he believes in justice, truth, and right; if he loves his brother, and helps his brother in this world, — then, whether he knows it or not, he belongs to Jesus, and he really believes in him. I do not mean to say that the historic faith is unimportant; quite the contrary: but, though important, it is not essential.

It belongs to theology: it does not belong to religion. It belongs to the intellect, not to the heart. It is a matter of correct thinking, not necessarily a matter of correct living.

Of the tens of thousands of sweet and holy souls which pass every year into the other world, how many have any clear or exact belief concerning the historic Christ? Of the thousands of Christians who pass away out of every church, how many know much, even about their own creed? But they believe that God, the infinite and unseen, is good; and they reverence him. They know that Christ is to them, somehow, a revelation of God as Father and Friend; and they believe that. They know that this life is sweeter and more heavenly in proportion as we put into it more of generosity, self-forgetfulness, and love. They feel very humbly that they do not do what they ought; but they try to do *something* for others. And so, not knowing it, they are already risen with Christ (as Paul says), and are seeking the things above. Christ is already their resurrection and life: and we feel concerning them, that they cannot die; that outward death is a mere transition for them to higher worlds.

No man fears *death*, or believes in *death*, when his soul is alive. When we are full of any lofty conviction, any great purpose, any self-forgetting love, death disappears: it ceases to be any thing. It is no king of terrors to us, except when we are in a low and selfish state. When we rise out of that with Christ, he is our resurrection, and we feel that we cannot die.

See that old man, whose life has been an earnest seeking after truth, an earnest striving to do good. He has, from time to time, caught a glimpse of great realities. Too honest to profess more than he is certain of, he has never had a very long creed: but he has always believed in goodness; he has always believed in honesty and truth; he has always been ready to help the helpless, and comfort the forlorn. He did not consider whether the poor man, who needed his help, was very good or not: he needed his help; so he tried to help him. He did not ask whether he was white or black or yellow or red; a foreigner or an American: he tried to help him. He did not exclude him from his sympathy because he was a negro, because he was an Irishman, because he was a Roman Catholic, or because he was an Atheist. If God could bear with him, he could. So, now, in the calm evening of life, he looks out on the sweet, sunny landscape before his door, and his heart brims over with God's love. He says to himself, "How good God has been to me!" He thinks of his boyhood, its hopes and hilarity. He sees the field where he played; where he rode the horse with a halter, without saddle; the wood where he went to get nuts; the pond where he fished and paddled in the water. All the kindly influences of Nature, he perceives, taught him; and all were God's messengers to his intellect and heart. He remembers the dawning affections of his soul, the sweet love-story of his youth, the struggles and sorrows of his manhood. He thinks of the hour when God gave him a kindred heart to be his companion and friend in life, and how his heart was opened and purified by that affection; and he thinks of the hour when he stood by the open grave, looked his last look at that calm, serene face, and saw all heaven opened, and immortality born out of death. So he sees God in every thing, and so he tranquilly awaits his own coming change. Christ is to him life and resurrection, and he does not fear death: he knows that what is good in him is real, and what is real cannot die.

See that youth, full of all good culture carefully acquired, full of all choice and rare ability carefully trained. He has studied; he has travelled; he has written books, not yet published, but such as will give him a reputation among the first writers of his land. He has studied man and nature, and his words flow rich in all happy expression to convince and charm. All life is before him, full of promise. But, at the first call of his country's need, he goes to war; in one of the first battles, he flings himself on the enemy's batteries, and dies, shot by a ruthless bullet in the front field. Did he not love life? Did he not fear death? He loved life, but did not fear death; because his soul was full of realities; because he was not living for a name or an appearance, but for duty and manly accomplishment. He has passed away from earth, apparently leaving his work unfulfilled. But

God has many mansions in his house; and every soul will find enough to do, and enough to be, somewhere in God's great heaven.

See, too, that woman who has been for long years a helpless invalid, with no ability (one would say) to learn or do any thing; useless (one would think) to herself and to others. Ah, no! She is learning in that helpless state new lessons every day of God's tender love; she is teaching every day, by her patience and goodness, new lessons to others; and when her time is fulfilled, and she is gently called away, no one thinks, that, because her body is feeble and her sensations imperfect, she is not ready to live on and to go on. The soul within is full of healthy life, and she cannot die.

These all die in faith, not having received the promises.

Even when a little infant goes, which has never done either good or evil in this world, its life's task all unlearned, its earthly work all undone: does any one doubt that it goes where better lessons will be provided, and a more suitable duty given? We say in our souls, while tears dim our eyes, "Let the little one go to Jesus, and forbid him not; for of such is the kingdom of heaven."

It is not accomplishment, it is not attainment, that fits us for a higher life: it is faith. That is, it is that spirit which trusts and hopes, and looks forward, and does not despair. It hopes for others as for itself. It is patient, and therefore strong.

Immortality and resurrection, therefore, begin here. We rise with Christ into a higher life with every right word, act, purpose, and affection. We sit with Christ Jesus now in heavenly places. We are in heaven already when we are full of love to God and man; in hell already when we lose that love. Heaven and hell are both in us, and all outward heavens and hells through which we may pass are only the reflections and supplements to our inward state. There is every variety, no doubt, of heaven and of hell in the other world; but they are all of them for our good. If we need hell, we shall go there; if we are fit for heaven, we shall go there. But God is in both, and both are his servants. He does not take away those whom he loves to be with himself in some separate heaven. He does not leave the bad, abandoned of all hope, to the Devil; but he himself cares for all, and loves all. Those who do not love him, he loves; those who do not know him, he knows; those who are as yet wilful, selfish, unreconciled, he remembers. No doubt there are lost souls in the other world, as there are lost souls in this world; but Christ, who came to seek and save the lost here, will seek and save the lost hereafter. Never was there a dogma more utterly baseless than that which teaches that this short life is all of trial allowed to us; that all the discipline, probation, and opportunity of the soul, is shut up in these few earthly years. Probably we shall need trial and probation for myriads of years; probably heaven itself shall not be free from trial and discipline. Even the angels and archangels may have their temptations, their difficulties, their great opportunities, their perpetual choice of freedom.

After all, nothing helps us so to believe in immortality and heaven as death. The man who is a sceptic and doubter in his study becomes a believer by the pale face of his darling child or the beloved bride of his heart. All which we see through a glass darkly, when we look at it merely with the intellect, we behold face to face when the heart is melted. As Stephen, stoned to death, saw heaven opened, so we, too, when we are beaten down by disappointment and disaster, often see heaven opened.

"Upon the frontier of this shadowy land,
We, pilgrims of eternal sorrow, stand:
What realm lies forward, with its happier store
    Of forests green and deep,
    Of valleys hushed in sleep,
And lakes most peaceful? 'Tis the land of *Evermore*.

Very far off its marble cities seem, —
Very far off, — beyond our sensual dream, —
Its woods unruffled by the wild winds' roar;
    Yet does the turbulent surge
    Howl on its very verge.
One moment, and we breathe within the *Evermore*.

And those we loved and lost so long ago
Dwell in those cities, far from mortal woe;
Haunt those fresh woodlands, whence sweet carollings soar.
    Eternal peace have they;
    God wipes their tears away;
They drink that river of life which flows for evermore."

XX.

POWER OF THE KEYS.

Rev. iii. 7: "THESE THINGS SAITH HE THAT IS HOLY, HE THAT IS TRUE; HE THAT HATH THE KEY OF DAVID; HE THAT OPENETH, AND NO MAN SHUTTETH; AND SHUTTETH, AND NO MAN OPENETH."

Luke xi. 52: "WOE UNTO YOU, LAWYERS! FOR YE HAVE TAKEN AWAY THE KEY OF KNOWLEDGE: YE ENTERED NOT IN YOURSELVES, AND THOSE THAT WERE ENTERING IN YE HINDERED."

Matt. xvi. 19: "I WILL GIVE UNTO THEE THE KEYS OF THE KINGDOM OF HEAVEN; AND WHATSOEVER THOU SHALT BIND ON EARTH SHALL BE BOUND IN HEAVEN, AND WHATSOEVER THOU SHALT LOOSE ON EARTH SHALL BE LOOSED IN HEAVEN."

A KEY is a very ancient invention. You find keys, in Egyptian museums, made three thousand years before Christ: so that locks and keys were common enough among the Jews to be made use of as an illustration and metaphor by Jesus. In fact, locks and keys mark an epoch in civilization. The savage has nothing to lock up. If he has any thing he wishes to keep to himself, he hides it, as a dog hides his bone. When he can lock it up, and trust to the sacredness of a lock, he has already ceased to be a savage. In a yet higher civilization, I presume we shall once again dispense with locks and keys, because we shall have respect enough for each other to consider that all which any one wishes to keep to himself is sacred, even without a lock. In fact, locks are not now as common as they were once, nor as elaborate. In our homes we do not need them. Only on front-doors and bank-safes, and trunks when we travel, and the like, we use them.

Now, there is a place which God has locked, and for which he has provided the keys: it is a place where he keeps his best treasures. But there is this peculiarity about it, that, whereas to each of *our* locks there is only a single kind of key, God's lock is so made, that a variety of keys will open it.

This SECRET PLACE OF THE ALMIGHTY is in the depths of the human soul, — the depths out of which we cry to him. It is a place of profound peace when storms rage above and without. It is a place of perfect love when passions chase each other, dark and violent, over the surface of our troubled life. It is the "kingdom of heaven," which Christ says is within us; the "kingdom of God," which Paul says is "righteousness, peace, and joy in the Holy Ghost."

Christ gave to Peter and to the apostles the keys to this kingdom of heaven. It is usually supposed that this refers to an outward heaven, to a heaven hereafter in the other world. The common Roman-Catholic idea is, that St. Peter sits at an outward gate, with the keys in his hand, and unlocks it to the good, but keeps it locked against the wicked;

unlocks it to the Orthodox, but keeps it locked against the heterodox; unlocks it to the members of the true Church, but keeps it locked against the heretics; unlocks it to the converted, but keeps it locked against the unconverted. But it is certain that the door to any outward heaven lies through an inward heaven. If we do not first enter "the kingdom of heaven which is within us," we shall not enter any heaven above us or outside of us. It is always so. We find outside of us only that which corresponds to what is within. We feel outside that which we have felt within. Outward knowledge attaches itself to inward. An outward heaven is for those who have already gone into an inward heaven.

Three men were riding on horseback through a romantic country on a summer's day. Their road wound up to the top of a hill; and, when they reached the summit, a great range of country lay before them. They stopped to look at it. "How very interesting and extraordinary!" said one. "So it is," said the others; "more so than any place we ever saw." — "What a splendid subject for a painting!" said the first. "Do you see this little hill, with its dark clump of trees in shadow for the foreground; and that beautiful middle distance, with the winding and reaches of the stream, and the village roofs all glittering in sunlight; and then that exquisite soft blue distance, and the pale mountains beyond?" — "I confess," said the second, "I did not see your picture; but I was struck with the extraordinary geological character of this interval, especially those terraces, one above the other, marking the heights at which the river used to stand." — "And I," said the third, "noticed neither; but I thought I had never seen a place better adapted for a military position. That opening in the hills is so defensible! those terraces are so adapted for batteries! Nature has already made the works which would require an army working for months to erect." Thus these three gentlemen — one an artist, one a geologist, and the third a general — saw in the landscape what they had in their own minds; and meantime their horses, I suppose, saw nothing in the valley but the probability of good pasture, with plenty of soft grass.

Thus the outward heaven opens directly for every man out of his inward heaven. There is no locked door between. It is an open way, directly in and up. The moment we enter the inward heaven in our own soul, we are on the way to the heaven beyond. If the inward heaven is locked, then the outward one is locked too. If the heaven in the soul is not open, the heaven beyond is closed. If the heaven here on earth is bound, then that is also bound. If this is loosed, then that. Peter, therefore, and the apostles, do not sit by the gate of any outward heaven, but by the gate of the heaven in the soul; and they hold the keys, and offer them to us. What are they? How did Christ give them to Peter and to the other apostles?

Let us consider these questions a little more carefully than usual.

The Roman-Catholic Church says that Christ gave to the Apostle Peter the keys of the kingdom of heaven. I agree that he did. The Protestant Church says that he also gave this same power to all the disciples, in that subsequent passage of Matthew, in which he says to all of them collectively what he before said to Peter individually. Roman Catholics argue that the popes, being the successors of Peter, inherit his power of binding and loosing. Protestants argue that all Christian ministers inherit the same power from all the apostles. I agree to all this; but I believe still more than this. These theories do not go far enough. Christ gave the keys to Peter; he gave the keys to all the apostles; he gave the keys to all the successors of Peter, and to all the successors of the apostles: but he gave the keys also to all Christians, in all places, and in all times; to all who have Peter's faith. Every Christian, in my judgment, has the key to the kingdom of heaven; and what he binds on earth is bound in heaven; what he looses on earth is loosed in heaven.

For what is meant by "the keys of the kingdom of heaven," and by "binding and loosing"? We have here three questions, concerning "the kingdom of heaven," concerning "the keys," concerning "binding and loosing." Let us look at each of these questions.

What is meant by the kingdom of heaven? We have already given our answer. It is the reign of God, first in the human heart, and then in the human life;

the reign of truth and love; the reign of the Messiah foretold by the prophets, when men should beat their swords into ploughshares, and when the desert should rejoice, and blossom as the rose; it is the reign of Christ here and now; it is Christianity in this world, beginning here, continued hereafter. The kingdom of heaven, then, is not heaven in the other world, but heaven in this world; not heaven hereafter, but heaven here. It is true that it is continued into the other world; but it begins in this world. When John the Baptist, when Christ, and when his apostles, preached, saying, "The kingdom of heaven is at hand," they meant a kingdom in this world. When we pray, in our daily prayer, "Thy kingdom come," we are praying for it to come here. In the parables which compare the kingdom of heaven to "leaven," to "mustard-seed," to "a net," &c., Christianity in this world is spoken of; and so, when Christ speaks of the keys of the kingdom of heaven, it is the key to the kingdom of heaven in this world which is referred to. Heaven itself is the invisible, spiritual world of God; but the kingdom of heaven is that world descending into this, God with us, the tabernacle of God with men. The kingdom of heaven, therefore, means Christianity here, or Christ reigning, first in the heart, then in the Church, next in society, and lastly in the State.

What are THE KEYS of the kingdom of heaven? The keys are the power by which the door into this kingdom shall be opened. The kingdom is Christianity; the door is Christ himself; and the key is whatever reveals Christ or opens him, so that men may pass through him into Christianity. Jesus says, "I am the door. Through me, if any man enter in, he shall be saved, and shall go in and out, and find pasture."

To "bind and to loose" means simply to open and shut the door. Doors were fastened anciently by ropes, and the key was used to fasten and to unfasten them.

This, then, is the answer to our three questions. The kingdom of heaven is Christianity; the key is that which opens the door of Christianity; binding and loosing is opening or shutting the door.

The mistake which the Church has made concerning this doctrine of the keys has been to make the power of the keys something arbitrary. It has been supposed that Christ gave to Peter the power of deciding, in an arbitrary way, as to who should be admitted into heaven, or excluded from it; or that he has given to the Church an arbitrary power of receiving members into it, or excommunicating them from it. But the power here given is not formal, but real; not depending on any man's will or pleasure, but fixed in the nature of things. It is a power universally given to knowledge and insight. It is "the key of knowledge." All true insight is a key, with which to bind or loose, with which to open and shut.

Two or three thousand years before the birth of

Christ, the Valley of the Nile was inhabited by a nation which had carried all the arts of life to a high state of perfection. One of their habits was that of writing. They kept a record of every thing. They had a rage for history. For thousands of years, the whole nation kept a diary of all events, great and small. They engraved, and painted over, the stone walls of their pyramids, temples, and tombs, with the most multitudinous details of public and private life. But what it all was, no one could tell. The key had been lost. But at last Champollion found the key, and opened the door; and now all men can go in and out amid that mysterious Egyptian knowledge, and understand it.

Knowledge in the mind of any one is a key by which he can open the door of science or of art to others. When the knowledge is only of facts or of laws, it can be communicated without enthusiasm or inspiration. But the higher kinds of knowledge require these. Spiritual and moral truth must be taught in a living way, not in the letter, but in the spirit. To bear witness to such truths no hearsay information will suffice, but only personal conviction. Flesh and blood cannot reveal it, but only "my Father which is in heaven."

It was this sort of knowledge concerning Christ which Peter at that moment possessed. He, like other Jews, was expecting the Christ to come in a grand outward way, with pomp and power, with signs from heaven; living in Jerusalem like a king; leading great armies against the Romans, and driving them out, and placing the Jewish nation at the head of mankind. All at once, it flashed into the soul of Peter that this Jesus of Nazareth, the carpenter's son, the poor peasant of Galilee, was the great Messiah who was to come. This holy love and truth in him, this heavenly goodness, this strange wisdom, which moulded all minds, was the true sign of his divinity. It was but a momentary glimpse of the truth, but a glorious one. It was swept away the very next moment by the returning wave of prejudice and old opinion; so that Jesus was obliged, directly after, to call Peter, Satan. But Jesus beheld in this momentary insight the germ of a living faith, and said, "On this rock will I build my Church."

Personal, living faith in Christ is the key to Christianity. All who have this faith, from the pope in the Vatican to the poorest slave on a Southern plantation, have the key to the kingdom of heaven; and what they bind on earth is bound in heaven, what they loose on earth is loosed in heaven: that is, when they open the door, it is opened; and when they shut the door, it is shut.

Any such authority as this, if it were arbitrary, would be dangerous. We could not trust any human being with such power, and God would not trust him. But the power to bind and loose is not arbitrary. It depends on no man's will. It is a power which God gives of seeing and uttering the truth. Nor is it confided to one man, or to one class of men; not to bishops, not to priests, nor to ministers. It is given to the pure in heart, who see God: the keys are taken from the hands of the wise and the prudent, and given to the babes. God enriches whom he will with utterance and knowledge. He reveals deep things by his spirit. He shows his truth to the humble and the sincere, and makes them able ministers of the new covenant. They are able, by manifestation of the truth, to commend themselves to every man's conscience. God shines in their hearts, to give the light of the knowledge of his glory, giving them the spirit of wisdom and revelation. Thus the power of the keys is the power given to all sincere hearts to see the truth and to utter it.

Thus we understand what is meant by the keys in regard to opening the kingdom of heaven. All Christians, when they speak out of their own Christian experience, open the kingdom of heaven. But how do they shut it?

All truth has two sides, positive and negative. It attracts and repels. It draws men toward itself, or sends them from itself. It is a savor of life or of death. It distinguishes good from evil, truth from error, right from wrong. When the sun rises, it not only makes lights, but also shadows. The side toward it is in light: the side turned away is in shadow.

All divine offers are with conditions. Every thing has its price. The conditions are simple, but absolute. An invitation may be free, and yet conditional. You are freely invited to a great feast; but there are conditions attached to the invitation. The first is, that you shall be willing to go, that you shall accept the invitation; the second is, that you shall go at the right time and to the right place; and the third condition is, that, when there, you shall be dressed suitably, and behave properly.

Christianity, like every thing else, has its limitations and its laws. "Except ye be converted, and become as little children, ye shall not enter into the kingdom of heaven." "Repent, and be converted, that your sins may be blotted out." "Believe on the Lord Jesus Christ, and thou shalt be saved." "If we confess with our mouth the Lord Jesus, and believe in our heart that God has raised him from the dead, we shall be saved." "Every one that loveth is born of God, and knoweth God." "He that loveth not, knoweth not God; for God is love." "If we confess our sins, He is faithful and just to forgive us our sins, and to cleanse us from all unrighteousness." Every one of these conditions is a key which turns two ways. Turn it one way, it locks the door; turn it the other, and it unlocks it.

It is, therefore, easy to see how every Christian has given to him, in his sight of divine truth, the keys of the kingdom of heaven; the power to bind and to loose, to open and shut; to judge the world, men and angels; to part the sheep from the goats. Whosesoever sins he remits, they are remitted; and whosesoever sins he retains, they are retained. When he utters the truth, if men are willing to accept it, they enter the kingdom; if unwilling, they turn away. Every true word makes a parting of the ways; compels us to decide which way we will go, — whether to the right, into spiritual life; or to the left, into spiritual death; and is, therefore, a savor of life or of death.

But human words have this great power only when they are the words of God, and not ours; only when God speaks through us. When they proceed from our own will, they are empty and insignificant.

But I have emphasized *keys*, in the plural. The text says *keys*, in the plural; and that plural is significant. We are apt to suppose that there is only one. It is very natural. It is our church; it is our creed; it is our experience: that is the only one. I recollect a young lady, who, having just been proselyted to the Roman-Catholic Church, wrote a letter to a friend, describing her satisfaction therein, and said, "Believe me, true happiness and real peace cannot be found anywhere else than in our church." In like manner, you will hear those just converted to some other faith say the same; or rather, let me say, *converted to God* by means of some other faith. I have heard the same sort of claim made, with perfect sincerity, for every church and for every creed. Each thinks the creed and church by which he has found heaven to be the *only* way to heaven. He does not know of any other. I have often thought that I should like to see a book written, to be called "The Book of Converts," containing the experiences, given by themselves, of those who have been converted from the Roman-Catholic Church to the Protestant, and *vice versâ;* from Orthodoxy to Unitarianism and to Universalism, and the contrary; from Episcopacy to Quakerism; to Swedenborgianism; yes, even from Christianity to Infidelity, as well as from Infidelity to Christianity. For, from all these, you can find perfectly sincere and honest statements of the joy and peace they have found in their new belief or unbelief. And such a book would tend to liberalize the Church; showing, first, that no such conversion proved any thing in regard to the abstract truth of the system renounced or accepted, because the same comfort and peace is found by those *going in* and those *going out;* and secondly, that, by all these various creeds and churches, God does teach something to the soul, and that all these experiences are *keys* to some one of the many mansions in God's heaven. God teaches us sometimes even by unbelief; and the way to heaven may descend through the dark, damp valley of denial and doubt, before it ascends into the region of upper light, life, truth, and joy. When any one is ready to collect such a book of experiences from such conversions, I shall be glad to furnish a motto for it out of Shakspeare. The motto is what the melancholy Jacques says at the end of "As you Like It," in regard to the duke: —

> "To him will I: out of these convertites
> There is much matter to be heard and learned."

Of these many keys, one is faith. This is the key which Peter had. But what sort of faith? That kind, says Jesus, which "flesh and blood" does not give, but my Father in heaven. The only faith which is a key to the kingdom within us is that of profound personal conviction. There are two kinds: first, that of hearsay belief, which flesh and blood gives us; secondly, personal conviction, or the original sight of truth. The first often produces unbelief instead of belief. Formal acceptance of hereditary opinions is a kind of dead faith which is not faith. The witnesses in our courts are obliged to testify to what they have seen themselves: all hearsay evidence is ruled out. I think that God *rules out* of his courts all hearsay evidence. I wish the Church would do the same. A great amount of infidelity is produced by the dead hearsay faith of Christians. Every creed was once alive. It sprang all alive from the heart or brain of some earnest soul, like Minerva from Jupiter, all aglow with inspiration; but too often it dies of routine.

The Church, frequently, instead of *conviction*, seeks *assent*. An earnest seeker, who doubts because he is seeking, is looked upon with fear; a sceptic, who is on his way to belief through doubt, is thought to be criminal in that; a person who loves truth so earnestly as not to be satisfied with words and phrases, who will not say that he believes till he does believe, — to him the Church turns the cold shoulder. But a man who does not care enough about it to know whether he believes or not; who is ready to accept thirty-nine articles, or three hundred and ninety-nine, just as it happens; who in Catholic countries is ready to be a Catholic, and go to mass; in Methodist countries, to shout and sing, and cry glory; who in Boston is a Unitarian, and in Washington a Presbyterian,—he is the well-beloved son of the Church. The Church, usually, is satisfied with assent: it does not ask for conviction.

But all sincere conviction is a key to open the door of the kingdom of heaven in the soul. It leads us to belief in the reality of truth: that is the good it does. It destroys that worst of all scepticisms,—doubt if any thing be true or right.

Again: the Church is a key. Its imposing ceremonies, its solemn sacraments, its majestic influences, bring peace to many souls, and educate multitudes to trust in God and to obedience. Yet it is the Church in the Church which does it. It is not the dead form, not the dead letter, but the life within. If the Church is only a form, then it is not a key. But, as long as you who are worshippers come together with serious hearts, this teaches others; and they feel and say that "God is with you of a truth." So it was in the early Church, when "the multitude who believed were of one heart and one soul; neither said any of them that aught that he possessed was his own, but they had all things common." Then "great grace was upon them all;" then they "did eat their meat with gladness and singleness of heart;" and *then* "the Lord added daily to the Church such as were saved."

In the Epistle to the Corinthians, Paul makes the earnest utterance of the whole Church, the united expression of their honest convictions, a key to the kingdom of heaven. The miraculous and wonderful gift of tongues he thinks less likely to convert men to Christianity than the prophecy or teaching of the Church. Prophecy is speaking the truth seen in the heart. He says, If the whole Church come together, and all speak with tongues, and strangers come in, they will think you crazy: but if you all teach, and a stranger comes in, he is convinced by what you say; he sees that you know what is in his heart; he falls on his face, and worships God, and declares that God is truly with you.

I shall never forget an evening which I passed in the Cathedral of Antwerp, one of the noblest of mediæval buildings.

It was Sunday evening. I was alone in the city of Antwerp. I knew no one in the place, and no one knew me. All day long, I had not spoken to a living soul. I had been visiting churches, and seeing altar-pieces; but my heart was lonely. In the evening, passing by the great cathedral, I saw a dim light issuing from a doorway. I went in. One part of the vast nave was lighted by a few candles hung against the columns. A few hundred people, clustered around the pulpit, were listening to a preacher speaking in Flemish. The light penetrated only a little way through the forest of columns into the solemn darkness of the interior. I took a chair, and sat near the little congregation. I understood scarcely a word of what was said; but I felt earnestness and sincerity in the tones of the speaker. I saw reverence in the faces of the worshippers. I was no longer lonely: I felt among friends. I felt the human hearts beating around me to the same tone as mine; and I was in communion with those worshippers and with God. Their service was to me *the key to the kingdom of heaven.*

Yet I recollect also how once, in Nice, I found a little body of Protestants worshipping in an upper chamber, without any solemn cathedral, majestic music, or ancient ceremony; but in their worship, too, being in spirit and truth, I found a key to the kingdom of heaven. I entered heaven with them in prayer and praise, in faith and gratitude.

But it is also true, that where two or three meet in the name and spirit of Christ, where two or three unite in any Christian work, there is also a door opening into heaven. Christ is with them, as he promised to be; and where he is, there is heaven. Have we not talked in days gone by with dear friends, some of whom have since fallen asleep? and as we spoke of earnest themes, as we talked of things divine, has not Jesus seemed to come and walk with us, and our hearts burn within us with a joy which was surely heavenly, and not earthly? And though these dear friends leave us, going on before into that higher world where they shall have more of heaven than here, it is yet the same kind of heaven they have had already. They have seen God here: they shall see him more nearly there. They have known Christ: they shall know him more intimately. They have had the joy of active usefulness, of living insight, of generous affection: they shall have more of it there, — more to know, more to do, more to love.

Nature is also a key to the kingdom of heaven; for Nature is God revealing himself to us in all its majestic order, all its boundless variety, all its transcendent beauty, all its deep peace. Who has not felt his heart drawn to God by the glory of morning, the charm of evening, the solemn night, the majesty of ocean, the serenity of the mountain, the tenderness of flowers, and the forest-depths, full of mysterious, inexplicable influences? "There are many voices in the world, and none of them without signification."

God sometimes touches a hard heart with the fragrance of a flower, or with a melody reminding it of childhood. You remember what Napoleon said to his marshals, when they were sneering at his encouragement of the Catholic worship: "Yesterday I was walking in my garden, and I heard the church-bell of Ruel; and involuntarily I was carried back for a moment to my innocent childhood. Now, gentlemen, if the mere sound of a bell affects thus a man like me, such a man as I am, what must be the influence of such associations on the general mind?"

How often does God send trial and sorrow as keys

to the kingdom of heaven! If even Jesus learned obedience by the things he suffered, if even that pure soul went deeper into the love of God by the path of trial, if *he* could only become *perfect* through suffering, let us not murmur at our trials, which are sent to us that we may be partakers of the holiness of God.

Sometimes little children come to us, bringing in their little hands the keys to the kingdom of heaven. The man whose heart was perhaps growing hard in the struggle of life; who, unconsciously, was becoming worldly; whose face, practised in meeting men, was gradually becoming rigid in its outlines; whose keen eye was losing its tenderness, — has had sent to him these sweet little angels as a voice from God: —

> "Trailing clouds of glory do they come
> From heaven, which is their home."

His heart grows young again with them; his soul is softened by their infantile caresses; his life is checked in its tendency; and they lead him to his Father and theirs. Nature's priesthood, these little children, in their innocence and simplicity, are evermore bringing back the hearts of fathers and mothers into a more simple and childlike trust and joy. Coming to us, they bring the keys of the kingdom of heaven. Going from us, they unlock those sacred doors; and we, in our bereavement, find our hearts drawn up after them to God. The heavens, into which they have gone, remain open; and the fragrance and melody of that upper world comes down to us here, and never leaves us again.

Thus God gives into our hands the keys with which we may open heaven to others. Not to Peter alone, not to the apostles alone, but to all of us, he says, "*What ye bind on earth* shall be bound in heaven; what ye loose on earth shall be loosed in heaven." Whenever we are faithful to our convictions, true to the light God shows to us, unselfish and generous, then we open the gateway of heaven to those who are with us. Whenever we are selfish and unbelieving and hard, we shut the gateway. The spirit we are in inevitably communicates itself even by our voice and tone, and preaches to others truth, generosity, humility, faith, or preaches unbelief, selfishness, doubt, despair. Influence falls from us, at every moment, for good or evil. We say, by our state of mind, that there is something real in truth, in virtue, in love; that immortality is not a dream; that heaven is close at hand; that life is rich in great opportunities. We say this every moment, when we are in a right state of mind; and, in saying this, we unlock heaven to others, and lead them in. Or we say to others, by our formality, by our coldness, by our self-seeking, that religion is empty; that Christianity is only a name; that life is a weariness; that all things are vanity; that love is an illusion; that the gospel is a cheat and a lie. And, saying this, we lock the doors of heaven; we turn away from God those who are seeking him; we make infidels and sceptics; we corrupt innocent and childlike hearts by our worldliness. Such eternal consequences follow our trivial earthly actions. So it is, that what we bind *on earth* is bound in heaven; that what we loose on earth is loosed in heaven.

Let us thank God that there are many keys by which to open the blessed door which leads into the heavenly kingdom. To one the door is opened in childhood; and the dear little feet go in, and the small curly head is already surrounded with the pure glory of a light beaming from the presence of God. Another, in youth, drops the trivialities and follies of youth, and lifts deep, earnest eyes toward the great truths of life and time, of death and eternity. One enters the kingdom by faithful work: loyalty to duty unlocks the door, and he goes in. One finds the key through temptation, sorrow, sin, remorse, penitence, turning to God in hopeless shame, but meeting hope and unexpected joy shed abroad in his heart. One rises from the bed of sickness with all of his past life closed behind him; and a new life, filled with purer hopes, opening upward into heaven. One is moved by the noble words, the holy life, and the rapt enthusiasm of the saints and martyrs, by the utterings of genius and the eloquence of fiery hearts; and follows, with enthusiastic love, their pathway, till they lead him to the mountain-heights of holy truth. The words of a dear mother, the loving kiss of a dying child, the never-fading remembrance of a departed friend, of a noble and generous sister or brother gone before us to God, raise some of us above ourselves. Such are the multitudinous paths which lead us to God: so we come, at last, to Christ, the image of the invisible God. The air of heaven, even here, begins to fan our heated brow; the music of heaven comes softly down, mingling with our daily life; the light of the upper world shines down into our poor human hearts. God be blessed for it all, — for all the sorrow, all the joy, all the experience of good and evil, light threads and dark threads shooting to and fro across the web of human life! Brothers and sisters, — dear friends of mine, fellow-workers in this wonderful world, — let us be fellow-helpers through it, till we meet on that higher shore, in that larger liberty, and with that fuller peace of rest and action, which remains for God's children, beyond the low-arched gateway that mortals call death.

XXI.

THE PROPER AND THE BECOMING.

Matt. iii. 15: "THUS IT BECOMETH US TO FULFIL ALL RIGHTEOUSNESS."

WHEN Jesus went to Bethabara to be baptized, John the Baptist refused to baptize him. John said, "I have need to be baptized of thee; and comest thou to me?" John had a profound feeling of the holiness and grandeur of Jesus. They were cousins; they had known each other as children, known each other in youth; and John felt that Jesus was so much holier and better than himself, that he was not fit to baptize him. Then Jesus made this answer: "Suffer it to be so now: thus it becometh us to fulfil all righteousness." What did he mean by it? Why was it becoming in him to do this?

There seemed to be no good reason why Christ should be baptized. The usual reasons do not, apparently, apply to Jesus. Many came to John because they thought him a very holy man, whose blessing would help them in some mysterious, perhaps magical way. This was not the reason of Jesus; for there is a slight tinge of superstition in this motive. Jesus did not expect to be made better by being touched with John's hands. Others came to John from a moral motive; came as sinners to confess their sin, to repent of it, to inaugurate a new life better than the old one. *This* was not the motive of Jesus: he needed not to repent, confess, or reform. He was free from sin, and needed no baptism to repentance. Another object of baptism is initiation. Proselytes were admitted into the Jewish Church by baptism; catechumens are admitted into the Christian Church by baptism. This was not Christ's object. He did not come to John to be admitted into the number of his disciples. Some say that he was baptized as a consecration to his office, as an act of self-dedication to the work of the Messiah. This could hardly be, since he did not mean to be known as the Messiah until long after.

The only reason which Jesus had for being baptized seems to be the one which he gives in our text. It was becoming. It was not necessary for himself, nor for others; it was not a baptism of repentance, nor of initiation, nor of dedication. It was simply *becoming;* that is, handsome, suitable, in accordance with the circumstances, in harmony with the state of things. There was moral grace and beauty in it. That was all; but that was enough.

For in human actions, beside the element of necessity, of expediency, of duty, there is also the element of *beauty.* Some actions are morally beautiful, and are to be done for that reason. Such was that act of the woman in the gospel, who brought her alabaster box of precious ointment to Jesus, and anointed his feet therewith. There was no utility about it: it did no good, in any common sense. But it was "becoming;" it was beautiful; it expressed her intimate convictions, her love, her reverence, her devotion. Any thing which thus beautifully expresses a true and noble sentiment is *becoming;* and, because it is becoming, it is right. When David longed for the "water of the well of Bethlehem, which is by the gate," and his three mighty men brake through the enemy's ranks, and procured it for him, and he would not drink it, but poured it on the ground, saying, "Is not this the blood of the men who went in jeopardy of their lives?" that was not a very reasonable action; there was no use in wasting the good water which they all needed; but it was a very *becoming* action. Many actions are good because they are becoming, and for no other reason; actions which political economy and utilitarian morality would quite condemn. A clergyman in this city once declined an increase of salary. Twenty good reasons can be given why he ought not to have refused it: nevertheless, it was a *becoming* action. It had a moral beauty about it: no one can deny that. A butcher in Boylston Market declined selling a piece of meat to a United-States commissioner who had returned a fugitive, telling him that his money was "base money." So I knew a clergyman who sent back a part of his salary which had come from rum-sellers. Both of these actions have moral beauty, as expressive of strong convictions of right, though they may both be quite open to objections on the side of political economy or utility.

But, before going farther, let us stop a little, and analyze this term "becoming," and see precisely what it means. The Greek word *πρέπω,* — *το πρέπον,* — is used in half a dozen places in the New Testament, and always with the same sense. In one place it is translated "comely;" in all other places, "becoming." Now, the "becoming" or "comely" is that which *comes* to a thing; which *suits* it; which is fit, suitable, congruous, in harmony with it. The harmonies of time, place, circumstance, are conveyed by this term; and the English word hints at a law of Nature, a law of attraction which a thing exercises over other things that suit it, and are in harmony with it, so that they come to it. Like draws like: so harmonious persons, actions, and qualities come together. Perhaps this law includes that which causes planets to gravitate to their sun, and that which causes crystals to be elaborated slowly, through thousands of years, in the depths of the earth, — includes the chemical affinities which mingle and arrange the elements of earth; the law which makes seeds and plants to move toward the light and the moisture; which occasions society to organize itself in families, friendships, neighborhoods, and states; which causes truth, holy and sacred, to be felt in the depths of the soul; which makes the reason respond to it, the conscience move to it, the heart cleave to it; which, in fine, causes man to worship God, and to serve his neighbor, because he was made for this piety and charity, and because it *suits* his noblest instincts so to do. So the world becomes a *kosmos*, a beauty, when every part of it is filled with harmony.

And why was it *becoming* in Jesus to be baptized by John? In two ways,—as a testimony to John; and as an expression of his own inward purpose.

John was a true and a noble character; faithful and strong as steel; ready to act and to bear for what he thought the truth. Jesus, in coming to be baptized by him, took sides with him; showed that he believed him in the main to be right; manifested his sympathy with him; approved of his work; showed a modest willingness to receive all he had to give. This was a becoming act in Jesus; and it is always a sign of true greatness and nobleness thus to recognize desert, and bear a willing testimony to it. Not that John the Baptist had not great faults: but he was a noble person, and doing a right work; and Jesus, instead of any captious criticism of his manner of acting, took openly his side.

When a great controversy is going on, in which great principles of truth, justice, liberty, are involved, the noble-minded man wishes to act as Jesus acted; openly to take sides with those who are, in the main, in the right. A small-minded man, on the contrary, prefers to find petty faults, and refuses to co-operate, because some things are said or done which he thinks in bad taste or bad temper.

When ideas and principles are on one side, and what we consider culture, taste, gentlemanly conduct, on the other, some persons take the latter; but the highest souls choose the former.

Some years ago, in those days we all remember, when the abolitionists were very odious in Boston, the governor of the State recommended to the Legislature to pass a law to punish the writing and printing of what were called incendiary publications. The abolitionists asked to be heard in opposition to the passage of this law. A hearing was granted them; and Mr. Garrison, Dr. Follen, and others, appeared before the committee to argue against the proposed law. While the argument was going on, the door of the room opened, and Dr. Channing appeared in the entrance. He was then at the height of his fame, the most conspicuous citizen of Boston; having achieved a European reputation, and receiving visits every week from distinguished foreigners. Looking around the room, he discovered where Mr. Garrison was seated, — at that time, probably, the most unpopular and odious person in the State. Passing by the dignified representatives and respectable citizens present, Dr. Channing went up to Mr. Garrison, took him by the hand, and took a seat by his side. In doing so, he seems to me, unconsciously perhaps, to have followed the example of Jesus Christ in the case before us. Dr. Channing and Mr. Garrison differed from each other in many respects, and Mr. Garrison had not been sparing of his criticism of Dr.

Channing's views; but, feeling a profound sympathy with the main purpose and conviction which animated this reformer, Dr. Channing would not allow any minor differences, in matters of opinion or of taste, to prevent him from bearing his testimony to the essential justice of the cause. When an attempt was to be made to crush freedom of speech in Massachusetts, and to silence the voice which claimed liberty for the captive, Channing deemed it becoming to take his place by the side of this champion of the slave.

But almost every good thing has its counterfeit, and so the becoming has its counterfeit. The counterfeit of the becoming is the proper. The morally beautiful is replaced by the conventionally correct. Propriety is a kind of minor morality, and governs society in social life, as public opinion governs it in public life. Thus mothers say to their children, "You must not do that, my dear." — "Why not, mamma?" "Because it is not proper, my child." This argument is deemed final and unanswerable.

The most becoming things are not always the most proper things; for they are apt to be violations of etiquette. It was becoming of Jesus to be baptized; but it was hardly proper. John was not a fit person, in the view of propriety, to keep company with,— a mere fanatic; a man living in the wilderness; living on locusts and wild honey, and dressed not in soft raiment or broadcloth. He had a devil, so they said; was evidently crazy; was a mere enthusiast, if he was not an impostor. He probably wanted an office; or, at any rate, was preaching doctrines which led directly to riots and insurrections. He did not speak at all respectfully of the dignitaries and distinguished people. He called the scribes and Pharisees "serpents" and "a generation of vipers;" though they were, in fact, the chief people in Jerusalem. Under these circumstances, propriety evidently forbade Jesus from giving him any countenance: but it was becoming, nevertheless, to go, and share his unpopularity, and partake his odium; and so Jesus went.

The sources of the proper and the becoming are different. That which is becoming flows from an instinctive perception of what is morally beautiful. It leads us to fulfil all righteousness; for it penetrates to small things. It makes life graceful and gracious by the multitude of little acts and words of kindness which it inspires. It is an invisible spirit of sympathy, faith, reverence, and modesty, which informs the manners, and makes one courteous, taking out of life whatever is harsh and hard.

Seek, therefore, that which is becoming rather than that which is only proper; for the becoming includes the proper, but not the reverse. That which is truly becoming may indeed not always appear proper, though in the highest sense it may be so: for the *proper* means only that which is customary, or which other people do; but the *becoming* is that which is suitable to present circumstances and present needs, whether it has ever been done before or not.

Many things which Christ and his disciples did seemed highly improper to the Pharisees, who were men of religious punctilio and etiquette. They did not think it proper that he should cure a sick man on the sabbath, or that his disciples should pluck ears of corn on that day. They thought it improper for the disciples not to fast, and still more improper that they should sing hosannas on his entrance into Jerusalem. To drive the buyers and sellers out of the temple was not proper; and it was by no means proper to call the Pharisees serpents, and a generation of vipers. But, though these things were improper in view of religious pedantry, they were highly suitable under the circumstances, and therefore were becoming. For as propriety based upon custom is the highest law of conventionalism; so the becoming, founded on the harmony of things, is the largest and highest law of realities.

When Wesley began his great work, which revived the decaying religious life in the English nation, his course in many respects was thought very improper. In those days of drunken curates and fox-hunting rectors, when Paley had to advise the clergy not to drink and play cards in ale-houses, it shocked all England to hear of lay-preaching and services in the open air. I know not a more striking scene than that of John Wesley preaching at Epworth, in the churchyard, in the evening twilight, standing on his father's tomb, when he was shut out of his father's church. "They accuse us," said he, "of indecorum because we preach in the open air. I go into their churches, and find drowsy congregations and sleepy preachers: in that I see indecorum. But I have preached on the hill-side to many thousand people, who were so attentive, that when a wall fell down, upon which a great many people were sitting, it made no disturbance in the congregation."

Propriety in the pulpit is not always equivalent to what is becoming therein. If a minister wishes to do what is proper in the pulpit, he can very easily accomplish that task. All he has to do is to keep in the line of safe precedents, and do as others have done already. He may defend with some energy all the accepted and popular opinions of his church; he may wax warm against heretics, and may even be slightly and handsomely severe in speaking of them. He may also condemn as strongly as he will the Jewish scribes and Pharisees. He may be sarcastic against Pontius Pilate. He may denounce Roman Catholics and Infidels; and may say almost any thing he chooses against Hume, Voltaire, and Rousseau. But let him beware how he censures the vices of his own time and his own community. He may show the people the sins of their grandfathers, and they will listen; but, if he tries to show their own sins, some will always say it is improper to do so. Taking a man from Africa to make a slave of him, he may call piracy; but taking a man from Boston to make a slave of him, he must not call kidnapping: if he does, some alderman will walk out of church.*

I do not know whether the parishioner was convinced; but I know that Amasis, King of Egypt, was a much wiser man than some of these discontented parishioners. Before he became king, he was disposed to pilfer; and, when accused of taking people's property, he would appeal to the oracle of the place, which would sometimes acquit and sometimes condemn him. When, therefore, he became king, he paid no attention to the gods and oracles that had *acquitted him*, nor contributed to their temples; considering them of no consequence, and as lying oracles. But to such as convicted him of theft he paid the highest respect, considering them as truly gods and truth-tellers; for of what use are gods and pulpits that do not tell us the truth?

But I consider nothing more *becoming* in the pulpit than to speak the truth, — simple, pure, plain truth. It might have been quite improper in Nathan to rebuke the great King David, and to be guilty of the personality of saying, "Thou art the man!" but it was *becoming*. It was no doubt thought very improper in Jesus to drive the money-changers out of the temple, and to say harsh things about those highly respectable people, the scribes and Pharisees. It was not proper for Luther to burn the pope's bull, for Horace

* This sermon was preached in the bad days of 1851. Since then, what a change!

Mann to expose the iniquities of slavery, or for John Pierpont to set forth the miseries and woes which come from making and selling rum. These things were not thought proper; for you will observe, that, of all sticklers for propriety, those are the chief who make gain by any sort of wrong-doing.

Nations, as well as individuals, can do that which is *becoming*, sometimes transcending the limits of utilitarian prudence and propriety. When, in the Irish famine, the ship "Jamestown" crossed the ocean to carry food, political economy might not wholly approve it; but surely it was noble and becoming. And when the English nation, on the 1st of August, 1838, emancipated eight hundred thousand slaves, and gave a hundred millions of dollars to compensate their masters, it was not wise, perhaps, in the sense of political economy; but it was wise in the wisdom of heavenly truth and justice.

When Florence Nightingale found that the food and comforts destined for the sick soldiers were kept locked up and unused, because no one knew who had authority to dispense them, she ordered the doors to be broken open, and the provisions to be taken to the hospital. That was certainly improper: it was also certainly becoming.

It sometimes takes a high soul and a great nature to elevate the thing which is improper, and to make it becoming. What more improper than for Joan of Arc to ride in man's clothes at the head of an army, and offer herself to lead soldiers into battle? yet the act, so evidently improper, is the most beautiful event in the history of a thousand years. Yet to imitate that act would require another soul as pure and brave as hers.

The *becoming* flows, as we have seen, from an instinctive perception of what is morally beautiful. It leads us to fulfil all righteousness; it penetrates to small things; small acts and words of kindness flow out of it; it makes life graceful and gracious; it is an invisible spirit of sympathy, of love, of faith, of hope, of reverence, of modesty, of joy, which informs the manners, and makes one gentle, courteous, and kind; taking out of life all that is harsh and hard.

Instead, therefore, of aiming at what is proper, aim at what is becoming.

As regards children, what is becoming in them is to have a spirit of reverence and of confidence conjoined; a spirit which respects parents, teachers, superiors; which reverences all that is above them, but is not checked in that charming confidence and freedom which makes the grace of childhood. Instead of surrounding them with bristling proprieties, show them how to respect others; and teach them to be simple, sincere, and truthful themselves. These two graces are natural to childhood: only let them not be repressed.

In young men, the spirit which makes the becoming is a spirit of modesty and manliness, which, when combined, form the elements of moral beauty, — a modesty which avoids conceit, arrogance, and pretension; and a manliness which is ready to do its work bravely, and to take hold of life with courage and self-reliance.

In young women, the becoming spirit is the same. We wish to see in them freshness of thought, and openness of manner; we wish to see also the spirit of respect and consideration for all that is around them. The charm of womanhood is this combination of expansive sympathies and fresh impulses, with quick consideration for the feelings and rights of all others.

In all we do, the *becoming*, the beautiful, that element which makes heroes in heroic times, and gives romantic beauty to life, is the spirit of reverence and the spirit of freedom. Life is full of awe and mystery. God, the Eternal and Infinite, is always near. Death surrounds us and attends us; the inscrutable mysteries of a great hereafter are always close at the door. Therefore reverence and religious awe are *becoming* to man; reverence for God's presence everywhere, — for Him who filleth all in all. No one but respects the man who respects God; no one but sees the beauty of the truly religious character. The religion of propriety and of usage is cold and cheerless: but the religion which sees the wonders and glories of eternity gleaming ever through the portals of time — this commands the respect of all; is felt to be comely, heroic, and admirable.

"It becometh us to fulfil all righteousness;" to

respect every manifestation of the truly religious life; to give our testimony to all parts of Christian faith and action; but especially to live in that spirit of mingled reverence and freedom which shall enable us to comply with propriety or to transcend propriety; always to live near to God; and always to do that, and speak that, which is beautiful, gracious, and of good report.

XXII.

THE FAVORITE TEXTS OF JESUS.

Luke iv. 17: "HE OPENED THE BOOK, AND FOUND THE PLACE."

WHEN you read an interesting book, it becomes more interesting if you find that some one whom you love and respect has read it before you, and has marked, here and there, any favorite passages. The first time I read Spenser's "Fairy Queen," it was in Kentucky, and in a copy which had belonged to the poet John Keats. It was marked all through with his pen at those places which especially interested and pleased him. I enjoyed the book all the more for those marks. The pleasure you find in this, arises, I think, from the fact that you are reading *two* minds at the same time, — the mind of the author, and that of the previous reader. You seem to look into the heart and thought of him who has gone before you; and, whenever you come to his pencil-mark, you say, "Why was he interested in this?" and you stop a moment to read in your friend's mind what *his* thought was about the author.

Now, suppose that we could have the very copy of the Hebrew Scriptures which was used by Jesus when a child, a boy, a man, at Nazareth, — the very rolls, marked in the margin with his hand at his favorite passages: could any thing be more interesting than this? Would it not let us into the mind of Christ to see what texts he loved the most in all the volume? How very interesting, how deeply affecting, would it be to see the Bible which our Lord used! I was interested in John Keats's marks in "Spenser," because he was a poet too. A poet reading a poet seems to be a good guide; but Jesus, the prophetic soul, reading the books of the great prophetic souls who went before him, interprets them to us best of all.

We have not the Bible that Jesus used; but we have almost the same thing: we have his *favorite passages* in the Old Testament given to us in another way. We have his quotations from it preserved for in us the New Testament. All may not be preserved; but we have about forty passages, quoted by Jesus from the different Jewish Scriptures.

I have thought it might be interesting and useful to look at these, or at some of them, and so get a glimpse into the mind of Jesus through this little window.

Jesus has quoted about thirty-nine passages from eleven books of the Old Testament. From each of the five books of Moses, Genesis, Exodus, Leviticus, Numbers, and Deuteronomy, fifteen passages; nine passages from the Psalms; seven from Isaiah; eight from Jeremiah, Hosea, Malachi, and Zechariah.

He has quoted nothing from the historical books, from Joshua to Esther inclusive; nothing from Job, Proverbs, Ecclesiastes, or the Song of Solomon; nothing from twelve of the prophets, including Ezekiel and Daniel.

Let me remark, before proceeding further, that, in quoting from the Old Testament, our Lord thinks more of the spirit than of the letter. He quotes sometimes from the Hebrew, and sometimes from the Septuagint Greek translation; and of some passages it is hard to say whence they are quoted. Sometimes he puts together two texts from different places, as when he says, "It is written, My house shall be called a house of prayer for all nations; but ye have made it a den of thieves." The first half is from Isaiah, the last from Jeremiah. Therefore he has not any idea of using these passages logically as proof-texts, or controversially as arguments adapted to convince doubters; for, in such a case, it would have been necessary for his purpose to quote with precision. The object for which he adduces these passages is moral and spiritual, for which no such accuracy is needed.

CHRIST FULFILLING SCRIPTURE.

He sometimes spoke of himself as *fulfilling* these Scriptures. I think we often have a false idea of what is meant by this. We suppose that it means to adduce a prediction which is literally accomplished by a fact. We suppose that Jesus did certain things merely to fulfil the predictions of Scripture. Thus we might suppose that Jesus healed diseases to fulfil one prophecy of Isaiah; that he kept silence about himself to fulfil another; and spoke in parables to fulfil a third.*

But this is not the Scripture meaning of "fulfil." Such a fulfilment of prophecy as this would have no value, and reflect no honor on prophecy. When an astronomer predicts an eclipse to take place on a certain day, at a particular hour and minute, and it does happen at that very time, we see in it a proof of knowledge on his part; but if God should interfere, and cause an eclipse to happen then, merely to confirm the astronomer's prediction, it would *not* be any proof of his science. So, if Jesus worked miracles or spoke parables merely because it had been predicted that he would do so, it would not redound to the credit of the prophecy. If you predict, that, on a certain day, I shall preach a sermon on a certain text, and I select that text in order to fulfil your prophecy, do you not see that it would not give any one faith in your prophetic talent?

There is another sense in which the word "fulfilled" is used in the New Testament. Jesus fulfilled Scripture in another way. To "fulfil," in the Scripture sense, is "to carry out perfectly:" it is to develop a principle or truth to its ultimate result.

* The usual formula on these occasions is, "All this was done, that it might be fulfilled which was spoken by the prophet," &c.

Thus "love is the fulfilling of the law;" that is, it carries law out to its last results. "*Fulfil* ye my joy;" that is, carry it fully out. "He will *fulfil* the desire of them that fear him;" that is, give them all they desire. "It becometh us to *fulfil* all righteousness;" *i.e.*, carry it all out perfectly. Thus the law is fulfilled, obedience is fulfilled, joy is fulfilled, in this way, by being carried to perfection.

Jesus fulfils all things in the law and the prophets by carrying each thing fully out to its perfection. "I came not to destroy, but to fulfil." He sees a germ of good in all things: he comes to fulfil it. He destroys nothing. He does not destroy any thing in nature or in man, or in human life, or in the religions of the world: he fulfils them all.

Thus it was that Jesus did not destroy, but fulfil, the Hebrew law. He took up its essence into his own doctrine, and dropped its accidental form. He fulfilled its morality by a higher morality. The law written on stone was fulfilled by a law written in the heart. He changed it from a law of negation and prohibition into one of attraction, of positive good. Thus, when the law said, "Do not murder," Christ fulfilled it by saying, "Love your enemy."

MERCY, AND NOT SACRIFICE.

One of his favorite passages — which he quotes, indeed, twice, and in reference to two different matters — is from Hos. vi. 6: "I desired mercy, and not sacrifice; and the knowledge of God more than burnt-offerings." The first time was when Jesus was reproved for eating with publicans, and said, "Go, and learn what that meaneth, I will have mercy, and not sacrifice." The other time was when his disciples plucked ears of corn on the sabbath-day. The Pharisees blamed them; but Jesus said, "If ye had known what this means, I will have mercy, and not sacrifice, you would not have condemned the guiltless." Evidently, he had thought of it often, and deeply. What does God wish of us? Does he wish any thing from us? Does he wait and long to have any thing? He wishes for mercy to man, not sacrifice to himself; good-will to our brethren, not worship to himself. Sabbath-keeping is good; but love is better, — care for man is better. Do we realize this? I am afraid, not. We do not know now, eighteen hundred years since Christ said it, twenty-six hundred years since Hosea said it, what it means. There is meaning in it yet, which the Church has not exhausted. Jesus was deeply convinced that good to man was the best worship of God. God is wishing for this; God is wishing that you and I should do more for those who need than we now do.

MAN LIVES BY TRUTH, NOT BY BREAD.

Another favorite passage of Jesus is found in Deut. viii. 3. It teaches that God led the Jewish nation forty years in the wilderness, to humble and prove it, and to know what was in its heart; and goes on thus: "He humbled thee and proved thee, and suffered thee to hunger, and fed thee with manna, which thou knewest not, neither did thy fathers know; that he might make thee know that man doth not live by bread only; but by every *word* that proceedeth out of the mouth of God doth man live." In the Hebrew text, the original expression is "every thing;" in the Septuagint it is "every word." Jesus here follows the Septuagint.

In reading Deuteronomy, his eye caught at this. How does man live? What is man's true life? Not of the body, but of the soul. What is his real food? *Truth*, the sight of truth, coming from God,—this is his real life.

If, then, he must sacrifice every thing else,—all comfort, success, appreciation, reputation; if he must be laughed at, set aside, counted as nothing; if his life seems a failure; if he have many enemies and few friends,—all this is nothing, if he really sees the truth; for this will make him strong and happy. He can live on this, and live joyfully. He will have no sense of sacrifice: all will be glad and joyful in his heart while he sees the truth.

In the hour of his great temptation, these words of Moses came to him; and it had become an intimate conviction with him, so that he resisted the temptation easily, and said to Satan, "I do not need bread: I need to be right. I am not hungry for any thing this world can give; I am hungry for truth: my longing is for that."

So afterward he said to the Jews (with a reference

to this passage in his mind), "Moses gave you not *that* bread from heaven: my Father giveth you the true bread from heaven." Miraculous bread does not come from heaven; for, after all, it is material food, not spiritual. Nothing comes from heaven but what is spiritual.

This quotation also illustrates his meaning in the petition, "Give us this day our daily (necessary) bread." Truth is daily bread, more necessary even than earthly food; and is always to be understood as included in this petition.

GOD THE GOD OF THE LIVING.

The passage (Matt. xxii. 32; Mark xii. 26; Luke xx. 37) quoted from Exod. iii. 6, 16, is very interesting and important.

God in this place says to Moses, "I am the God of Abraham, and the God of Isaac, and the God of Jacob." Jesus takes this as the proof-text of immortality in the Old Testament. Why did he do so?

It is well known that there is little to be found in the Old Testament concerning a future life. Some writers say that nothing is there. All that the Jews learned about it they are said to have learned in the Babylonish captivity. Yet some other passages Jesus might have quoted. There is, for instance, the famous passage in Job, "I know that my Redeemer liveth," &c. There is that in Daniel, "Many of them who sleep in the dust of the earth shall awake, some to everlasting life, and some to shame and everlasting contempt. And they that be wise shall shine as the brightness of the firmament; and they that turn many to righteousness, as the stars for ever and ever."

But Jesus passed by these texts, which are commonly quoted as proof-texts of immortality, and took this one. Why? If God is our God, he says, we cannot die. He is a living God. He speaks of Abraham, Isaac, and Jacob as being *his.* The moment he calls them *his,* they must be alive. For God to *think* of them would make them alive, if they had been dead a thousand years.

Is not this the only guaranty of life? It is the interest felt by God in each particular soul, the love of God for each soul. If every soul is a separate being to God, with a separate, special value, a name of its own, then each soul must live. If *he knows* you and me, knows us as he has made us, and made us for himself, then we cannot die.

Why, if you have taken pains to carve a figure, or draw a man's face with a pencil, you do not quite like to destroy it. *You have put some of yourself into it.* God has put something of himself into each of us. We, therefore, all live *to* him; for we all live *from* him.

This is the highest proof of immortality; but it is a proof not addressed to the logical understanding, but to the higher reason. It shows us what Jesus regarded as the true authority of the Old Testament in proof of doctrine.

The common mode of proof by theologians is to

say, "Here are so many texts in which such a doctrine is stated by Moses, Job, Solomon, and Micah: but these are inspired men; therefore God says it; therefore, whether you can understand it or not, you must believe it." This is arguing like a pedagogue, not like a Christian teacher.

But Christ does not quote Scripture thus. He does not concentrate a battery of texts, torn from their contexts, with which to confuse and prostrate an opponent. Instead of this, his argument demands the presence of some religious insight in order to be understood, and it is convincing in proportion to the amount of faith in the hearer. The word of Jesus profits only when mixed with religious faith in those to whom he speaks. To feel the force of this passage, for example, one must know something of the nature of love, human and divine; something of the nature of the human soul, and its worth; something also of what life really is.

THE MESSIAH.

There is a peculiar interest in noticing the passages which Jesus quotes from the Old Testament, in regard to the Messiah, as applied to himself.

Luke iv. 18, 19,— taken from Isaiah (lxi. 1, 2). Jesus quotes the following passage: "The Spirit of the Lord is upon me, because he hath anointed me to preach the gospel to the poor: he hath sent me to heal the broken-hearted, to preach deliverance to the captives, and recovering of sight to the blind; to set at liberty them that are bruised; to preach the acceptable year of the Lord."

In this passage, which Jesus selected from the book of Isaiah to read at Nazareth among his own people, and which he applied to himself after having read it, we gather the view he himself took of his own work.

There are many other passages in Isaiah, usually applied to Christ, and supposed to be predictions of the Messiah, which Jesus might have quoted, but did not. There is the passage concerning "Immanuel," in the seventh chapter. There is the passage (Isa. ix. 6) in which Christ is usually believed to be predicted, and in which he is called "Wonderful, Counsellor, the mighty God, the everlasting Father, the Prince of peace;" but Jesus does not select this passage.

Then there is the famous passage (in Isa. xi.) in which is described the Branch that was to grow out of the stem of Jesse, — a passage which contains a beautiful description of the coming of Christ, and of his kingdom of peace; but even this he passes by. More remarkable is it that he entirely omits to notice the famous prophecy (in Isa. liii.) of the man of sorrows, except by a casual allusion. Still less does he refer to the prophecy of a triumphant and conquering Messiah, who overcomes his enemies, and subdues nations; but he selects this passage, in which the Messiah is described as sent to preach to the poor and to heal the broken-hearted. Evidently he had often dwelt in his mind upon this view of the Christ. He saw himself called to be the Messiah in this high sense; and in this sense he really became the Messiah.

There is another passage concerning the Christ, which he quotes (Matt. xxii. 44) from the hundred and tenth Psalm. In this Psalm, David calls the Christ, whose coming he foresees, "my Lord." Jesus asks the Pharisees how David could have called his own descendant "my Lord." This question, which is left unanswered both by the Pharisees and by Jesus himself, shows that he had meditated upon its meaning. He saw that the Messiah was not to be merely a continuation of David, or a reproduction of David: he was to go on from the standpoint of David to a much higher one. David was already so glorified in the Jewish mind, that the Jews mostly expected in the Messiah only another David; but Jesus had seen intimations in the Old Testament itself of that which he saw clearly in the prophetic instincts of his own soul, — that the day of the Messiah was to transcend by a long interval that of David.

Put together these two passages, in one of which Jesus had found from Isaiah that the work of the Messiah was to comfort and help the lowly; and in the other, that by this work he was to become David's Lord. The two, thus united, result in the central idea of Christ's teaching, that he who humbles himself shall be exalted; that the work of the Messiah is to seek and save those who are lost. Thus, no doubt, by the revelations made to his own soul, and by meditations on these profound passages of Scripture, Jesus gradually formed in his mind the idea of the true Messiah, and saw that he was sent to fulfil it. This was his mission in the world; for this God had sent him. He did not accommodate Scripture to his idea, as is the fashion sometimes to say; nor did he change his idea to suit the Scripture: but he saw that in essence and spirit they were identical. When he said, "Your father Abraham rejoiced to see my day; and he saw it, and was glad;" and then added, "Before Abraham was, I was the Christ,"—we see that Jesus, meditating on the promise to Abraham, that in his seed all the nations of the earth should be blessed, saw that this prophecy could only be fulfilled by a Jew, who, like himself, had risen wholly above the distinction of Jew and Gentile, and to whom all mankind were brethren, because children of one Father.

Observe also the authority which the Master claims for himself as the Son of man,—that is, as the man in whom humanity took its full development; who, because perfectly Son of man, is therefore Son of God. For that which is perfectly human comes into a perfectly filial relation to the Father. He who stands in this relation to God and man stands higher than the Scripture, because at the source from whence the Scripture came. He has the same spirit from whence the Scripture proceeded. Hence Jesus considered himself to be, not the servant, but the master, of the sabbath; not the servant, but the master, of the ten commandments. In Matt. xix. 18, he re-arranges them, putting "Honor thy father and mother" after the rest, instead of before them; and adding an eleventh commandment, out of Lev. xix. 18: "Thou shalt love thy neighbor as thyself." Evidently, our Lord, in reading Leviticus, had seen this command shining like a star in the midst of the ceremonial and ritual ordinances. It left its place in Leviticus, and joined the ten great commandments, at his behest; for he was Lord of the Scripture as of the sabbath, because he was the Son of man.

This very phrase — "Son of man" — was taken by Jesus from Dan. vii. 13. In this passage, the Messiah is represented as "*a man*," coming "with the clouds of heaven," and standing before the "Ancient of days" to receive an everlasting dominion which shall never pass away. There Jesus could see himself to have been foretold by the prophets. He saw himself as a *man*, receiving an everlasting dominion, but coming "in the clouds of heaven;" for the "clouds of heaven," in the language of the Old Testament, indicate the obscurity which surrounds the providences of God. When Jesus predicts his future coming as to be "in the clouds of heaven," he means that it will be without "observation."

The subject I have spoken of is one for a book, not for a sermon.

These thirty-nine quotations from the Old Testament deserve to be weighed carefully, till we learn what Jesus found in each of them. His meditations on them are full of light for us all. We shall find that to him the Old Testament was a book most valuable, not for what it said, but for what it suggested; that he searched in it for the spirit, and not for the letter; that he did not value its prodigies and wonders; that he did not regard its long procession of marvels and portents; that all its savage wars he omits to notice; and that of the worldliness, infidelity, and unbelief of its people and princes he says nothing. Solomon, for example, who is to the Mahommedans so much, to Jesus is nothing.

The texts most quoted by our modern Orthodox teachers and writers, Jesus never quotes at all.

Jesus took *the best* out of the Old Testament as out of every thing. This is the lesson of his quotations. He passes by the low, the mean, the false, and finds the good. Finding the good, he found the true; for only that which is good is really true.

How differently have others studied the Old Testament! Some study it to find *proof-texts* of this or that doctrine; some to find arguments in favor of old abuses, slavery, intemperance, polygamy, despotism, persecution, war, witchcraft; some to find faults, errors, contradictions, absurdities, in its letter; some to justify low views of God as an arbitrary Being, of man as a degraded being. But Jesus studies these inspired writings to find the best, highest, and purest in all things. So he finds in them a divine spirit; he searches in them for a profounder sense of God's love; he develops them all to a higher point; and he thus *fulfils* every thing which they contain. He makes them full of meaning and full of life. He takes out of the hard shell its living kernel; he supersedes much of them, and values always the practical part more than the ceremonial.

XXIII.

DIARY OF 1863.

2 Cor. iii. 3: "YE ARE MANIFESTLY DECLARED TO BE THE EPISTLE OF CHRIST, WRITTEN NOT WITH INK, BUT WITH THE SPIRIT OF THE LIVING GOD; NOT IN TABLES OF STONE, BUT IN FLESHLY TABLES OF THE HEART."

AT the beginning of the year, one of the usual actions is to provide one's self with a diary,—a little blank volume, with each day of the year having a space arranged for it, in which its engagements may be written beforehand, and its events afterward. Many persons have, for years, found it convenient to keep such diaries. Formerly, they were obliged to prepare them for themselves; but now, blank journals of this kind are for sale in every bookstore. Evidently the practice of keeping such journals has greatly increased, or there would be no demand for such a supply. Is it that men value time now more than formerly? Is it that the historic element of our nature is taking a fuller development? It is evident that some periods and some nations tend more to this habit of recording events than others. The ancient Egyptians, for example, carved and painted on stone all the actions of their lives: so that the traveller to-day can read on walls, built four thousand years ago, what men did then every day; how they hunted and fished, and hatched birds by artificial heat, and beautified their gardens with summer-houses, flower-stands, and vases; how they kept accounts; went to ride in chariots and litters; carried parasols to keep off the sun; taught monkeys to hold torches for them at a feast; made music on harp, pipe, and drum; anticipated the pirouettes of the modern ballet; played games of checkers; played with dice, with balls, and the like. Thus they wrote down every day on tables of stone, moved by some instinct to journalize all their life. Other nations did nothing of the sort. The Greeks, for example, were so occupied with *living*, that they could not stop to describe their lives. This historic impulse apparently comes as the activity of man abates. The greatest men and the greatest nations have not been given the most to minute journalizing. Mr. Samuel Pepys is like an Egyptian in keeping his diary; but who ever saw Shakspeare's diary? It is all in "Hamlet" or "Othello,"—nowhere else. Men who are thinking the highest thoughts and doing the noblest actions do not usually stop to record them: they leave it to others to do so. He who lived the noblest human life on earth never but once, so far as we know, wrote a line; and that line he wrote, not on imperishable stone or perennial brass, or even on parchment which may last a thousand years, but on the sand: "He stooped down, and wrote on the ground."

But the advantage to most of us of keeping a watch over our fleeting days is so great, that I think this invention of printed diaries will improve the character of our people. We are active enough, full enough of outgoing life: the objective element is sufficiently strong; we need, perhaps, the antagonist tendency to balance it. We need to stop, and watch ourselves; to stand still, and consider. Keeping a diary, even of outward events, is a good habit for a young person to acquire. Better if a little reflection on what we do makes a part of our journal. It helps us to keep the reins in our hands, and prevents our being swept away by events. A record of facts is good: a record of ourselves is better. Watch the outward life; but watch the inward life also.

The modern invention is merely to have the days of the week, month, and year printed beforehand; to have places prepared in which to enter every thing. But I suppose no one buys such a blank diary without getting one use out of it which the publisher never thought of. Is it not a very serious thing to buy a diary of the coming year; to look forward, and make arrangements for three hundred and sixty-five more days of coming life? Does it not seem presumptuous to take this thought beforehand, not for the morrow, but for so many morrows? Shall we live to the end of the year? Will not our diary stop somewhere in it, and the last part of it remain for ever blank? Some time, it must be so. Some year, our diary will end long before the year ends. Will it be this one? Such thoughts are wholesome, if not too gravely dwelt upon.

But, beside this *diary of life* which we keep ourselves, there is another diary which God keeps for us. Every thing which we do, feel, and think, — all acts and all impressions, — are instantly daguerreotyped, as soon as they occur, in those wonderful tablets which we call *memory*. There they are written down, and packed away in every man's soul, — a whole library written full of past transactions. There are the faces of all the people we know, the names of multitudes more; the books we have read; pictures of the places we have seen; memories of all the moments, sad and bitter, with which our days have been crowded. There they are, hidden away perhaps, forgotten by the consciousness, but still latent in the memory. Some day they will come up again. It seems probable that we never really forget any thing. The very effort to *recollect* shows it. We know that the fact is *in* our memory, though we cannot bring it up to clear, conscious knowledge. We dive into our memory for it, as, by the fragrant coast of Ceylon, men dive for Oriental pearls. We did not go deep enough this time: dive a little deeper, and we shall find it. You recollect the story of the servant-girl, who, in her fever, began to speak in an unknown language, and spoke, hour after hour, with great fluency. At last, some one was found who pronounced it to be Hebrew, and said that she was reciting chapters out of the Hebrew Bible. Then it appeared that she had once lived with a clergyman who was in the habit of reading aloud from his Hebrew Bible. She had heard him, though she did not listen. It went into her memory below the region of conscious recollection. There it remained, latent knowledge, till the excitement of the fever broke up the habits of thought, and this came to the surface. After such a fact as that, who shall say that we ever actually and wholly forget any thing?

When parchment was scarce, it often happened that the writing would be erased from a manuscript, and something else written over it. This is called a palimpsest. But the erasure was only partial; and, as the original book is often more valuable than that which is written over it, means have been found to recover the underlying manuscript. Thus have been recovered some of Cicero's lost works, which were erased in favor of monkish legends. But what palimpsest is like the human soul? This may contain innumerable rescripts, one above the other; and yet the lowest of all, written in youth, sometimes comes out in age the clearest and most distinct of any.

These diaries of the soul the Apostle Paul speaks of, when he says, "Ye are our epistle, written not with ink, but with the spirit of the living God; not in tables of stone, but in fleshly tables of the heart." Every day, something is written down in the diary of the soul. In it events write themselves good and evil, joyful or otherwise. What deep impressions are made upon it by passing events, of which we are not conscious at the time, but the results of which we see long after! As the soldier in the heat of battle may receive a sharp cut, and not be conscious of the wound at the time, but long afterward it shall pain him; so it is with the events of life. We carry to our grave the scars of wounds received in our childhood. We come out of the battle of life covered with these scars, maimed and helpless invalids, veterans of many a stormy battle. How many mistakes we have made, what errors, what follies, what sins! and these are all written down in the diaries of each year. The soul of man is the book of judgment for him, to be opened on the last day. It is a palimpsest in which many things have been written. Sometimes a noble and beautiful work is erased, that a worthless one may be written over it. But that which seems to be erased may still be there; and, at last, the letters may be restored.

What shall be written during the coming year in the diary of the soul? Every day before us is now blank, innocent of any evil, empty of any good. At the end of the year, the diary will be full. Every day will have its mark. The coming year will be better or worse than the last. It is not likely to remain the same. Let us make it better. Let us write something good in each day's empty spaces. Let us gain some new knowledge each day, do some good action each day, receive some good influence from God's spirit into our souls each day.

But, beside what we receive, — the inward diary of

the soul, — we keep another by means of what we do. All our life goes out of us, and leaves an impression. Some years ago, a man of science came to this city, and showed some curious experiments allied to mesmerism. It appeared from these, that some persons of great nervous sensibility were endowed with the power of reading the character of a man merely by holding in their hands a scrap of his writing. It seemed that something of his life went out of him, through his pen, into the paper. Who knows? Stranger things than these we know to be true. Is not the photograph as strange? In every photograph the face has gone, and left itself on the negative. Your face has painted for me your picture. Part of yourself is there. Some effluence from your own thought, love, life, has come to me, and will stay with me in this little mysterious drawing.

So we write our diaries, — the diaries of the soul. What have we written during this past year? It has brought to us an infinite store of life. God has given to us all the magnificence of Nature, — his suns and storms; the divine beauty of the long summer day; the exuberance of flowers and foliage; the changing seasons, with all their variety. In all this he has come near to us to touch our hearts. Then he has sent to us human friendship and love; he has drawn out of us our best thoughts, by teaching us to confide in others; he has sent to us dear little children to charm away all that is austere in life by their trusting, playful tenderness; he has given to us wise friends, who have guided us better than we knew ourselves; he has sent to our souls aspirations, hopes, and good purposes. We have all had hours, some few at least, during the year, in which life seemed all good and fair, heaven around us, and God and his angels near at hand. Christ was then as a brother and a friend, and perfect love cast out all fear.

And what if the dark hours returned? What if we found ourselves again lonely and empty, without God and hope in the world? These moods of the soul are like days of storm, like this sharp cold which bites so nigh. It sends us back upon ourselves; teaches us to summon our powers, to bear and to wait; teaches endurance, patience, submission. The sun is there behind the cloud: God is there behind this desolate emptiness of your being. Your friends have left you alone; but whatever was divine in their friendship remains. Truth and love never deceive us, never depart from us. They seem to go; but they have not gone. When God has once visited the human heart, and touched it with holy purpose, with tender penitence, with earnest aspiration, with self-forgetting love, those gifts of his "are without repentance." It is impossible for us ever wholly to forget or wholly to forsake any really good experience of our soul. It is there, covered up, perhaps hidden, beneath the ashes left by burning passions, beneath the dust which has been drifted over it from worldly pursuits and anxieties; but it is there. In the heart of the hardened pirate lingers a tender spot, consecrated to the memory of his mother's love. Legree could not help shuddering at the floating curl which brought back his innocent youth. Good is stronger than evil; for evil passes away, but good remains. "The things which are seen are temporal: the things *not* seen are eternal."

Therefore, if, in the diary of your soul during this year, God has written any sincere conviction, any moment of pure love, any hour in which you determined to live for good ends, any day in which you did a kind act for another in the name of Christ, these moments, few though they be, are like the imperishable jewels, — the rubies, emeralds, diamonds, which men put away in caskets, and hand down as an ancestral inheritance from mother to daughter. So small, and seemingly so exposed to loss and disaster, they are safer than palaces, more permanent possessions than broad acres. God's love and truth in our souls are like the diamonds and Asiatic gems which glittered three thousand years ago on the dusky brow of Semiramis, and which adorn the fair-haired Northern maiden to-day.

During this year, God has also taught us to believe in heaven. We have seen dear friends pass away; and as we looked at the calm, serene face of death, we have followed them into the world beyond with our faith and our longing. We have stood by the brave young soldier, who, led by the earnest purpose of duty, went out from his home, and died as easily and sweetly on the bloody field as ever he fell asleep, a tired child, in his mother's arms. We have followed to the grave the man of experience, for years the energetic man of business, and long the centre of great activity, who passed from thence into quiet age, as the summer mellows into autumn. We have stood by the cradle-coffin of the little boy, whose soul, all overflowing with life, seemed made to be at home in this world, but who, like little Samuel, heard God's voice calling in the night, "Samuel!" and went and stood before God, saying, "Here am I; for thou didst call me." We have seen the mother, who, for long years a helpless invalid, sent from her sick-room holy influences of patience and sweetness to all that came near; teaching them the realities of life. We have looked on the worn face, pallid and faded with long disease, but always cheerful with an inward peace, of one who would be called a saint, if we, in our prosaic churches, gave that name to any one. So we have bidden them farewell, one by one; the father, the husband, the mother, the little child, the young woman, the noble young hero, — we have bidden them all farewell: but as we said, "Go to God," a voice in our heart replied, "Till we see each other again."

Every church, this year, has had its diary; not so much, however, of its meetings, its discussions, its contributions to good objects, its generous activities, its Sunday school and Bible class, or its efforts for the poor. But if it is really a church of Christ, then it has every year brought Jesus nearer to some souls. Some have therein found inward peace and hope; some have been drawn nearer to God and to heaven; others have been led to turn from empty lives to generous efforts and earnest aspirations. As I look on your faces to-day, I know this is true of some of you; but of whom? *That* we do not know now, but shall know hereafter.

History also has kept its diary during the past year, and has written in it the most extraordinary events. Let us look at some of them.

When the last year began,* a great battle was raging at Murfreesborough; a battle which lasted four days, but ended with the repulse of the rebels. On the same day, the President of the United States issued his proclamation, declaring all the slaves in the rebel States free; an act which was worth more than many victorious battles. The President of the Confederacy replied to this by declaring that he would give up all United-States officers taken prisoners, to be dealt with as criminals; but the threat has never been carried out. During the year, we have had the great and bloody battles of Chancellorsville (May 1–4), Gettysburg (July 1), Chicamauga (Sept. 20), and Lookout Mountain. Vicksburg and Port Hudson have

---

* Jan. 1, 1863.

been taken, and the Mississippi opened. East Tennessee has been occupied, and the attempt to retake it defeated. The great policy of enlisting negro troops has been begun as an experiment, and is already an admitted success.

This has been a memorable year to our nation. It has been our true *annus mirabilis*. When it began, Europe was sure that the Union was destroyed. Europe thought the Northern people mad in fighting to maintain their national existence and honor. To-day Europe has learned to look at us with different eyes. She begins to see to-day that we have a determined purpose, and that this must conquer. She sees the Rebellion split into three great fragments, — the United States in the very heart of it; its finances broken down by the stringency of our blockade, the slaves emancipated, and slavery virtually at an end. She sees the freedmen industriously laboring, or courageously fighting on the side of the Union; the Border States on the point of emancipating their slaves by law; great Southern cities like St. Louis, Nashville, Baltimore, New Orleans, clamoring for immediate emancipation. This year has been the turning-point in our history. God and the angels have looked upon us, and said, "You are a nation fit to be free; fit to become the leading republic of the world; fit to inaugurate the Christian democracy which is to come."

God be thanked for it all! God be thanked for our

country's noble diary during the past year! God be thanked for the wisdom higher than our own which has guided our counsels; for the firmness which has led our soldiers to stand against reverses in the field, and mistakes in the cabinet! God be thanked, especially, that this year has seen the downfall of a prejudice no less fatal to our own prosperity than hateful in the sight of God and man! The disgraceful riots in New York were like the rending of the possessed man by the evil spirit, before it took its final departure. When the Fifty-fourth Massachusetts Regiment, colored troops, went through Boston on Anniversary Week, and we looked in their serious faces, we felt in our souls that the crisis had come. When they stormed the bloody intrenchments of Fort Wagner, then we knew that the lives laid down there had set the seal to the regeneration of a race.

Blessed be God, then, for this year; for all its joy and all its sorrow; for its triumph and its disaster; for its hours when love and truth came to our hearts; for its hours when our hearts seemed empty and desolate! Let us bless him for it all; for all is good.

And now let me make some suggestions in regard to the improvement to be made of the year which is before us. In offering them to you, I also offer them to myself. The suggestions which suit one will suit all.

The first maxim which I offer to you and to myself is, that we should *try to do some one good thing every day.* Let us, every day in the year, do some kind act, or speak some one kind word. Help somebody; comfort some one. Do not wait till you can do some great thing, but do some little thing. Condescend to men of low estate, and to things of little consequence. Be faithful in few things. The probability is, that, if you propose to yourself to do a *single* good action each day, you will do more than one. While looking for one, you will see another. But do something. If your motive is to do good, that motive will glorify the most trivial action, and make it important.

The next maxim which I offer to you is, that you should *do every thing as serving Christ.* The essence of Christianity is amazingly simple, though it has been thought mysterious. Jesus says, "Follow me:" that is the whole of it. Christ desires that the same thing shall be done in the world now which he did himself. He wishes the blind to see, the lame to walk, the sick to be visited, the strangers to be taken in, the hungry to be fed, the prisoners to be cared for, the poor to have the gospel preached to them. When we are doing these things, we have a right to feel that we are serving him. "Repentance," "conversion," "regeneration," "coming to Jesus," are all included in the simple act of doing any thing in his name. If you wish to come to Jesus, you will find him in the first little child whom you meet, and whom you can help in any way. Christ is not in heaven, that we should say, "Who shall go up to heaven, and bring him to us?" nor beyond the sea, that we should say, "Who shall go over the sea, and find him for us?" but he is very nigh to us. He is in the next street, in that sick man's chamber, in the jail with that prisoner. He came to your door this morning with that poor boy who wanted a warm coat. While you are visiting these in his name, and for his sake, you find him. We are like the disciples on their way to Emmaus. Jesus walks with us, and our heart burns within us with a sense of his presence; but our eyes are holden, that we do not know him.

The third maxim is, *to have some plan* for our spiritual and moral life, and arrange each day accordingly. Let the plan be simple, so as to be practicable. Do not attempt too much; but, having formed a plan, keep to it. Shakspeare says, —

> "Stick to your journal-course. The breach of custom
> Is breach of all."

Regularity and perseverance are just as important in the care of the soul as in the care of material interests. Character can only be formed as cotton is manufactured. You have a building where the bales are taken in at the basement, and the cotton is picked apart, and cleaned. It is taken up one flight of stairs, and carded; it is taken up another flight, and spun; it is taken up another, and woven. Every working-day in the year, the bells ring at a certain hour for work; and, at a certain hour, to finish the work.

Without this regularity, there would be no profits. Paul describes the training of gladiators: "Every man that striveth for the mastery is temperate in all things: but *they* do it to obtain a crown of oak-leaves, which will fade; but we, one which will never fade."

The most brutal prize-fighter knows that he must lead a strictly temperate life, and be a perfectly virtuous man, if he wishes to win the purse. He must keep under his body, and bring it into subjection.

That life only is worth living which is devoted to some lofty aim. All our lives may be so devoted. But it is not enough to have a high aim: we must also have practical methods. It is melancholy to see persons, sincerely desiring improvement, with good purpose, and the best intentions, wasting their lives for want of some practical method. Have a plan, then, and keep to it. What you have to do, do at once. Finish every thing, and so have the joy which only comes with accomplishment.

But as every good thing has an opposite good thing to balance it, without which it is imperfect; so *plan* is imperfect, unless married to its opposite, *inspiration.* With plan alone, life becomes too mechanical, and we tire of its routine. My fourth maxim, then, is, *have faith in inspiration.* Believe that God is ever present in your soul, to inspire you for each duty, and to change routine and drudgery into life and love. While undertaking any thing, look up for a moment, and open your hearts to God. This is prayer. Essentially there is no other prayer than this, — to look up to God for strength with which to do God's work. As the flowers lift their cups to the sunshine, and the trees hold up their multitudinous leaves to the driving summer shower; so the human heart must evermore lift itself to God for strength, insight, and love. This is the daily bread of the soul, without which life becomes very meagre and poor. The human heart is never, indeed, without God. In a total eclipse of the sun, at the moment of entire darkness, when the last bead of light is cut off by the interposing planet, a corona of rays bursts out, encircling the moon, and indicating the place in the darkened sky where the sun is hidden. So, in that atheistic mind which is most without God, there are still some rays of a higher than earthly glory, indicating the place in the soul where God is hidden. But how joyful the moment when the unnatural eclipse is over; when the sudden sunbeam, shooting from the midst of the heavens, re-awakens the blessed noon; when the birds begin again to sing, the insects spring again from the ground, the cattle lift their drooping heads, Nature puts on her robes of color, the little hills rejoice on every side, and the lively din of the cock scatters the thin rear of darkness! With equal joy does the soul receive God again, after its dark eclipse of sin, of ignorance, or of unbelief. When we believe in the inspiration of God, it comes with equal blessing to the heart in all its states. In our summer hours, — when we are glad and happy and hopeful, when the soul is covered with leaves and flowers, — God's blessing falls like the dew and the rain, feeding the roots of our life, and making it bring forth and bud more abundantly. And in its wintry moments of sorrow or remorse, in our hours of disappointment and failure, when tormented with the sense of sin, God's blessing falls, like the soft snow of last week, covering the dark earth with its charitable mantle, and adding a fairy beauty to the bare branches and gray forests. The forgiving love of God hides our sins as this fair sheet of snow covers the cold earth.

THE END.

www.ingramcontent.com/pod-product-compliance
Lightning Source LLC
LaVergne TN
LVHW010151110826
845151LV00002B/482

* 9 7 8 1 4 2 5 5 3 8 0 7 1 *